JESUS AND THE WORLD OF JUDAISM

0334020948

JESUS
and the
World of Judaism

GEZA VERMES

SCM PRESS LTD

334 02094 8

First published 1983
by SCM Press Ltd
26–30 Tottenham Road, London N1
Third impression 1993

Phototypeset by Input Typesetting Ltd, London
Printed and bound in Great Britain by
Mackays of Chatham PLC, Chatham, Kent

Contents

Preface

The title, *Jesus and the World of Judaism*, chosen by the publishers, seems to summarize very suitably the topic common to eight out of the ten papers included in the present volume (chapters 8 and 10 being concerned with the world of Judaism rather than with Jesus). I fear, however, that some readers may be misled by the conjunction 'and'. This little word must not be taken to signify that the two halves of the title constitute two separate 'worlds': my whole approach demands that that 'and' be interchangeable with 'within'.

All ten contributions, originally delivered as public lectures, have already appeared in print, but they have now been revised to a greater or lesser extent. The three articles on the Dead Sea Scrolls and the Essenes (chapters 8–10) represent my latest views on the impact of Qumran on the study of the Old and New Testament and on Jewish historiography. The 'son of man' lecture (chapter 7), read in Oxford to an international New Testament conference in 1978, offers a fairly up-to-date version of the current state of a continuing debate.

The two essays on the relationship between post-biblical Jewish literature and the New Testament, the first (chapter 5) laying greater stress on the historical aspects of the issue, the second (chapter 6) on methodology, are intended to define a fresh scholarly stance towards gospel exegesis by postulating that the only (apparently) valid approach to Jesus' teaching is one that envisages it as part and parcel of the complex universe of first-century Palestinian Judaism, itself belonging to the even larger Graeco-Roman world and to the dynamic flow of Jewish civilization of the preceding and following periods.

'Jesus the Jew' (chapter 1), the earliest of the studies, originally the 1974 Claude Goldsmid Montefiore Lecture given in the Liberal Jewish Synagogue in London, sums up the thesis of my book of the same title, but adds here and there to the argument developed in it (e.g. the sketch of the attitude of the Jewish establishment towards real or potential political troublemakers, or the inappropriateness of Jesus' moral teaching to social ethics) and surveys some of the Jewish and Christian reactions to the theories expounded there.

From my historian's point of view, the most substantial contribution to the quest for the 'real' Jesus is offered in the three Riddell Memorial Lectures, delivered at the University of Newcastle upon Tyne in March 1981 (chapters 2–4). They represent a prolegomenon to the second part of the Jesus trilogy announced at the end of the Preface to the first paperback edition of *Jesus the Jew* (1976). These three talks contain (1) an outline of methodology for the rediscovery of the authentic teaching of Jesus; (2) a sketch of his central religious vision, and (3) a portrayal of the religion preached and practised by him, contrasted with that of which he has been made the object.

In the course of addressing academic and lay audiences in the British Isles and in the United States of America, I have noted three principal types of objection to the lectures on the Gospel of Jesus, and in particular the final one, 'Jesus and Christianity'.

The most commonly voiced critical query concerns what appears to be for many an absence of correlation between the Jesus depicted here as a man steeped in Jewish piety and fundamentally non-political in his outlook, and the hostile attitudes towards him on the part of the representatives of Judaism (or at least some of them) and of Rome. I believe the difficulty springs from a misreading or misinterpretation of the evidence. Violent reactions by Jewish religious authorities towards one of their subjects, and their handing over of him to the jurisdiction of the Romans, do not necessarily imply that in their judgment a religious or political crime has *actually* been committed. The offence may have simply been irresponsible behaviour *likely* to lead to popular unrest. Those in charge of the maintenance of law and order could easily have believed it to be their duty, in view of the common good, to prevent dangerous situations developing in a society already racked with revolutionary fever. The case of John the Baptist, as depicted in Josephus' *Antiquities*, viz. of an influential, hence *potentially* dangerous, preacher (see p. 12 below), gives already a good insight into the case of Jesus as seen by the Jewish leadership. However, the less familiar account, equally by Josephus, of an apocalyptic 'prophet' also called Jesus, provides an even more telling parallel.

In AD 62, four years before the outbreak of the first revolution against Rome, during the feast of Tabernacles, the Jewish leaders of Jerusalem arrested Jesus son of Ananias for uttering ill-omened prophecies in the city. He was apparently proclaiming woe to the sanctuary and the people. In order to stop him, they dealt him a severe beating. But Jesus son of Ananias suffered the strokes silently, without a word of protest, and did not desist from prophesying. This placed the leaders into a real quandary; some of them are said to have wondered whether Jesus son of Ananias was inspired by God (cf. Acts 5.39). Nevertheless, persuaded that the source of a possibly serious disturbance had to be neutralized, they chose to hand the man over to the Roman governor and Jesus son of Ananias was 'flayed to the bone with scourges'. When not even this torture was effective, and when, examined by the Procurator, he still persisted with his laments and refused to answer Albinus' questions, the latter released him. He believed that the man was mad.[1]

There is a *prima facie* similarity between the case of Jesus son of Ananias and that of Jesus of Nazareth.[2] Their conduct was likely to cause a breach of the peace and might have occasioned a massive Roman intervention: a situation to be averted at all cost. Yet instead of acting themselves, the Jewish magistrates were quite prepared to deliver the 'troublemaker' to the Romans. In doing so, they protected themselves against the accusation of having neglected their duty, and at the same time saw to it that they were excused from having to pass and execute sentence in an embarrassing case which they no doubt would have preferred not to have encountered. The trial of Jesus son of Ananias ended in an acquittal on the grounds of lunacy, that of Jesus of Nazareth, a much more serious affair because of the actual affray which he caused in the Temple, and because of the suspicion that some of his followers were Zealots,[3] led to a miscarriage of justice and to one of the supreme tragedies in history.[4]

The second objection that I have frequently encountered from professional New Testament scholars is that my selection of what constitutes a genuine teaching of Jesus is haphazard. In particular, they criticize a lack in my study of sufficient attention to a theory (any theory) of relationships between the synoptic gospels. I recognize a saying as authentic, they claim, if it has Jewish parallels. Although there is a grain of truth in this statement, it does not describe my stand correctly. I have not yet had the opportunity to expound the system to which I adhere – it will be done in the promised book on the teaching *of* and on the teaching relating to Jesus in the New Testament (both issues are now planned to be discussed in a single volume), but I trust that chapters 2 and 6 may be considered as a start towards a full exposition.[5]

Meanwhile it may be of some use to emphasize that two historical conclusions clearly stated in chapters 3 and 4 (pp. 30f., 37f., 50f.), have a considerable impact on matters of authenticity. The first concerns the definition of Jesus as a teacher. If it is agreed that he was not only a charismatic exorcist and healer but also a charismatic master, who taught with authority, in a manner different from that of the scribes, then it is not unreasonable to treat with reserve polemical passages in the gospels which portray him as a proto-rabbi cleverly manipulating convincing, or not so convincing, scriptural proof-texts.

The second historical stand with interpretative repercussions is connected with the notion of eschatological urgency. In chapters 3 and 4, I state firmly that, in my view, Jesus definitely expected the imminent arrival of the kingdom of God and was convinced that he would play an important part in its triumphal establishment. Now if we believe that this is how his mind worked, we have to accept that a man living under the paramount pressures of eschatological enthusiasm will necessarily concentrate all his physical and spiritual energies on the task immediately before him; he will have no time for planning for the future. If the concept of a close and coming End lay at the centre of Jesus' concern, we are bound to treat with some incredulity sayings attributed to him in the gospels having to do with the foundation and organization of an institutional church.[6]

A third criticism cavils at my portrayal of Christianity on the basis of a mere (and allegedly biased) sketch of the thought of St Paul. Here again, I must plead for time to explain more thoroughly my view of his teaching. I know very well that a schematic description of the religion deriving from his letters can scarcely do justice to the apostle's complex mentality, but I still submit that the picture drawn in chapter 4 is a fair reflection of the ancient, and not so ancient, understanding of the faith preached by Paul and professed by the Christian church. Also, I continue to maintain that as far as Jesus' own thought and message are concerned, Paul – who did not know him – should not, indeed cannot, be treated as a principal witness.

These are, needless to reiterate, only preliminary replies to serious questions aroused by my presentation of the message of Jesus. As soon as the third and last volume of the revised Schürer is completed (*The History of the Jewish People in the Age of Jesus Christ*, now under way), I hope and intend to return to the unfinished task and produce, after all these years of gestation, *The Religion of Jesus and Christianity*.

1

Jesus the Jew

'Jesus the Jew' – which is also the title of a book I have written[1] – is an emotionally charged synonym for the Jesus of history as opposed to the divine Christ of the Christian faith that simply re-states the obvious fact, still hard for many Christians and even some Jews to accept, that Jesus was a Jew and not a Christian. It implies a renewed quest for the historical figure reputed to be the founder of Christianity.

In one respect this search is surprising: namely that it has been undertaken at all. In another, it is unusual: that it has been made without – so far as I am consciously aware – any ulterior motive. My intention has been to reach for the historical truth, for the sake, at the most, of putting the record straight; but definitely not in order to demonstrate some theological preconception.

Let me develop these two points.

If, in continuity with medieval Jewish tradition, I had set out to prove that Yeshu was not only a false Messiah, but also a heretic, a seducer and a sorcerer, my research would have been prejudiced from the start. Even if I had chosen as my target the more trendy effort of yesterday, the 'repatriation of Jesus into the Jewish people' – *Heimholung Jesu in das jüdische Volk* – it is unlikely to have led to an untendentious enquiry, to an analysis of the available evidence without fear or favour, *sine ira et studio*.

By the same token, when a committed Christian embarks on such a task with a mind already persuaded by the dogmatic suppositions of his church which postulate that Jesus was not only the true Messiah, but the only begotten Son of God – that is to say, God himself – he is bound to read the gospels in a particular manner and to attribute the maximum possible Christian traditional significance even to the most neutral sentence, one that in any other context he would not even be tempted to interpret that way.

My purpose, both in the written and the verbal examination of

'Jesus the Jew', has been to look into the past for some trace of the features of the first-century Galilean, before he had been proclaimed either the second Person of the Holy Trinity, or the apostate and bogey man of Jewish popular thought.

Strangely enough, because of the special nature of the gospels, a large group of Christians, including such opposing factions as the out-and-out fundamentalists and the highly sophisticated New Testament critics, would consider a historical enquiry of this sort *ipso facto* doomed to failure. Our knowledge of Jesus – they would claim – depends one hundred per cent on the New Testament: writings that were never intended as history but as a record of the faith of Jesus' first followers. The fundamentalists deduce from these premises that the pure truth embedded in the gospels is accessible only to those who share the evangelists' outlook. Those who do not do so are – to quote a letter published in *The Guardian*[2] – 'still in the night . . . and so (have) no title to write about things which are only known to (initiates)'.

At the other extreme stands the leading spokesman of the weightiest contemporary school of New Testament scholarship, Rudolf Bultmann. Instead of asserting with the fundamentalists that no quest for the historical Jesus *should* be attempted, Bultmann is firmly convinced that no such quest *can* be initiated. 'I do indeed think', he writes, 'that we can know now almost nothing concerning the life and personality of Jesus, since the early Christian sources show no interest in either.'[3]

Against both these viewpoints, and against Christian and Jewish denominational bias, I seek to re-assert in my whole approach to this problem the inalienable right of the historian to pursue a course independent of beliefs. Yet I will at the same time try to indicate that, despite wide-spread academic scepticism, our considerably increased knowledge of the Palestinian-Jewish realities of the time of Jesus enables us to extract historically reliable information even from non-historical sources such as the gospels.

In fact, with the discovery and study of the Dead Sea Scrolls and other archaeological treasures, and the corresponding improvement in our understanding of the ideas, doctrines, methods of teaching, languages and culture of the Jews of New Testament times, it is now possible, not simply to place Jesus in relief against this setting, as students of the Jewish background of Christianity pride themselves on doing, but to insert him fair and square within first-century Jewish life itself. The questions then to be asked are where he fits into it, and whether the added substance and clarity gained from immersing him in historical reality confers credibility on the patchy gospel picture.

Let us begin then by selecting a few non-controversial facts concerning Jesus' life and activity, and endeavour to build on these foundations.

Jesus lived in Galilee, a province governed during his lifetime, not by the Romans, but by a son of Herod the Great. His home-town was Nazareth, an insignificant place not referred to by Josephus, the Mishnah or the Talmud, and first mentioned outside the New Testament in an inscription from Caesarea, dating to the third or fourth century. Whether he was born there or somewhere else is uncertain. The Bethlehem legend is in any case highly suspect.

As for the date of his birth, this 'is not truly a historical problem', writes one of the greatest living experts on antiquity, Sir Ronald Syme.[4] The year of Jesus' death is also absent from the sources. Nevertheless the general chronological context is clearly defined. He was crucified under Pontius Pilate, the prefect of Judaea from 26 to 36 CE; his public ministry is said to have taken place shortly after the fifteenth year of Tiberius (28/29 CE), when John the Baptist inaugurated his crusade of repentance. Whether Jesus taught for one, two or three years, his execution in Jerusalem must have occurred in the early thirties of the first century.

He was fairly young when he died. Luke reports that he was approximately thirty years old when he joined John the Baptist (Luke 3.23). Also one of the few points on which Matthew and Luke, the only two evangelists to elaborate on the events preceding and following Jesus' birth, agree is in dating them to the days of King Herod of Judaea (Matt. 2.1–16; Luke 1.15) – who died in the spring of 4 BCE.

Let me try to sketch the world of Jesus' youth and early manhood in the second and third decades of the first century. In distant Rome, Tiberius reigned supreme. Valerius Gratus and Pontius Pilate were governing Judaea. Joseph Caiaphas was high priest of the Jews, the president of the Jerusalem Sanhedrin, and the head of the Sadducees. Hillel and Shammai, the leaders of the most influential Pharisaic schools, were possibly still alive, and during the life-time of Jesus, Gamaliel the Elder became Hillel's successor. Not far from Jerusalem, a few miles south of Jericho, on the shore of the Dead Sea, the ascetic Essenes were worshipping God in holy withdrawal and planning the conversion of the rest of Jewry to the true Judaism known only to them, the followers of the Teacher of Righteousness. And in neighbouring Egypt, in Alexandria, the philosopher Philo was busy harmonizing the Jewish life-style with the wisdom of Greece, a dream cherished by the civilized Jews of the Diaspora.

In Galilee, the tetrarch Herod Antipas remained lord of life and death and continued to hope (in vain) that one day the emperor might end his humiliation by granting him the title of king. At the same time, following the upheaval that accompanied the tax registration or census ordered in 6 CE by the legate of Syria, Publius Sulpicius Quirinius, Judas the Galilean and his sons were stimulating the revolutionary tendencies of the uncouth Northerners, tendencies which had resulted in the foundation of the Zealot movement.

Such was the general ambience in which the personality and character of Jesus the Jew were formed. We know nothing concrete, however, about his education and training, his contacts, or the influences to which he may have been subjected; for quite apart from the unhistorical nature of the stories relating to his infancy and childhood, the interval between his twelfth year and the start of his public ministry is wrapped in total silence by the four evangelists.

Jesus spent not only his early years, but also the greatest part of his public life in Galilee. If we adopt the chronology of the synoptic gospels (Matthew, Mark and Luke) with their one-year ministry, apart from brief excursions to Phoenicia (now Lebanon) and Perea (or present day northern Transjordan), he left his province only once – for the fateful journey to Jerusalem at Passover. But even if the longer time-table of John's Fourth Gospel is followed, the Judaean stays of Jesus corresponded to the mandatory pilgrimages to the Temple, and as such were of short duration. Therefore, if we are to understand him, it is into the Galilean world that we must look.

The Galilee of Jesus, especially his own part of it, Lower Galilee around the Lake of Gennesaret, was a rich and mostly agricultural country. The inhabitants were proud of their independence and jealous of their Jewishness, in which regard, despite doubts often expressed by Judaeans, they considered themselves second to none. They were also brave and tough. Josephus, the commander-in-chief of the region during the first Jewish War, praises their courage, and describes them as people 'from infancy inured to war' (*BJ* iii.41).

In effect, in the mountains of Upper Galilee, rebellion against the government – any government, Hasmonean, Herodian, Roman – was endemic between the middle of the first century BCE and 70 CE, from Ezekias, the *archilēstēs* (the chief brigand or revolutionary) whose uprising was put down by the young Herod, through the arch-Zealot Judas the Galilean and his rebellious sons, to John the son of Levi from Gush Halav and his 'Galilean contingent', notorious in besieged Jerusalem for their 'mischievous ingenuity and audacity' (*BJ* iv.558) at the time of the 66–70 CE war. In short, the Galileans were admired as staunch fighters by those who sympathized with their rebellious aims; those who did not, thought of them as dangerous hot-heads.

In Jerusalem, and in Judaean circles, they had also the reputation of being an unsophisticated people. In rabbinic parlance, a Galilean is usually referred to as *Gelili shoteh*, stupid Galilean. He is presented as a typical 'peasant', a boor, a *'am ha-areẓ*, a religiously uneducated person. Cut off from the Temple and the study centres of Jerusalem, Galilean popular religion appears to have depended – until the arrival at Usha, in the late 130s CE, of the rabbinic academy expelled from Yavneh – not so much on the authority of the priests or on the scholarship of scribes, as on the magnetism of their local saints like Jesus' younger contemporary, Hanina ben Dosa, the celebrated miracle-worker.

These lengthy preliminaries done with, it is time now to turn to the gospels to make our acquaintance with Jesus the Jew, or more exactly, Jesus the *Galilean* Jew. I intend to leave to one side the speculations of the early Christians concerning the various divinely contrived roles of Messiah, Lord, Son of God, etc. that their Master was believed to have fulfilled before or after his death. Instead, I will rely on those simple accounts of the first three gospels which suggest that Jesus impressed his countrymen, and acquired fame among them, chiefly as a charismatic teacher, healer and exorcist. I should specify at once, however, that my purpose is not to discuss his teachings. Few, in any case, will contest that his message was essentially Jewish, or that on certain controversial issues, for example whether the dead would rise again, he voiced the opinion of the Pharisees.

His renown, the evangelists proclaim, had spread throughout Galilee. According to Mark, when Jesus and his disciples disembarked from their boat on Lake Kinneret,

> he was immediately recognized; and the people scoured the whole country-side and brought the sick on stretchers to any place where he was reported to be. Wherever he went, to farmsteads, villages

or towns, they laid out the sick in the market places and begged him to let them simply touch the edge of his cloak; and all who touched him were cured (Mark 6.54–56).

Similarly, Mark, referring to events in Capernaum, writes:

> They brought to him all who were ill and possessed by devils . . . He healed many who suffered from various diseases, and drove out many devils (Mark 1.33–34).

And both Luke and Mark report Jesus himself as saying:

> Today and tomorrow, I shall be casting out devils and working cures (Luke 13.32).

And

> It is not the healthy that need a doctor but the sick; I did not come to invite virtuous people but sinners (Mark 2.17).

My twentieth-century readers may wonder whether such a person should not properly be classified as a crank. We must, however, bear in mind, firstly that it is anachronistic and, in consequence, wrong to judge the first century by twentieth-century criteria, and secondly, that even in modern times, faith-healers and *Wunderrebbe* and their secular counterparts in the field of medicine, can and do obtain parallel therapeutic results where the individuals who ask for their help are animated by sufficient faith.

To assess correctly Jesus' healing and exorcistic activities, it is necessary to know that in bygone ages the Jews understood that a relationship existed between sickness, the devil and sin. As a logical counterpart to such a concept of ill-health, it was in consequence believed until as late as the third century BCE that recourse to the services of a physician demonstrated a lack of faith since healing was a monopoly of God. The only intermediaries thought licit between God and the sick were men of God, such as the prophets Elijah and Elisha. By the beginning of the second pre-Christian century, however, the physician's office was made more or less respectable by the requirement that he, too, should be personally holy. The Wisdom writer, Jesus ben Sira, advised the devout when sick to pray, repent, and send gifts to the Temple, and subsequently to call in the physician, who would ask God for insight into the cause of the sickness and for the treatment needed to remedy it. As Ecclesiasticus words it:

The Lord has imparted knowledge to men
that by the use of His marvels He may win praise;
by employing them, the doctor relieves pain (Ecclus. 38.6–7).

Jesus' healing gifts are never attributed to the study of physical or mental disease, or to any acquired knowledge of cures, but to some mysterious power that emanated from him and was transmitted to the sick by contact with his person, or even with his clothes. In the episode of the crippled woman who was bent double and unable to hold herself upright, we read that

He laid his hands on her, and at once she straightened up and began to praise God (Luke 13.13).

Sometimes touch and command went together. A deaf-mute was cured when Jesus placed his own saliva on the sufferer's tongue and ordered his ears to unblock, saying:

Ephphetha (*'eppatah*): Be opened! (Mark 7.33–34).

There is nevertheless one story in which Jesus performs a cure *in absentia*, that is to say without being anywhere within sight, let alone within touching distance, of the sick man. Matthew's account of the episode reads:

When (Jesus) had entered Capernaum a centurion came up to ask his help.
Sir – he said – a boy of mine lies at home paralysed . . .
Jesus said, I will come and cure him.
Sir, – replied the centurion – who am I to have you under my roof? You need only say a word and the boy will be cured. I know, for I am myself under orders, with soldiers under me. I say to one, Go! and he goes; to another, Come here! and he comes; and to my servant, Do this! and he does it.
Jesus heard him with astonishment, and said to the people following him,
I tell you this: nowhere, even in Israel, have I found such a faith.
Then he said to the centurion,
Go home now. Because of your faith, so let it be.
At that moment the boy recovered (Matt. 8.5–13).

I quote this in full not only because of its intrinsic interest, but also in order to compare it with a Talmudic report concerning one of the famous deeds of Jesus' compatriot, Hanina ben Dosa. It will be seen from the second story how closely the two tales coincide.

It happened that when Rabban Gamaliel's son fell ill, he sent two
of his pupils to R. Hanina ben Dosa that he might pray for him.
When he saw them, he went to the upper room and prayed. When
he came down, he said to them,
> Go, for the fever has left him.

They said to him,
> Are you a prophet?

He said to them,
> I am no prophet, neither am I a prophet's son, but this is how
> I am blessed: if my prayer is fluent in my mouth, I know that
> the sick man is favoured; if not, I know that the disease is fatal.

They sat down, wrote and noted the hour. When they came to
Rabban Gamaliel, he said to them,
> By heaven! You have neither detracted from it, nor added to
> it, but this is how it happened. It was at that hour that the fever
> left him and he asked us for water to drink (*bBer.* 34b).

Instead of ascribing physical and mental illness to natural causes,
Jesus' contemporaries saw the former as a divine punishment for
sin instigated by the devil, and the latter as resulting from a direct
demonic possession. Therefore, by expelling and controlling these
evil spirits, the exorcist was believed to be acting as God's agent in
the work of liberation, healing and pardon.

Jesus was an exorcist, but not a professional one: he did not use
incantations such as those apparently composed by king Solomon,[5]
or foul-smelling substances intolerable even to the most firmly
ensconced of demons. He did not go in for producing smoke, as
young Tobit did, by burning the heart and the liver of a fish (Tobit
8.2), or for holding under the noses of the possessed the Solomonic
baaras root, the stink of which, so Josephus assures us, drew the
demon out through the nostrils.[6] Instead, Jesus confronted with
great authority and dignity the demoniacs (lunatics, epileptics, and
the like) and commanded the devil to depart. This act is usually said
to have been followed by relief, and at least a temporary remission
of the symptoms. (Even in the gospels, the demons seem to have
had an uncanny facility for finding their way back to their former
habitats (Matt. 12.34–44).)

So – we read in Mark – (Jesus and his disciples) came to the other
side of the lake, into the country of the Gerasenes. As he stepped
ashore, a man possessed by an unclean spirit came up to him from
among the tombs where he had his dwelling. He could no longer

be controlled; even chains were useless; he had often been fettered
and chained up, but he had snapped his chains and broken the
fetters. No one was strong enough to master him. And so,
unceasingly, night and day, he would cry aloud among the tombs
and on the hill-sides and cut himself with stones. When he saw
Jesus in the distance, he ran and flung himself down before him,
shouting loudly, . . . In God's name, do not torment me!

For Jesus was already saying to him,

Out, unclean spirit, come out of this man!

. . . The people . . . came to Jesus and saw the madman who had
been possessed . . . sitting there clothed and in his right mind;
and they were afraid (Mark 5.1–15).

Once more I must parallel the gospel narrative with one concerning
Hanina ben Dosa and his encounter with the queen of the demons.

Let no man go out alone at night . . . for Agrath daughter of
Mahlath and eighteen myriads of destroying angels are on the
prowl, and each of them is empowered to strike . . . Once she
met R. Hanina ben Dosa and said to him,

Had there been no commendation from heaven, 'Take heed of
R. Hanina ben Dosa . . .', I would have harmed you.

He said to her,

Since I am so highly esteemed in heaven, I decree that you shall
never again pass through an inhabited place (*bPes*. 112b).

Jesus, curing the sick and overpowering the forces of evil with the
immediacy of the Galilean holy man, was seen as a dispenser of
health, one of the greatest blessings expected at the end of time,
when 'the blind man's eyes shall be opened and the ears of the deaf
unstopped'; when 'the lame man shall leap like a deer, and the
tongue of the dumb shout aloud' (Isa. 35.5–6).

But in this chain of cause and effect, linking, in the mind of the
ancients, sickness to the devil, one more element remains, namely
sin. Besides healing the flesh and exorcizing the mind, the holy man
had one other task to perform: the forgiveness of sin. Here is the
famous story of the paralytic brought to Jesus in Capernaum.

Four men were carrying him, but because of the crowd they could
not get him near. So they opened up the roof over the place where
Jesus was . . . and they lowered the stretcher on which the

paralysed man was lying. When Jesus saw their faith, he said to
the paralysed man,
     My son, your sins are forgiven.
Now there were some lawyers sitting there and they thought to
themselves.
     Why does the fellow talk like this? This is blasphemy! Who but
     God alone can forgive sins?
Jesus knew in his own mind that this is what they were thinking,
and said to them,
     Why do you harbour thoughts like these? Is it easier to say to
this paralysed man, 'Your sins are forgiven', or to say, 'Stand up,
take your bed and walk'? But to convince you that the son of man
has right on earth to forgive sins – he turned to the paralysed
man –
     I say to you, stand up, take your bed and go home!
And he got up, and at once took his stretcher and went out in full
view of them all (Mark 2.3–12).

'My son, your sins are forgiven' is of course not the language of
experts in the law; but neither is it blasphemy. On the contrary,
absolution from the guilt of wrong-doing appears to have been part
and parcel of the charismatic style; this is well illustrated in an
important Dead Sea Scrolls fragment, the Prayer of Nabonidus,
which depicts a Jewish exorcist as having pardoned the Babylonian
king's sins, thus curing him of his seven years' illness. In the
somewhat elastic, but extraordinarily perceptive religious terminology of Jesus and the spiritual men of his age, 'to heal', 'to expel
demons' and 'to forgive sins' were interchangeable synonyms.
Indeed, the language and behaviour of Jesus is reminiscent of holy
men of ages even earlier than his own, and it need cause little
surprise to read in Matthew that he was known as 'the prophet Jesus
from Nazareth in Galilee' (Matt. 21.11), and that his Galilean
admirers believed he might be one of the biblical prophets, or
Jeremiah, or Elijah *redivivus* (Matt. 16.14). In fact, it could be
advanced that, if he modelled himself on anyone at all, it was
precisely on Elijah and Elisha, as the following argument with the
people of his home-town Nazareth, would seem to bear out:

Jesus said,
No doubt you will quote the proverb to me, 'Physician, heal
yourself!' and say, 'We have heard of all your doings in Caper-

naum; do the same here, in your own home town.' I tell you this – he went on – no prophet is recognized in his own country. There were many widows in Israel, you may be sure, in Elijah's time . . . yet it was none of these that Elijah was sent, but to a widow at Sarepta in the territory of Sidon. Again in the time of the prophet Elisha there were many lepers in Israel, and not one of them was healed, but only Naaman, the Syrian (Luke 4.23–26).

Jesus was a Galilean Hasid: there, as I see it, lie his greatness, and also the germ of his tragedy. That he had his share of the notorious Galilean chauvinism would seem clear from the xenophobic statements attributed to him. As one review of *Jesus the Jew* puts it – a review written, interestingly enough, by the Gardening correspondent of the *Financial Times*! – 'Once he called us "dogs" and "swine" and he forbade the Twelve to proclaim the gospel to . . . Gentiles.'[7] But Jesus was also, and above all, an exemplary representative of the fresh and simple religiousness for which the Palestinian North was noted.

And it was in this respect that he cannot have been greatly loved by the Pharisees: in his lack of expertise, and perhaps even interest, in halakhic matters, common to Galileans in general; in his tolerance of deliberate neglect in regard to certain traditional – though not, it should be emphasized, biblical – customs by his followers; in his table-fellowship with publicans and whores; and last but not least, in the spiritual authority explicitly or implicitly presumed to underpin his charismatic activities, an authority impossible to check, as can be done when teachings are handed down from master to disciple. Not that there appears to have been any fundamental disagreement between Jesus and the Pharisees on any basic issue, but whereas Jesus, the preacher of *teshuvah*, of repentance, felt free rhetorically to overemphasize the ethical as compared with the ritual – like certain of the prophets before him – he perhaps could be criticized for not paying enough attention to those needs of society which are met by organized religion. As a matter of fact, this Pharisaic insistence on the necessity of faithfulness towards religious observances as well as of a high standard of ethics, has as it were been vindicated by a Christian *halakhah*, evolved over the centuries, that is scarcely less detailed and casuistical than our Talmudic legislation!

Nevertheless, the conflict between Jesus of Galilee and the Pharisees of his time would, in normal circumstances, merely have resembled the in-fighting of factions belonging to the same religious body, like that between Karaites and Rabbanites in the Middle Ages, or between the orthodox and progressive branches of Judaism in modern times.[8]

But in the first century circumstances were not normal. An eschatological and politico-religious fever was always close to the point of eruption, if it had not already exploded, and Galilee was a hotbed of nationalist ferment. Incidentally, there is no evidence, in my reading of the gospels, that would point to any particular involvement by Jesus in the revolutionary affairs of the Zealots, though it is likely that some of his followers may have been committed to them and have longed to proclaim him as King Messiah destined to liberate his oppressed nation.

But for the representatives of the establishment – Herod Antipas in Galilee, and the chief priests and their council in Jerusalem – the prime unenviable task was to maintain law and order and thus avert a major catastrophe. In their eyes, revolutionary propaganda was not only against the law of the Roman provincial administration, but also murderously foolish, contrary to the national interest, and liable to expose to the vengeance of the invincible emperor not only those actively implicated, but countless thousands of their innocent compatriots. They had to be silenced one way or another, by persuasion or by force, before it was too late. As the high priest is reported to have said of Jesus – and it is immaterial whether he did so or not – 'It is more to your interest that one man should die for the people, than that the whole nation should be destroyed' (John 11.50). Such indeed must have been the attitude of mind of the establishment. Not only actual, but even potential leadership of a revolutionary movement called for alertness and vigilance. John the Baptist, who according to Josephus was 'a good man' and 'exhorted the Jews to live righteous lives', became suspect in Herod's eyes because of an 'eloquence' which might 'lead to some form of sedition . . . Herod decided therefore that it would be much better to strike first and be rid of him before his work led to an uprising'.[9] Jesus, I believe, was the victim of a similar preventative measure devised by the Sadducean rulers in the 'general interest'.

As Jesus hung dying on a Roman cross, under a *titulus* which read, Jesus of Nazareth, king of the Jews, he cried out with a loud voice:

Eloi eloi lema shevaqtani?
'My God, my God, why hast thou forsaken me?' (Mark 15.34).

Nothing, to my mind, epitomizes more sharply the tragedy of Jesus the Jew, misunderstood by friend and foe alike, than this despairing cry from the cross. Nor was this the end of it. For throughout the centuries, as age followed age, Christians and Jews allowed it to continue and worsen. His adherents transformed this lover and worshipper of his Father in heaven into an object of worship himself, a god; and his own people, under the pressures of persecution at the hands of those adherents, mistakenly attributed to Jesus Christian beliefs and dogmas, many of which – I feel quite sure – would have filled this Galilean Hasid with stupefaction, anger and deepest grief.

I recognize that this sketchy portrait, and even the somewhat more detailed one given in my book, *Jesus the Jew*, does him – and you – less than justice. In particular, no biography of a teacher of the past can come alive if it is unaccompanied by a discussion of his essential message. As the Dean of Christ Church told me the other day in front of Thornton's bookshop in the Broad:

> My dear fellow, you are like an examination candidate who must answer several connected questions. So far you've only dealt with the first one: 'What kind of a Jew was Jesus?' You have advanced a theory. But I won't know whether it's true or not until you reveal your solution to the remaining parts of the puzzle.

Henry Chadwick was, of course, correct; *Jesus the Jew*, whether printed or spoken, is but the first part of a trilogy. I have the title for the second part: *The Gospel of Jesus the Jew*. But the rest has still to be written! The third will explore the metamorphosis of Jesus the Jew into the Christ of Christianity in the works of Paul, John and the rest of the New Testament writers. In the meanwhile I must accept that some of my listeners will prefer to suspend judgment on my assessment of this remarkable man.

As I have already said, I began my search for the Jesus of history for its own sake, to prove that, by employing the right methods, something of the authentic image of the Master from Galilee can be recovered from the dark historical past. To my surprise and pleasure, however, at least one of my readers feels that the work may have some interesting side-effects. It has been said of *Jesus the Jew* by an anonymous reviewer that it

> poses a challenge to Christianity, though it may not be its primary

purpose, or intended at all. The implied challenge is that, if Christians wish to return to the historical Jesus, they must also return, in some measure, to the Judaism in which he lived and moved and had his being. [10]

Rather less sure, but still encouraging, David Daube, perhaps the most influential Jewish voice on this subject, after assessing the book's contribution to the 'quest for the historical framework of Jesus's activity' and 'for his own concept of his vocation', goes on:

Whether it will do much towards removing ill-will and distrust may be doubted. These attitudes are largely independent of scholarly data. Still with luck, it may do a little. The present climate gives some ground for hope. [11]

On the Christian side, reactions have been varied.

'Vermes's own "historian's reading of the Gospels" . . . is presented lucidly, persuasively and with humour' – writes William Horbury of Cambridge – 'but its cheerful elimination of *mysterium Christi* again and again raises the question whether the author is not neglecting evidence that cries out for historical interpretation.' [12]

A well-known English Jesuit, the late Father Thomas Corbishley, described *Jesus the Jew* as 'overcrowded' and its learning as 'oppressive'. [13] And one of his less prominent brethren finds, rather depressingly – in a review entitled 'Minus the Resurrection' – that this 'learned but tedious book' is a 'disappointment'. [14] An American Bible expert, reacting sharply to my comment that professional New Testament scholars often wear the blinkers of their trade, concludes his piece with the words: 'Jesus the Jew deserves better than this.' [15] A French lady, writing in an extreme right wing periodical, calls the book 'scandaleux et blasphématoire'. [16] On the other hand, the editor of a French theological quarterly ends his positive evaluation with an exclamation: 'Jésus ne sera plus le même pour moi après la lecture de (ce) livre.' [17]

In general, however, Christian academic opinion has been sympathetic yet not wholly convinced. As A. R. C. Leaney has put it in Oxford's own *Journal of Theological Studies*:

The result is a valuable contribution to scholarship, but it is hard to assess exactly how successful it is. [18]

2

The Gospel of Jesus the Jew I
A Historian's Reading of the Gospels[1]

Videtur quod non: such was the formula used by mediaeval theology in launching a debate. The schoolmen frequently initiated their discussions with arguments militating *against* their thesis.[2] In our case too, this *videtur quod non* – roughly, 'it would appear that such and such is *not*' – would seem most appropriate. Specifically, it would appear that the gospel of Jesus the Jew is *not* a suitable subject for historical enquiry.

The first, and on the face of it more reasonable, objection raised against pursuing such an undertaking is that a historical approach to the teaching of Jesus is unlikely to lead to any insight substantially new and worth while. A topic investigated and studied so intensely and constantly for some nineteen centuries must already have yielded everything accessible to the understanding.[3] If any further research is made, if it is sensible the outcome is likely to be commonplace; and if it is in any respect out of the way, its results cannot but be suspect.[4]

There is no theoretical answer to give to this, but the following considerations may be borne in mind by way of a preliminary defence. The bulk of New Testament research has been carried out by Christian theologians. In the present instance, it is conducted within a context of Jewish history, independent of later demands of creed and tradition, Christian or Jewish.[5] Again, contemporary New Testament study, unlike the broader theological scholarship of former centuries, views the pocket-book containing the sacred writings of Christianity as an autonomous object of study to which all other relevant ancillary material – i.e., the whole of Judaism and Hellenism – must be subservient.[6] It speaks of the *world* of the New Testament, to which Judaism and Hellenism furnish the *background*. Here, by contrast, Jesus and the gospels are regarded as parts and products of first century AD Palestinian Judaism. And since during the last three decades fresh archaeological and manuscript discoveries, as well as substantial progress in the reassessment of the classical sources of Judaism, have greatly improved our grasp of the society, culture and religion to which Jesus belonged, a new look at the gospels from this angle, by a Judaica specialist, should certainly add to what was known previously.[7] One other justification for my choice of subject is that a scholarly evaluation of the gospel of Jesus the Jew entails above all a balanced synthesis of the many known data; and here again, our new knowledge of the civilization into which Jesus was born opens up distinctly fresh possibilities.[8]

The second objection current among gospel specialists may astonish the non-initiate. Arising from the acute pessimism of twentieth-century New Testament exegesis, it expresses with multiple variations a basic distrust of the interpreter's ability to establish the historicity of gospel pronouncements, and in particular to trace to Jesus himself words placed on his lips by the evangelists. For many New Testament scholars, a historical exploration of Jesus' teaching is and must be essentially speculative.

On this point I am faced with a problem of presentation, for I have to deal with it in some detail and at the same time not lose the good-will and attention of the non-experts who read this book. I will do my best.

The key issue is the nature of the evidence supplied by the New Testament. In the old days, that is to say from the late first to the eighteenth century, people could speak without hesitation of 'the gospel truth'. It was inconceivable that anything in Matthew, Mark, Luke or John should be inaccurate or false; the veracity of the evangelists, in their story-telling and in their reports of Jesus' sayings, was guaranteed by heavenly warrant. Unlike Herodotus or Thucydides, Livy or Tacitus, the four narrators of the life of Christ bore the seal of God's approval. Indeed, for many, the evangelists were God's mouth-pieces; their gospels were a divine dictation.[9]

The trouble is: we have not one gospel but four. And not only do the accounts given by these four represent four points of view; again and again they seem to vary in actual substance. The difference between the synoptics – Matthew, Mark and Luke – on the one hand, and John on the other, is particularly noticeable: two of the most glaring discrepancies are the duration of Jesus' ministry – given as one year in the synoptics, with a single Passover, and two or three

years in the Fourth Gospel – and the date of the crucifixion, which
according to the synoptics followed the evening of the Passover
supper, but according to John, preceded it.[10] Had the law commonly
regulating the development of religious traditions been operative in
the case of the gospels, these divergences would have succumbed to
the trend towards unification.[11] The same would have happened to
them as to the four sources or traditions underlying the Pentateuch
in the Hebrew Bible which, incorporated to form a single work,
needed the brilliant scholarship of the nineteenth century before
they were discovered. But although attempts made in the second
century to merge all four gospels into a single narrative known as
the *Diatessaron* met with ephemeral success in Syria,[12] this *Four in
One* failed in the long run to replace the separate original works. The
principle of harmonization triumphed nevertheless. Discordances
between the evangelists were carefully muted by means of an
exegesis which took it for granted that the spokesmen of God could
not possibly contradict one another. In the age of enlightenment
and liberalism of the late eighteenth century, however, this attitude
of mind was replaced by a spirit of criticism. Variants, and the
concept of development in the gospels, were no longer rejected in
advanced scholarly circles, and from then on research concentrated
on discovering the earliest, least evolved, and consequently most
reliable of the differing accounts.[13] As you know, this turned out to
be the Gospel of Mark. But since this slender volume includes a
very limited amount of doctrinal matter, a separate source of sayings,
one that had been used each in his own way by Matthew and Luke,
was given the name of Q (short for the German Quelle = source)
and proclaimed an additional document with a standing roughly
equal to that of Mark.[14]

In other words, nineteenth-century New Testament scholarship,
pursuing the old quest for 'gospel truth' with the help of critical
tools, concluded that it can be found only in parts of the sources,
and in a considerably reduced quantity.

With the turn of the present century, the spirit of criticism gave
way to one of scepticism. It began now to be argued by Christian
New Testament experts, starting with Wilhelm Wrede, that not even
Mark may be accepted as an unbiased reporter. His gospel, too, is
dominated by purposes of theology.[15] Its material is arranged to
conform with doctrinal aims and is therefore not trustworthy as a
historical framework.

Then, between the wars, any hope of recovering the historical

Jesus apparently received its death blow, chiefly at the hands of Rudolf Bultmann, who categorically asserted the impossibility of reaching back to the teacher of Nazareth via the gospels. These church documents, Bultmann said, afford no direct access to Jesus. Jesus was not a Christian; he was a Jew.[16] (The great Julius Wellhausen was of the same opinion.[17]) In an oft-quoted passage from his book, *Jesus*, published in 1926, Bultmann writes: 'I do indeed think that we can now know almost nothing concerning the life and personality of Jesus, since the early Christian sources show no interest in either.'[18] According to this leader of the school of form criticism, the gospels represent, not the aims, aspirations and thought of Jesus, but doctrine to meet the spiritual needs of the primitive church, which actively participated in its formation. In particular, it is often alleged – though without much justification I think – that utterances in the name of the 'risen Lord' pronounced at liturgical gatherings by Christian 'prophets' – St Paul refers to such individuals a number of times[19] – are added by the evangelists to the sayings actually spoken by Jesus himself. The task of the form critic is therefore to detect in the gospel-accounts the discrete original literary units; to define their nature; to discover their *Sitz im Leben* (the particular church circumstances responsible for their formation); and to investigate, by comparing parallel attestations, the pre-history of the tradition, which may occasionally lead to the Palestinian church, or even to Jesus. In his classic *History of the Synoptic Tradition*, Bultmann devises a tentative method by means of which words or *logia* may, as he says, 'in a very few cases' be ascribed to Jesus with 'some measure of confidence'.[20]

The practical consequence of the impact of form criticism was to advise against, and even discredit, historical enquiry proper. Gone now were the days when serious New Testament exegetes could compose without scruple comprehensive presentations of the life and teaching of Jesus. The last characteristic example of this favoured genre was *L'évangile de Jésus-Christ* by the famous French Dominican, Marie-Joseph Lagrange, which was published in 1929. After Bultmann's *Jesus*, another thirty years were to pass before one of his pupils, Günther Bornkamm, could summon up courage to write his *Jesus of Nazareth*. Even so, Bornkamm's opening sentence, 'No one is any longer in a position to write a life of Jesus',[21] bears the stamp of *Formgeschichte*.

Gone, too, were the days of full expositions of Jesus' message. The British scholar, T. W. Manson, who never subscribed to form criticism, could still produce a major work of this kind in the thirties[22] but his 'old-fashioned' approach was superseded in influential German circles by New Testament theologies. Again, the original impetus came from Bultmann who, typically, dared to allot, out of a total of 620 pages in the 1965 fifth edition of his *Theologie des Neuen Testaments*[23] a mere thirty-four pages (thirty in the 1952 English translation) to the preaching of Jesus on the grounds that it is a *presupposition* of New Testament theology but does not actually belong to it![24]

It will seem from what has been said so far that in persisting in my search for Jesus' authentic religious thought I am running against the tide. But form criticism, for all that it has enriched New Testament study with profound insights and sophisticated analyses, contains some fundamental flaws. In fact, several of Bultmann's more recent followers have themselves recognized the fragility of his historical scepticism and tried to correct it. But their improvements still leave much to be desired. The system's chief weakness lies, I think, in the absence among its developers and practitioners of any *real* familiarity with the literature, culture, religion and above all spirit, of the post-biblical Judaism from which Jesus and his first disciples sprang. Instead, it is in the Hellenistic world of early Christianity that Bultmann and his pupils are at home.

I need hardly say that I am not in total disagreement with present-day New Testament scholarship, with form criticism, tradition criticism,[25] redaction criticism[26] and the rest. I concede that none of the evangelists were professional historians, not even the synoptists. I also grant that each had his own theological vantage-point and told his story with a specific end in view. But a theological interest is no more incompatible with a concern for history than is a political or philosophical conviction. As long as this interest is recognized, and as long as the interpreter realizes that it is likely to affect the whole work under scrutiny, he ought with a minimum of critical skill to be able to make allowance for it. In this connection, the fact that we have *three* theologically motivated accounts, and not just *one*, is in a sense fortunate and helpful because those elements which are common to them all are thus easily detectable and the historian is enabled to exercise his judgment on these basic data. Where the life-story of Jesus is concerned, for instance, no serious scholar of today would query the main threads of the narrative: Jesus entered into his public ministry during the mission of repentance preached by John the Baptist; he enjoyed a greater measure of success in

Galilee; he clashed with the authorities in Jerusalem; he died there on a cross; and all this took place during the middle years of the prefecture of Pontius Pilate, who governed Judaea between AD 26 and 36.[27]

On the other hand, one of the chief theories of the form critics calls for serious reflection. Is it really, as they assert, self-evident that the composition of the gospels is due entirely to the didactic-theological requirements of the primitive church? If the evangelists were primarily preoccupied with teaching Christian doctrine, how are we to explain their choice of *biography* as their medium? They cannot have been influenced by tradition; no Jewish convention exists that the sayings of the sages should be transmitted in this way. Anecdotes conveying them abound in rabbinic literature, but nothing by way of any similar biography has been handed down and there is no reason to imagine that one ever existed. The authors of the Qumran scrolls record no life-story of the Teacher of Righteousness, or of any other member of the sect for that matter. They do not even disclose the real names of people, but allude to them by means of cryptograms. So if the church opted for that particular literary form to expound its message, we have to ask ourselves what it can have hoped to gain from it. Liveliness and colour? But to amplify the account of Jesus' life by introducing Palestinian ideas and customs, and by including Semitic linguistic peculiarities and oriental realia of all sorts, will have rendered it largely incomprehensible to non-Jewish Hellenistic readers and have demanded continuous interpretative digressions bound to have been catechetically harmful and counter-productive. Other first-century Christian teachers, in any case – Paul, James or the author of the first church manual, the *Didache* or Doctrine of the Twelve Apostles – saw no advantage in a life-story as the vehicle of theological doctrine, moral exhortation, and disciplinary of liturgical rules, but like the Essenes and the Palestinian rabbis chose to communicate their religious thoughts directly.[28]

Again, if the raison d'être of the gospels was to provide for the doctrinal needs of the churches, how are we to understand the insertion into them of sayings of Jesus, and attitudes of mind, which actually conflict with essential teachings of primitive Christianity? The evangelists note that Jesus made disparaging remarks about Gentiles.[29] They observe that he was apparently unwilling to allow his followers to announce him as the awaited Messiah.[30] Neither of these matters can have greatly suited the first promulgators of the gospels, whose main task was to convince non-Jews of the truth that 'Jesus is the Christ' (John 20.31; cf. Acts 2.36).

It is consequently difficult to avoid concluding that if the evangelists chose to tell the story of Jesus' life, it was because, whatever else they may have intended, they wished also to recount history, however unprofessionally. And if they included circumstances which were doctrinally embarrassing, it was because they were genuinely believed to be part of the narrative. In that case, Bultmann's dictum about the impossibility of knowing anything about Jesus or his personality, 'because the early Christian sources show no interest in either',[31] becomes a plain misjudgment.

If the extreme, but highly influential, wing of contemporary New Testament criticism is distinguished by its almost all-inclusive historical scepticism, it must in fairness be recognized that when German theorizing marches alongside British (and occasionally American) common sense, the outcome is compromise. In a work entitled *Rediscovering the Teaching of Jesus*, the late Norman Perrin,[32] though a whole-hearted form critic, advanced various criteria by which a scholar may determine whether a gospel saying or parable is authentic. The first is the principle of *dissimilarity*. If a teaching has no parallel in Judaism or in the primitive church, it most probably originates in Jesus. The second is *coherence*. Material from the earliest layers of gospel tradition may be classified as genuine if it is consistent with a doctrine already established as authentic through the principle of dissimilarity. A third and auxiliary criterion is *multiple attestation*. The discovery of a doctrinal motif in more than one source (e.g., Mark and Q), as well as in a variety of literary contexts (sayings, parables, stories, proclamations, etc.), postulates authenticity.[33] In a later publication Perrin added a fourth principle to these three: *linguistic suitability*.[34] For a saying surviving in a Greek gospel to be associated with Jesus, who did not teach in Greek, it must be susceptible to a Semitic rendering.

Perrin's criteria – which are shared by a number of scholars all over the world – are valid as long as they are accompanied by *caveats*. Dissimilarity is certainly significant; but if it implies an entire absence of antecedents, it will be rarely found. Originality in the field of religion mostly consists in giving a new twist, lending a fresh understanding, to ideas that are in themselves age-old. Also, it should be remembered that today's originality may appear less striking tomorrow, as has been amply shown by the Dead Sea discoveries. Above all, care must be taken never to base an assertion

32 (1967) Perrin

of uniqueness on incomplete knowledge and information. This is a constant danger where New Testament scholars – the majority – have no direct independent access to the vast Hebrew and Aramaic sources of post-biblical Judaism. Their dependence on secondary sources is fraught with hazard.[35] The principle of coherence is self-explanatory. Its specific gravity is less than that of dissimilarity; at the same time it is applicable to a much broader range of cases. Multiple attestation is an external literary manifestation of consistency. For instance, the fact that Jesus' love and kindness towards the outcasts of Jewish society appears in stories, sayings, parables etc., is a safe indication of valid historical evidence.[36] As for linguistic suitability, I would refer in this connection to the second half of *Jesus the Jew*, where Jesus' various titles of prophet, lord, messiah, son of man and son of God, are subjected to a thorough analysis within the appropriate Aramaic-Hebrew philological context with a view to discovering their historical significance.[37] Interestingly, this often turns out to be very different from the meaning attached to the terms by Christian tradition.[38] The most striking finding is that the celebrated epithet 'son of man', on which so much modern christological speculation has been based, does not in fact represent an established concept in post-biblical Judaism and cannot be applied as a title in Aramaic. It cannot, therefore, be accredited to Jesus as such.[39]

To these criteria devised by New Testament exegetes who are as a general rule scholars and churchmen, the independent historian is able to add several of his own. When he deals, for example, with contradictions in the gospels, he will not try to reconcile them. Bearing in mind that the brevity of Jesus' career will have allowed him no time for his ideas to evolve, it will seem no more than sensible to conclude that if one saying ascribed to Jesus appears to be sharply at variance with another, they cannot both be authentic.[40] His xenophobic utterances and his institution of an apostolic mission to the nations cannot both be accepted as genuine.[41] Nor for that matter can the sympathy with the tax-collector evident in, 'The tax-collectors and the harlots go into the kingdom of God before you' (Matt. 21.31), be judged to tally with the contempt for tax-collectors and Gentiles apparent in the advice, 'If (your brother) refuses to listen even to the church, let him be to you as a Gentile and a tax-collector' (Matt. 8.17). The same man, in such a brief period of teaching, cannot have been responsible for both these remarks.

Most importantly, no objective and critical evaluation of the gospels can overlook the impact of Jesus' tragic fate on the first chroniclers of his story and on the evangelists themselves. They present him as God's emissary, as God's son, sent to usher in the kingdom of God; yet beyond a tiny area of rural Palestine his word went largely unheeded. From the Judaean leaders he encountered nothing but hostility. And when he was finally brought before the Roman governor and sentenced to die by crucifixion, even his own deserted him, even, so he felt, his heavenly Father himself. '*Eloi*', he cried, '*Eloi, lema shevaqtani?*', 'My God, my God, why have you forsaken me?'[42] Could a failure such as this ever be recognized as the ultimate spiritual teacher, the elect of heaven, lord and Messiah? Without eliminating the scandal of the cross, clearly no.[43] The historian's eye will therefore inevitably look for the hand of early Christian apologists in those parts of the story which first imply, and subsequently try to prove, that contrary to common Jewish expectation,[44] the violent death of the Messiah was divinely fore-ordained. Furthermore, he will apply, *pace* C. H. Dodd, the great British New Testament specialist, the same treatment to the tales of the resurrection transforming disaster into triumph.[45] In Mark, the earliest of the gospels, he will find merely a simple insinuation of a happy ending, and he will notice that subsequently this implication becomes more and more fully elaborated by the later evangelists. He will observe, moreover, that on this topic also the gospels display intrinsic contradictions.[46] On the one hand, they assert that Jesus repeatedly foretold his resurrection on the third day following his death. On the other, they describe the total disarray of the apostles and disciples immediately after the crucifixion and their startled perplexity at hearing that Jesus had risen from the grave. The evangelists themselves, in fact, testify to a progressive development, refinement and reinforcement of the evidence concerning the resurrection. In the first version it is based on hearsay: the report is brought by untrustworthy female witnesses whose words strike the apostles as 'an idle tale' in which they do not believe.[47] In the next version the news is confirmed by the trustworthy Peter, or by Peter and another disciple (Luke, John). Elaborated still further, the resurrection testimony becomes evidence at first hand: apparitions of the risen Jesus are seen by the eleven apostles either in Jerusalem (Luke) or on a Galilean mountain (Matt.), and subsequently (Paul) by a crowd of over five hundred brethren, many of whom are said by the apostle to be still alive (in faraway Galilee?) in the mid-fifties

of the first century, at the time of writing his first letter to the
Corinthians (I Cor. 15.6).

Gospel references to the *parousia*,[48] Christ's glorious return, have
also to be viewed in the setting of a career terminating in seeming
humiliation and ignominy. The resurrection argument is addressed
to believers only, to initiates. There is no suggestion in the New
Testament that the risen Jesus was encountered by outsiders. To
tell the truth, not even the apostles and disciples seem to have
recognized the person who joined them on the road to Emmaus and
who entered the room where they were hiding.[49] The majestic
second coming, by contrast, was to be the vindication and triumph
of Jesus in the eyes of the whole world, the whole of mankind (Matt.
25.31–32). In its earliest stage, this *parousia* tradition expects the
day of the Lord to come very soon, even during the lifetime of Jesus'
own generation; members of the church in Thessalonica have to be
advised to keep strict control of their enthusiasm.[50] But only a
little later, Christians are being encouraged to be watchful; the
bridegroom's coming may be delayed until midnight (Matt. 25.6;
cf. Luke 17.34). And a little later still, they are exhorted to cultivate
the great virtue of endurance (II Peter 3). Then, with the *parousia*
still not realized the apocalyptic momentum flags, and soon after
the completion of the New Testament, the end-time, the *eschaton*,
is deferred *sine die*, relegated to the remotest future.[51]

Although I myself think it incompatible with Jesus' essential
religious outlook, it can doubtless be argued that the *parousia*
speculation originated in his own eschatological and apocalyptic
teaching rather than in later Christian apologetics.[52] The apologetic
nature of the *parousia* expectation is moreover strongly supported
by the eschatology of the Dead Sea Scrolls. In Essenism, the
consecutive postponements of the day of the Lord are also attended
by exhortations to patience and perseverance. The Habakkuk
Commentary reads: 'The final age shall be prolonged and shall
exceed all that the Prophets have said; for the mysteries of God are
astounding. *If it tarries, wait for it, for it shall surely come and shall
not be late* (Hab. 2.3). Interpreted, this concerns the men of truth
who keep the Law, whose hands shall not slacken in the service of
truth when the final age is prolonged. For all the ages of God reach
their appointed end as He determines for them in the mysteries of
His wisdom.'[53]

In sum, if we accept that in reporting the life and message of
Jesus, the intention of the evangelists was, to some extent at least,

to recount history, and if it seems reasonable to assume that the resurrection and *parousia* material is attributable to the doctrinal and apologetic needs of the early church, it becomes as clear *a posteriori* as it has been *a priori* that our understanding of the real Jesus must derive basically from an analysis of the synoptic data relating to his actual ministry and teaching that are unaffected by accretions deriving from the creative imagination of nascent Christianity.[54]

The main force of the New Testament representation of the 'Christ-event' (*Christusereignis*) – to use the jargon of contemporary theologians – still embryonic in the synoptic gospels but fully developed in the letters of Paul, is directed towards providing a history of salvation. It sets out to announce the redemptive function and effect of the suffering, death and resurrection of Jesus. In the Pauline writings, the ordinary details of Jesus' life and teaching receive negligible attention compared with the stress laid on the ultimate purpose of his mission. Indeed, it is sometimes held that since all the New Testament writers without exception stand on a central theological platform, so that the 'dogmatic' approach dominates the Jesus story at every level of its transmission, it is unscholarly to disregard it and to attempt to reach behind the screen of the primitive Christian 'myth'. Anyway, it is asked, is it likely that every single one of the first-century spokesmen misrepresented most of the major issues, and that the twentieth-century historian, after a lapse of some nineteen hundred years, is able to correct their tendentious distortions and draw a more reliable outline of the happenings of their times, offer a more authentic version of a message nearly two thousand years old?

The answer is that on the face of it success would appear unlikely. But it is not impossible. And methodologically, the endeavour is perfectly legitimate. The very fact that the synoptic portrait of Jesus as a person and the synoptic character of his teaching are so manifestly and radically at variance with the figure and message found in the theological canvas of Paul itself guarantees that, notwithstanding all the redactional and editorial manipulation carried out by the primitive church and the evangelists, a concrete basis exists on which to reconstruct history. In addition, the critical student of the gospels will be aware of the cultural cataclysms which took place during Christianity's earliest period. The civilization to which Jesus and those who heard and followed him belonged was Jewish; their provenance and province was Palestinian-Galilean;

their language was Aramaic-Hebrew. From the middle of the first century onwards, by contrast, Christianity was transplanted and took root in Graeco-Roman soil, in a Graeco-Hellenistic civilization.[55]

In parenthesis, I am of course acquainted with the recent tendency in New Testament scholarship to seek to efface the differences between Judaism and Hellenism by blurring the frontiers dividing them. But I am firmly convinced of the untenability of Martin Hengel's statement that from 'the middle of the third century BC *all Judaism* must really be designated "Hellenistic Judaism" ', and that 'the differentiation between "Palestinian" and "Hellenistic" . . . proves no longer adequate'.[56] Fergus Millar, one of our leading ancient historians, is fully justified in asserting that no reader of inter-testamental Jewish literature, and of the Dead Sea Scrolls in particular, 'will be readily disposed to assent without severe qualifications to the proposition that Palestinian Judaism was as Hellenistic as that of the Diaspora'. 'On the contrary,' he adds, 'what we should emphasize is the uniqueness of the phenomenon of an original and varied non-Greek literary activity developing in a small area only a few miles from the Mediterranean coast.'[57]

Returning to the upheaval caused by the migration of Christianity from a Jewish milieu to pagan Syria, Asia Minor, Egypt, Greece and Rome – there can be little doubt that if in one sense some continuity persisted, in another, the uprooting was so thorough that as a source for the historical understanding of Jesus of Nazareth, the reliability of the Gentile church, together with all the literature composed especially for it, can be ruled out.[58] In many respects, the Hebrew Bible, the Apocrypha, the Pseudepigrapha, the Qumran writings, and the enormous body of rabbinic literature, are better equipped to illumine the original significance of words and deeds recorded in the gospels.[59]

Another historical consideration remains, involving the question of why the Judaeo-Christians, the first of Jesus' followers, withdrew so relatively fast from the main body of the church. Rarely confronted, this problem is nevertheless of methodological importance because the most likely reason was that the Ebionites became convinced that they were witnessing in the Hellenistic communities a fatal misrepresentation of Jesus, a betrayal of his ideals, and their replacement by alien concepts and aspirations.[60]

Dealing now with a preliminary issue of a different kind – nobody doubts that the Jesus of history was a teacher, but to understand his teaching function properly, together with the lesson itself, we need to consider them against the backcloth of his other activities, in the context of his ministry as a whole. As well as a teacher, Jesus was a physician of the body and the mind. Curing physical ills and disabilities and 'exorcizing' sick spirits, ministering to the diseased in the name of God, his place was in that stream of Judaism inherited from the prophets and exemplified by such figures as Elijah and Elisha which I have termed 'charismatic'.[61] Here, in a genre of popular piety which has endured for centuries, the hero is neither priest nor sage but the *ish ha-elohim*, the man of God. In his excellent paper, 'Popular Religion in Ancient Israel', J. B. Segal writes: 'The "man of God" performed miracles – not grandiose affairs, but acts within the context of everyday life that the people could understand . . . In times of famine he assured the return of food in plenty . . . A small quantity of grain would suffice to feed . . . a hundred men. Elisha not only healed the great Naaman from leprosy, but restored from death a small child. And it was when Elijah had resuscitated her son that the widow of Zarephat knew that he was a "man of God".'[62]

In an age and society in which the combination of sanctity and the miraculous was considered normal, Jesus' talents and activities fitted the image of the holy man. Authority, as in the era of the prophets, frowned on charismatic acts as potential or actual threats to religious order, but it could usually do little to stop them because of the high esteem in which the man of God was held. The rabbis themselves were ambivalent about them. The various manifestations of the miraculous in the Bible could hardly be ignored, and the many *obiter dicta* in Talmud and Midrash demonstrate that even in post-biblical times supernatural occurrences were still recognized. But among the learned, their importance was played down.[63] The childlike confidence of the 'men of deed', the *anshe ma'aseh*, offended the conventional standards of many of the sages.[64]

That Jesus was a renowned exorcist is well attested in the synoptic gospels, though this function of his ministry goes unmentioned in the rest of the New Testament. Inheriting the inter-testamental notion of a world ruled by spirits of light and darkness, he rejected the opinion of apocalyptic circles that in the struggle against evil, human beings have only to act as insignificant aids to a heavenly host of angels, powers and dominations. He injected reality into the fight against the devil. When nervous and mental disorders were

attributed to demonic possession, he cured them by himself over-
coming the evil spirits believed to be inhabiting the minds of the
sufferers. And he mended the bodies of men and women sure that
illness is the result of sin by loosening Satan's grip on them with a
declaration of forgiveness.[65] The same understanding of healing,
but divested of its eschatological associations, and without any
mention of a mediator, survives in the later Talmudic saying: 'No
sick man shall recover from his illness until all his sins have been
pardoned' (*bNed.* 41a). But the principal distinguishing feature of
Jesus' activity as exorcist and healer was his assumption that his
work heralded the coming of the kingdom.[66]

'A prophet mighty in deed and word' (Luke 24.19), is how Jesus
is depicted in the gospels; and in the Greek phraseology of Josephus'
renowned *Testimonium Flavianum* the partial authenticity of which
is increasingly recognized, as a 'wise man' famous for his *paradoxa
erga*, his 'marvellous deeds'.[67] In this guise, as one who converted
into reality his convictions and beliefs, Jesus appears to represent a
Jewish piety more typical of rural Galilee than of the sophisticated
Judaism of the south, and of Jerusalem in particular.[68] I am not
alone in emphasizing this. In the paper already referred to, Professor
Segal comments: 'It should be remarked that, like Elijah and Elisha,
Jesus came from northern Palestine . . . Perhaps . . . most significant
is the bond of sympathy between the womenfolk and Jesus, reminiscent of that between women and the "man of God" in North Israel.'[69]

Jesus the teacher cannot properly be understood without taking
into simultaneous account Jesus the man of God, Jesus the holy
man of Galilee, Jesus the *Hasid*. With this firm statement, I realize
that I expose myself to the charge, actually voiced by Seán Freyne
in a recent monograph, of partially prejudging the issue.[70] I assure
him, and those among you who may share his concern, that I
have been watching this carefully, but have never noticed any
incompatibility between the *Hasid*-concept and Jesus' teaching. But
I am also sure that if I had neglected to bring out this aspect of his
character and ministry, Professor Freyne, or someone else, would
have been quick to point out that the social and religious setting of
the doctrinal message of Jesus the Jew was missing from the
synthesis.

By now, I trust that I have made plain the nature and difficulty of
the task facing the historian in search for Jesus' gospel, and the
various ways in which his approach differs from that of the theologian. I will aim at determining the principal features and motives of

his preaching, his thought rather than his specific words. Once the real qualities of his vision of God are identified – and this will be the purpose of the next chapter – we shall be able to reconstruct the spiritual aspirations which that vision inspired. We shall in other words come closer to grasping the piety taught and practised by him. In the third chapter on this theme of 'the Gospel of Jesus the Jew' I shall try to express my understanding of the piety characteristic of Jesus and to compare it with Christian religion as we know it.

The Gospel of Jesus the Jew II
The Father and His Kingdom

In addition to his ministry as healer and exorcist, Jesus also taught.[1] Disciples, sympathizers and even passers-by regularly address him as teacher or master, *rabbi* or *rabbuni* in Aramaic, rendered as *didaskale* or *epistata* in Greek.[2] But what kind of teacher was he? The Semitic title might suggest that he was regarded as a 'scribe',[3] the contemporary equivalent of what later became the office of 'rabbi'. No less an authority than Bultmann categorically asserts that this was so. Jesus, he maintains, 'actually lives as a Jewish rabbi. As such he takes his place as a teacher in the synagogue. As such he gathers around him a circle of pupils. As such he disputes over questions of the Law . . . He disputes along the same lines as Jewish rabbis, uses the same methods of argument, the same turns of speech.'[4]

As so often happens, Bultmann's view has been taken up and repeated so frequently that it has come to be accepted as the established truth. But it is in fact somewhat misleading. The title of rabbi does not seem to have acquired by Jesus' lifetime the meaning attached to it in later ages of a fully trained exponent of scripture and tradition. None of his predecessors or contemporaries, not even the great Hillel or Shammai, or the elder Gamaliel, are referred to as rabbi in the Mishnah or the Talmud.[5] *Rabbi*, signifying literally 'my great man', must be taken here in its broader sense, without prejudging the type and style of either the teacher or his teaching.

On the other hand, since the evangelists so often depict Jesus involved in scholarly controversy and exegetical debate[6] with Pharisees, Sadducees, and lawyers, should we not assume that he too belonged to the intellectual élite, and as he always wins the argument, that he was more learned and possessed greater expertise than his opponents? Perhaps. But again, perhaps not, for our knowledge – which although admittedly imperfect is knowledge all the same – of Galilean culture of the late Second Temple era, and the New Testament evidence itself, support to some considerable extent the opinion that Jesus was an amateur in the field.[7] In the first place, although it was normally the speciality of the Pharisaic scribes to expound and interpret the Bible, not only is there no mention in the gospels of Jesus belonging to their ranks; neither Josephus nor rabbinic literature indicate any noticeable Pharisee presence or impact in Galilee at all prior to AD 70.[8] The village scribes[9] whom Jesus met regularly were men able to draw up contracts, marriage settlements, bills of divorce, and to teach children in the schools, but are not to be confused with the luminaries of Jerusalem Pharisaism. Also, there is no hint in the New Testament of Jesus having received any specialized training – not to mention the fact that rabbinic sources go out of their way to describe the Galileans as being in any case not conspicuous for their erudition.[10]

Moreover, reflecting on the doctrinal sections of the gospels, particularly the bulk of the literary forms in which Jesus' teaching is expressed – words of wisdom, prophetic warnings, and above all parables – we are bound to notice that they demand no skill in Bible interpretation proper, or particular familiarity with the intricacies of Jewish law.[11] More positively, all three synoptic evangelists assert at the outset of his preaching career that his style *differed* from that of the scribes. Their prime concern was to invest all religious doctrine with the sanction of tradition as being part of a strictly defined chain of transmission originating – in fact, or by means of exegetical ingenuity – in scripture, and preferably in the Pentateuch.[12] Jesus, by contrast, is said to have taught with *exousia*, with authority, without feeling the need for a formal justification of his words.[13] Some of the most authentic of the controversies in which he was involved, such as the discussion whether his powers of exorcism derived from Beelzebub or 'the finger of God', and another on the true cause of defilement, include no scriptural proof-texts at all.[14]

The proposal advanced by the form critics that many of the scholastic debates and arguments between Jesus and the Pharisees should be postdated and identified as exchanges between the leaders of the Jerusalem church, the 'Judaizing' circles of Palestinian Christianity, and their Pharisee opponents, appears in consequence very persuasive.[15] Jesus was a charismatic holy man, a Hasid, not only as an exorcist but also as a teacher. He did not sit in a schoolhouse[16] reading and interpreting Holy Writ, or analysing and reconstructing the tradition of the elders. His existence was rather that of an itinerant preacher and healer.[17] And such was the force of his personality that those whom he treated, and to whom he spoke, sensed that his lessons possessed great driving-force and that they were listening to a man of God, a 'prophet mighty in deed and word before God and the people' (Luke 24.19), to repeat the quotation cited in the previous chapter.

Jewish religious teachers did not excel in creating doctrinal systems.[18] The prophets, sages and rabbis associated God with the reality which they knew. They did not go in for abstract speculation. Jesus was cast in the same mould. Analysis of the divine nature and of the divine mysteries was not for him. Not for him was God a transcendent idea, an eternal and boundless absolute, an *ens per se*. God was thought of, and spoken of, by him, not in philosophical or theological terms, but in existential language.

For Jesus, God was King and Father: implicitly King and explicitly Father, both divine forms inherited from scripture. Whether the famous synagogal prayer beginning, 'Our Father, our King', *avinu malkenu*,[19] already existed in the first decades of the Christian era, is uncertain. The Talmud ascribes it to Rabbi Akiba in the early second century (*b.Taan.* 25b), but the phrase itself is included in one of the benedictions preceding the recitation of the *Shema*, 'Hear O Israel, the Lord our God, the Lord is one!', and according to some liturgical experts may go back to the days of the Temple.[20] These two notions of God as King and Father must in any case have been widely current in Jesus' time.

Let us think first about king and kingdom. Jesus' teaching on the kingdom of God is generally thought to be the heart of his doctrine. To quote a recent writer, 'Jesus' teaching was focused . . . upon what he referred to again and again as the reign of God'.[21] For another modern scholar the kingdom of God is 'the central aspect of the teaching of Jesus . . . All else in his message and ministry serves a function in relation to that proclamation and derives its meaning from it.'[22]

The concept of the kingdom of God has a long history reaching from rabbinic and inter-testamental literature back to the Old Testament. To determine Jesus' precise understanding of it, we must therefore compare the gospel usage with the rest of the Jewish evidence. A number of modern and easily accessible studies of the subject are available,[23] so I will not enter here into the history of the idea but limit myself to outlining the four ways in which it is formulated.[24]

The feature common to them all is that the kingdom of God relates to God's sovereignty itself rather than to the realm over which he governs. When the Jewish nation was a monarchy, divine sovereignty was the counterpart of earthly kingship. The king was designated 'son of God', his representative on earth. Israel believed that it enjoyed a privileged position in the economy of providence and salvation and constituted the *de facto* province over which God was ruler. But it is believed also that his *de jure* kingdom extended far beyond Israel's boundaries and that one day a powerful king would subjugate the wicked Gentiles and compel them to pay homage to the one true God. The psalms are full of such themes. God promises power and conquest to the king of Israel.

> Ask of me, and I will make the nations your heritage,
> and the ends of the earth your possession . . .
> Now, therefore, O kings, be wise . . .
> Serve the Lord with fear (Ps. 2.8–11).

Elsewhere, the divine king is portrayed as a source of awe and dread to the Gentiles.

> The Lord reigns; let the people tremble! . . .
> The Lord is great . . . over all the peoples.
> Let them praise thy great and terrible name! (Ps. 99.1–3).

With its loss of independence in the sixth century BC, Israel looked to a new David to re-establish God's visible and institutional rule over Jews liberated from the foreign empires, and to impose this rule over mankind as a whole. Thus biblical messianism came into being, increasing in strength with the passage of the centuries to reach its apogee during the inter-testamental era. The most powerful expression of royal messianism appears in one of the Psalms of Solomon from the middle of the first pre-Christian century, in the early days of the Roman occupation of Palestine, conquered in 63 BC by Pompey.[25]

> Behold, O Lord, and raise up unto them their king, the son
>   of David . . .
> And that he may purge Jerusalem from nations
> that trample her down to destruction . . .
> And he shall have the heathen nations to serve him . . .[26]

The same figure of a victorious and holy king appears in a Qumran composition known as the Benediction of the Prince of the Congregation, a sectarian title for the royal Messiah.[27] It is also mentioned in the synagogal prayer *par excellence*, the *tefillah*, which has been in daily use since the first century AD, if not earlier:[28]

> Cause the shoot of David to shoot forth quickly,
> and raise up his horn by thy salvation.[29]

In addition to the notions of king and Messiah, a third concept emerged in Jewish apocalyptic milieux during the same inter-testamental period,[30] namely that the kingdom of God was to ensue from the victory on earth of heavenly angelic armies over the hosts of Satan. Israel's final glorious triumph was to be the corollary in this world of God's total dominion over the world of the spirits. Such a kingdom was of course not to be built. It was to irrupt into the world here below, annihilate it, and set itself up in a new heaven on a new earth. The Dead Sea Scroll's Community Rule and War Rule afford a perfect insight into the ideology of the extremist dreamers who looked forward to a kingdom of this kind. For the members of the Qumran sect, the universe was divided into the dominion of the Prince of Light at the head of the spirits of truth and the just among mankind, and that of the Angel of Darkness leading the spirits of iniquity and the wicked among mankind.[31] Their struggle would be without end because the spiritual hosts would equal each other in strength.[32] But the 'great hand of God' was to intervene and the stalemate then be broken.[33] Victory was to fall to Michael the archangel in the realm of the spirits, and Israel was to achieve dominion over 'all flesh'.[34] Apocalyptic visions of this type may or may not include a messianic figure, but even when they do, he is, like Qumran's Prince of the Congregation, a shadowy, and on the whole secondary and unimportant, character.

The fourth concept of the kingdom is quite different, with no associations whatever with violence or war. It was largely an exilic and post-exilic phenomenon, attested already by Deutero- and Trito-Isaiah in the second half of the sixth century BC. The pagans, suddenly realizing that Israel's God is the only Saviour, were all to flock to Jerusalem to offer worship to him and submission to his people.

> The nations shall come to your light . . .
> The wealth of the nations shall come to you . . .

They shall bring gold and frankincense
And shall proclaim the praise of the Lord . . . (Isa. 60.1–6).

A pure and sanctified Israel was to draw the Gentiles to God. The manifestation of God's sovereignty over his own was to serve as a magnet to the rest.

The recognition of this sovereignty was viewed by the rabbis of the post-biblical era as manifested through personal obedience to God's Law, i.e., through the acceptance of 'the yoke of the Torah' (*mAb*. 3.5) described also as 'the yoke of the Kingdom of Heaven'. Listing the various uses of the phrase in his renowned monograph, *Die Worte Jesu*,[35] the great Aramaic scholar, Gustaf Dalman, shows that according to rabbinic exegesis of Leviticus 20.26, the assumption of this yoke by the Israelites demands that they should set themselves apart from wrongdoing.[36] The link between submission to God's supreme authority[37] and obedience to the divine precepts is asserted in the Mishnah in connection with the *Shema'*, Judaism's confession of belief in God and his unity: 'A man should take upon himself first the yoke of the kingdom of heaven and thereafter the yoke of the commandments'.[38] Nevertheless, the Bible's concept of the nations' acknowledgment of God's rule coincides with rabbinic thought when it suggests that the Gentile convert, the proselyte, is one who has taken on himself the yoke of the kingdom of heaven.[39]

Now how does Jesus' view of the kingdom of God relate to those already current? The first, which in its time was an actual political-religious reality, would obviously have been irrelevant to him. Throughout his adult life, Judaea was administered directly by Rome, and his own Galilee was governed by a Herodian prince. As far as the second idea is concerned, that of the King-Messiah, there is little evidence in the gospels of a kingdom of God to be established by force. There was no plan for Jesus to reconquer Jerusalem, or any indication that he intended to challenge the power even of Herod, let alone that of the emperor of Rome.[40] This leaves us with the apocalyptic imagery on the one hand, and on the other, the prophetic and rabbinic conception of a quiet and willing submission to the yoke of God the King.

When the gospel teaching of the kingdom is considered in its entirety – or more exactly, with the omission of the Matthean passage concerning the last judgment, which in its present form is bound to be secondary[41] – one feature stands out: Jesus' representation of it includes little that is specifically royal. Some parables

introduce a monarch as the central figure, but they are few and
belong uniquely to the style of Matthew. Thus, 'The kingdom of
heaven may be compared to a king who wished to settle accounts
with his servants' (Matt. 18.23). And, 'the kingdom of heaven may
be compared to a king who gave a marriage feast for his son' (Matt.
22.1). But in neither case is royalty an essential element. The quasi-
parallel to this parable in Luke speaks simply of 'a certain man',
anthrōpos tis, described later more precisely as the 'landowner',
oikodespotēs, which is intended in its turn to correspond to the
Hebrew, *ba'al ha-bayith* (Matt. 14.16, 21). And in the story of the
servants required to justify their handling of money entrusted to
them, 'king' in Matthew 18 is replaced in Matthew 25.19 by 'master',
and in Luke 19.12 by 'nobleman'. Even more interesting, whereas
in a talmudic parable it is a king who hires workers for his vineyard,[42]
in the gospel it is once more a landowner: 'For the kingdom of
heaven is like a landowner who went out early in the morning to
hire labourers for his vineyard' (Matt. 20.1).

In the same way that Jesus, by practising and thereby sanctioning
the powers of exorcism and healing, tended to locate in this world
the fight of good against evil instead of in a mythical arena outside
the world,[43] so he also transforms into reality the 'unreal' ingredients
of the inherited imagery of the kingdom. The royal theme belongs
to this category. In the kingdom as he envisages it there are no
thrones, no courtiers, no heavenly choirs, no clashing hosts with
chariots, swords or javelins. In their place we encounter the land-
scapes, worktools and inhabitants of the Galilean country and its
lakeside life. The kingdom of heaven is like a field.[44] The kingdom
is like a vineyard in which day-labourers are treated fairly and even
generously by their employer.[45] The kingdom is like a tiny seed of
mustard which grows into a plant so large that birds are able to nest
in its branches.[46] Or again, Jesus associates the kingdom with the
fish, the net, the catch (Matt. 13.47ff.) and with the cook who adds
leaven to her flour to make dough for her bread (Matt. 13.33; Luke
13.20–21). The kingdom of heaven belongs to the little children,
and to those who resemble them, the humble and the trusting (Matt.
18.3–4; Mark 10.13ff. par.). It belongs to the poor; the rich will find
it more difficult to enter than the camel to pass through a needle's
eye, i.e. they will find it impossible.[47]

But when was this kingdom of Jesus' parables to come about?
Fairly soon, as contemporary apocalyptics thought? Very soon?
Was it conceived by him as close and already tangible? The gospel

When?

evidence shows this is changed to suit literary style

evidence appears inconclusive. Occasionally, the evangelists seem to establish the kingdom in a world to come, in a new age, as when Jesus is depicted as prophesying, 'Truly, I say unto you, I shall not drink again of the fruit of the vine until that day when I drink it anew in the kingdom of God' (Mark 14.25 par.). Elsewhere, the kingdom belongs to the here and now. Like the seed planted in the ground, it is already coming into being. Like the leaven in the dough, it is already at work.

see JL in NJ notes

This situating of Jesus' kingdom of God in a context of time has been the subject of much learned, and to my mind futile, controversy.[48] Albert Schweitzer's 'consistent eschatology' (*konsequente Eschatologie*) assigns it to the near future.[49] C. H. Dodd places it in the present time in the form of a 'realized eschatology'.[50] Joachim Jeremias compromises, and with his '*sich realisierende Eschatologie*', eschatology in process of being realized, allots it partly to the present and partly to the future.[51] Many New Testament scholars, furthermore, compound the difficulties facing them by taking it for granted that Jesus, for all his eschatological convictions, looked towards a temporal future. His ethical teaching was to serve as a pattern of life for his disciples during the interval between his first and his second coming: an irrational attitude of the eschatological mind, in the opinion of Rudolf Otto.[52]

Math urged Luke slow.

One of the methodological principles proposed in the previous chapter is that a doctrine which includes the notion of a *parousia* is likely to reflect church apologetics and not Jesus' own ideas. If he was convinced, as he undoubtedly was, of the imminence of the coming of the kingdom, he would not have exhorted his followers to settle down to wait for the day of the Lord.[53]

important

But to dismiss the problem thus summarily would be high-handed. Staying with it a little longer, I would therefore remark as a first point that the chief weakness of the Schweitzer–Dodd–Jeremias school of thought is that it applies ordinary time-concepts to Jesus' eschatological outlook. Admittedly, modern scholarship thereby merely follows ancient Jewish and Christian eschatological speculation. In the former, historical periods are distinguished from the beginning to the epoch of consummation. To take one of the best known examples, Daniel divides the age extending from the Babylonian exile to the moment of final salvation into seventy 'weeks of years' (or seventy seven-year periods), and sees his own time as falling within the last of these sabbatical cycles.[54] His principal chronological landmark is the erection in the Jerusalem

Temple of the 'abomination of desolation' in the form of a pagan god (Dan. 9.24–27). In early Christian apocalypticism, on the other hand, the history of salvation is represented as evolving in three stages. The first, subdivided into three times fourteen generations, reaches from Abraham to Jesus.[55] The second corresponds to the public life of Christ. And the third leads to the *parousia*, the approach of which is signalled by Daniel's 'abomination of desolation' (Mark 13.14; Matt. 25.15). Paul provides a still more detailed schedule of events heralding the second coming. 'That day will not come', he tells the Thessalonians, 'unless the rebellion comes first, and the man of lawlessness is revealed, the son of perdition, who opposes and exalts himself against every so-called god or object of worship, so that he takes his seat in the temple of God, proclaiming himself to be God . . . And then the lawless one will be revealed, and the Lord Jesus will slay him and destroy him by his appearing and his coming (i.e. *parousia*)' (II Thess. 2.3–4, 8).[56]

Jesus himself holds out no such promise of warnings or portents but says the very reverse: 'The kingdom of God is not coming with signs to be observed' (Luke 17.20). In other words, its hour is unknown; even he does not know it. It is God's secret (Mark 13.32; Matt. 24.36). He and his followers, inspired by faith and unaffected by the spirit of speculation, have entered the eschatological age and now perceive a fundamental difference between their own time and the preceding centuries. From the day when Jesus is moved by the Baptist's call to repentance, time for him is no longer time as we know it but has acquired a quality of finality. 'Repent, for the kingdom of heaven is at hand' (Matt. 4.17; Mark 1.15). The moment of his turning, his *teshuvah*, is the turning-point of his life, as it is of those who afterwards answer his own call to *teshuvah*, to turn back decisively and irrevocably to God. Making their choice, God's kingdom comes, and they enter in. A new era, or rather a new aeon, begins for them, which in Jesus' case manifests itself in powers of healing and powers of communication (sensed by the crowds flocking after him in their effort to storm the kingdom, in the picturesque idiom of the gospel). In the words of Matthew, 'From the days of John the Baptist until now, the kingdom of heaven has suffered violence and men of violence take it by force' (Matt. 11.12), a paradox which becomes more easily understandable in Luke's version: 'The law and the prophets were until John; since then, the kingdom of God is preached, and every one enters it violently' (Luke 16.16).[57]

If my interpretation of Jesus' eschatological mentality is valid, queries concerned with whether the kingdom had come, was on the way, or would come later, must be irrelevant. At issue in New Testament eschatology is the actual movement itself of turning back, of entering into the kingdom. It is in the surrender of the self to God's will that his sovereignty is realized on earth. Does this correspond accurately to Jesus' teaching? The Lord's Prayer, believed to summarize his authentic thought, seems to support such a reconstruction. Both the shorter (Lucan) and the longer (Matthean) recensions of the 'Our Father' give the petition, 'Thy kingdom come', Matthew following on immediately with the paraphrastic explanation: 'Thy will be done on earth as it is in heaven!' (Luke 11.2; Matt. 6.10).[58]

Despite the many references to God's kingdom in the gospels, there is, as I have said, surprisingly little use of royal imagery in Jesus' language. In particular, he nowhere alludes to, or addresses, God as King, a fact all the more remarkable in that, together with its synonym 'Lord', *adonai*, 'King' occurs frequently in ancient Jewish prayer and continues to do so to this day.[59] Jesus' only mention of God as 'Lord of heaven and earth' appears in a passage of dubious authenticity (Matt. 11.25; Luke 10.21).[60] In all but one of his other recorded prayers, and in his habitual speech, he uses 'Father'.

Father as a divine form has a long biblical and post-biblical history and has been studied extensively by scholars. I have myself dealt with it indirectly in *Jesus the Jew* in connection with the title, 'son of God'.[61] God is represented metaphorically in biblical and apocryphal literature as Father of the chosen people. 'I am a father to Israel and Ephraim is my first-born', declaims Jeremiah (Jer. 3.9). God is invoked as Father by the community, in the words of the Third Isaiah, 'Yet O Lord, thou art our Father . . . we are the work of thy hand' (Isa. 64.8). In the inter-testamental period, however, relation with the Father grows to be less of a privilege conferred on Israel as a people, and increasingly dependent on merit. It is those Jews whose hearts are circumcised who receive the divine promise, 'I will be their Father and they shall be my sons, and they shall be called the sons of the living God' (*Jub.* 1.24–25).[62] Kinship with the Father is accounted the privilege of the holy, and of people like the Qumran sectaries who regarded themselves as holy, and of those who suffered and died for their faith. Interpreting Ex. 20.6, 'those who love me and keep my commandments', Rabbi

Nathan, a second century AD sage, explains that the supreme proof
of devotion to God is total obedience, even to the sacrifice of one's
life. The martyr's wounds cause him to be loved by his 'Father who
is in heaven'.[63] A parallel version transmitted anonymously in
Leviticus Rabbah reads: 'I have done the will of *Abba* who is in
heaven' (*Lev. R.* 32.1). But this assurance of filial kinship was of
course applied *a fortiori* to the royal Messiah, as is particularly clear
from the Qumran explanation of the text, 'I will be his father and
he shall be my son' (II Sam. 7.14). Interpreted, so we are told, this
alludes to 'the Branch of David who shall arise . . . in Zion (at the
end) of time . . .' (*4QFlor* i, 11–12).[64]

Prayer in ancient Judaism is rich in invocations to God the Father.
In the Greek version of Ecclesiasticus, 'Father' is preceded by 'Lord'
and followed by 'Ruler' or 'God': 'O Lord, Father and Ruler (or
God) of my life' (Ecclus. 23.1, 4). Again, in the Greek text of III
Maccabees – a majestic roll-call of titles – 'O sovereign King, Most-
High, Almighty God' – ends with 'Father' (III Macc. 6.2–4). The
Hebrew Ben Sira imitates the simple biblical style: 'Thou art my
Father, for thou art the Hero of my salvation' (Ecclus. (Heb.) 51.10).
Similarly, 'Father' appears unaccompanied by other appellations in
the Greek Book of Wisdom, where a traveller preparing to set out
to sea in a ship, prays: 'It is thy providence, O Father, that is its
pilot' (Wisdom 14.3).

Where synagogal prayer is concerned, with its frequent use of
'Our Father', I must confess that it is not possible to prove that even
the earliest form extant represents anything actually current during
the age of Jesus. It may nevertheless be of interest to recall that,
according to the late Joseph Heinemann, author of the influential
Prayer in the Talmud, while most private and public prayer takes the
form of servant–master communication, a number of supplications
addressed to 'Our Father, our King' and to 'Our Father who art in
heaven', are likely to be 'based on very ancient models', possibly
originating in the Temple before AD 70.[65] The Palestinian version of
the Eighteen Benedictions, presumed to be the oldest recension of
these blessings, includes two petitions invoking the fatherhood of
God: 'Grant us, *our Father*, the knowledge (which comes) from
thee . . . Forgive us, *our Father*, for we have sinned against thee'.[66]

A word must finally be added relating to the prayer characteristic
of the ancient Hasidim.[67] According to the Mishnah, they were
accustomed to spend a full hour in recollection before they even
began to pray, 'in order to direct their hearts towards their Father

Hasidim / – saw God as Father

who is in heaven' (*mBer.* 5.1). And in the years of distress and misery following the destruction of the Second Temple, the saintly rabbi Eliezer ben Hyrcanus (around AD 100), and the Hasid, Pinhas ben Yair (second century), comfort themselves with: 'On whom can we rely now? On our Father who is in heaven' (*mSot.* 9.15; *bSot.* 49b).

Such is the literary and religious background against which I will now endeavour to reconstruct Jesus' own version of God the Father.

Beginning with his style, we shall concern ourselves in our final lecture with the implication of the varied *terminology*, 'my Father', 'your Father', 'our Father' and 'the Father'. For the present, we shall concentrate primarily on the *notions* 'Father' and 'heavenly Father', in passages recording his preaching and instructions, and on the invocation, 'Father!', which appears in nearly all of Jesus' prayers.[68]

The phrase, 'the Father who is in heaven', *ho patēr ho en (tois) ouranois*, or 'the heavenly Father', *ho patēr ho ouranios*, appears frequently in Matthew, once in Mark (Mark 11.25) and not at all in Luke, apart from the somewhat unusual expression, 'the Father from heaven', *ho patēr ho ex ouranou* (Luke 11.13). That Matthew's imputation to Jesus of this manner of addressing God may not always be genuine but his own invention, is perfectly possible,[69] bearing in mind that to his Judaeo-Christian readers such an idiom would be quite familiar. The substitution by Mark and Luke of 'God' for Matthew's 'Father', and 'Father in heaven', is best explained as an adaptation of Jesus' phraseology for the benefit of non-Jews, to whom the Semitic nomenclature would have seemed alien. For the same reason, Matthew's Hebrew-Aramaic 'kingdom of heaven' is replaced by the other two synoptics with the cosmopolitan 'kingdom of God'.[70]

Jesus' prayers present a different picture. With two exceptions, they use the short invocation, 'Father', the rendering, we can be reasonably sure, of Jesus' own Aramaic vocative, *abba*, which is itself preserved once in Mark (Mark 14.36) and in early Christian prayers cited by Paul (Rom. 8.15; Gal 4.6).[71]

Much has been written about the significance of the use by Jesus of the title *abba*, especially by Jeremias and his followers.[72] In the opinion of the late professor from Göttingen, this *ipsissima vox Jesu* is unparalleled in Jewish prayer. Compared with that of the ancient Jews, who, as one of Jeremias's pupils explains, 'maintained the dignity of God, in so far as they addressed him as Father at all, by scrupulously avoiding the particular form of the word used by children',[73] it is the 'chatter of a small child'.[74] Jeremias, that is to say, understood Jesus to have addressed God as 'Dad' or 'Daddy', but apart from the *a priori* improbability and incongruousness of the theory, there seems to be no linguistic support for it. Young children speaking Aramaic addressed their parents as *abba* or *imma* but it was not the only context in which *abba* would be employed. By the time of Jesus, the determined form of the noun, *abba* (= 'the father'), signified also 'my father'; '*my* father', though still attested in Qumran and biblical Aramaic,[75] had largely disappeared as an idiom from the Galilean dialect.[76] Again, *abba* could be used in solemn, far from childish, situations such as the fictional altercation between the patriarchs Judah and Joseph reported in the Palestinian Targum, when the furious Judah threatens the governor of Egypt (his unrecognized brother) saying: 'I swear by the life of the head of *abba* (= my father) as you swear by the life of the head of Pharaoh, your master, that if I draw my sword from the scabbard, I will not return it there until the land of Egypt is filled with the slain'.[77]

Jeremias's further thesis that since God is never called *abba* in ancient Jewish prayer, Jesus' usage of the title is unique, is also open to question. It would gain strength if he could point, first, to a representative sample of individual prayers in Aramaic and show that none of them include the vocative *abba*. But as far as I know, no such evidence exists. Second, it would help his argument if he could prove that the invocation was not part of the language of Hasidic piety. Here again, evidence is mostly lacking. To quote David Flusser: 'Jeremias could not find "Abba" used to address God in Talmudic literature; but considering the scarcity of rabbinic material on charismatic prayer, this does not tell us very much'.[78] We have, however, at least one indirect attestation in connection with the rain-maker Hanan, of the first century BC, the grandson of Honi the circle-drawer. Perhaps I should explain at this point that we know that a few holy men were given the honorific title of *abba*, the father.[79] Hanan was one of them, as was his cousin, Hilkiah. During one of the periodic droughts, when Hanan was chased by children in the street shouting, 'Abba, abba, give us rain!' his response was to entreat God to 'render service to those who cannot distinguish between the *abba* who gives rain and the *abba* who does not' (*bTaan.* 23b).[80]

So what do we find when we piece together the main features of God's form as Father as they emerge from the passages judged most likely to transmit Jesus' true teaching? Most of the texts derive, needless to say, from Matthew, but every dominant characteristic finds an echo in other sources also, with or without explicit mention of the word Father, and may be said to satisfy the authenticity criteria of multiple attestation and consistency.

As before, we have to return to the Lord's Prayer for a reliable insight into Jesus' mind. In the first half, he calls on God as Father, implying perhaps an individual supplication, or 'Our Father' suggesting communal prayer, and follows on in the pattern of the ancient hymn of praise, the *Kaddish*, which expresses the wish that God's Name may be sanctified and his sovereignty established.[81] The second half of the Lord's Prayer, in Luke and Matthew, is concerned to ask God to exercise the fatherly functions which are his attributes: to provide for essential needs, to forgive the repentant, to protect from evil. These are topics prominent in the remainder of the gospel material, in the teaching sections as well as in the parables. The Father knows the requirements of all his creatures, human, animal and vegetable, and bestows his paternal care on his 'little ones'.

To those whose instinctive reaction to this image is that it is an idealized dream having little in common with life as we know it, the reply is that Jesus seems to have been fully aware that all is not perfect in this world despite a heavenly Father who is perfect, generous, merciful. The fledgling falls from its nest (Matt. 10.29);[82] the little ones perish; the righteous suffer (Matt. 18.14; 5.10–11 par.). But as I have indicated earlier, Jesus propounded no syntheses. The unity and (illogical) logic of his teaching lies in the domain of subjectivity, in the inspiration and motivation of his religious action.

As I have suggested, he did not intend – and probably possessed no talent for it – to preach on God's nature and being as later theologians have done and continue to do. He tried to carry out his Father's will, to fall in with what he felt the Father demanded of him. And he taught his followers to devote themselves to the same task, irrespective of its outcome. The focus of his concern was not God as such, but himself, his disciples, and the world, in their relation to the Father in heaven and his kingdom.

Church's approach to Xist in conflict with historical evidence.

4

The Gospel of Jesus the Jew III
Jesus and Christianity

We are so accustomed, and rightly, to make Jesus the object of religion that we become apt to forget that in our earliest records he is portrayed not as the object of religion, but as a religious man.

These are not my words. They were written by the renowned New Testament scholar, Thomas William Manson.[1] But I could not have found a quotation better fitted to my theme. Whilst giving it his approval as a Christian, Manson understood that the church's general approach to Christ contains an ingredient in conflict with the best historical evidence.[2] My intention is to explore the gospels for that evidence and to piece it together so that, re-discerning the character of Jesus the religious man, we may subsequently contrast the essentials of his piety with the main spiritual thrust of the religion of which he has become the object. But we shall have first to enquire into the general religious climate of his place and time if we are to keep his particular contribution to it in perspective.[3]

In this larger setting, the notion of divine sovereignty, as we have seen in the discussion of the idea of the 'yoke of the kingdom', was associated and even interchangeable with, the 'yoke of the Law', the Torah.[4] Known in the Hebrew Bible as the Law of God or the Law of Moses,[5] it regulated every aspect of private and public existence – agriculture, trading and commerce, the choice and preparation of food, the intimacies of sexuality, and even occasionally the materials and styles of Jewish clothing. As a law-abiding person, Jesus may be presumed to have behaved in respect of these general rules and common customs like everyone else in Galilee.[6] Embracing the accepted way of everyday life, he will have conformed spontaneously to a number of biblical precepts. The gospels show him also complying with the laws regulating religious activities proper, participating in synagogue worship on the Sabbath (Mark 1.21; 6.2; Luke 4.16 etc.), visiting the Temple of Jerusalem as a pilgrim (Mark 11.15 par.), and celebrating the Passover (Mark 14.15–16 par.). Some scholars deduce from the references to the *kraspedon*, the hem or fringes of Jesus' robe, that he must have been a strict observer of the Torah,[7] but he may simply have dressed like his fellow-Galileans. If his own fringes or *ziziyoth* had been unusually long, he would hardly have been described as criticizing others for displaying them too ostentatiously (Matt. 23.5).[8]

More important, though still not particularly meaningful, is the selection Jesus makes of certain biblical commandments as summarizing the individual laws of the Old Testament. There was a general tendency among Jews in the early post-biblical centuries to discover a small number of all-inclusive precepts. The fullest illustration of this trend comes from Rabbi Simlai, a third century AD sage, who explains that all the six hundred and thirteen positive and negative commandments proclaimed by Moses were, according to David, contained in eleven (Ps. 15); according to Isaiah, in six (33.15); according to Micah, in three (to do justice, love mercy and walk humbly with God – Micah 6.8); according to Isaiah again, in two (to observe justice and do righteousness – Isa. 56.1); and according to Amos, in one alone, 'Seek me and live' (Amos 5.4).[9] Philo, Jesus' great Alexandrian Jewish contemporary, maintained that the Decalogue symbolizes all the 'special laws' of the Torah.[10] And when asked what must be done to inherit eternal life, Jesus merely recites from the Ten Commandments, 'Do not kill! Do not commit adultery! Do not steal!' etc. (Mark 10.19 par.)[11] Invited to reduce the many to one, he chooses the first or great commandment in its twofold aspect of love: 'You shall love the Lord your God . . . and your neighbour as yourself' (Mark 12.29–31 par.)[12] At the same time, when there is question of a comprehensive counsel of behaviour, his one-articled code – accredited also, though in a different form, to the great Hillel,[13] who may have been still alive when Jesus was born – explicitly prescribes the single duty, 'Whatever you wish that men should do to you, do so to them,' Matthew adding, 'For this is the Law and the Prophets' (Matt. 7.12; Luke 6.31)[14]

But has it not been asserted through the centuries that Jesus frees man from 'the curse of the Law',[15] that he substitutes for the Law a new dispensation of grace? Yes indeed, but in echo as we shall see

Jesus didn't offer a substitute 4 the law.

of the Diaspora Hellenist, Paul of Tarsus, not of the Galilean. He, as far as one may judge from reliable gospel evidence, excuses no neglect of the Law as such. Reminiscent of many a rabbinic dictum, his words as reported by Luke, himself a Greek addressing Gentiles, leave no room for doubt: 'It is easier for heaven and earth to pass away than for one tittle of the Law to fall' (Luke 16.17; Matt. 5.18).[16]

The controversial sayings attributed to Jesus in the gospels have to be considered against this faithfulness to the Torah. Some of the arguments turn on the interpretation of customs such as hand-washing before meals (Mark 7.15 par.);[17] others are associated with the Sabbath and its observance.[18] Jewish legal teaching – *halakhah* – was still in a fluid state in his time; the great endeavour of unification and definition resulting in so-called 'orthodoxy' was not made until after AD 70. He is admittedly often represented by New Testament exegetes, mostly on the basis of a gloss appended by Mark to a paradoxical question posed by Jesus, as having rejected the dietary laws.[19] 'Do you not see that nothing that goes from outside into a man can defile him?' Mark gives Jesus to enquire, adding as his own observation, 'Thus he declared all foods clean' (Mark 7.18–19).[20] But on reflection are we not bound to conclude *a priori* that in a Palestinian environment the abolition of all distinction between pure and impure food is almost inconceivable? Besides, what about the historically dependable claim in the Acts of the Apostles that Jesus' immediate followers found the very idea of touching forbidden food horrible and scandalous? (Acts 10.13–16). For them, as appears from Paul's angry criticism of Peter, Barnabas and other 'Judaizers', table-companionship even with Gentile Christians was intolerable and shameful (Gal. 2.11–14). The Marcan comment will have catered for non-Jewish members of the church unprepared to be bothered with such rules.

Again, the gospels themselves often involve Jesus in polemics over observance of the Sabbath.[21] Here, the main point to remember is that in Judaism the saving of life overrides the Sabbath laws.[22] During the bloody Hadrianic persecution, a hundred years after the time of Jesus, the rabbis recognized it as taking precedence of *all* laws with the exception of idolatry, incest and murder. The text from Leviticus 18.5, 'You shall keep my statutes . . . by which a man shall live', was interpreted to mean that observance of the Torah should not lead to death.[23] In the case of Jesus' Sabbath debates, where the subject at issue is almost always the healing of the sick, the principle emerging from them appears to be that every cure, great or small, is life-saving.[24] The restoration to health of a man with a paralysed hand is as serious as deliverance from death and as cogent a justification for infringing the Sabbath (Matt. 12.9–14; Luke 14.1–6)[25] – if, that is to say, such justification is necessary where the cure is performed by word of mouth and without any accompanying 'work' such as carrying or administering medicines.

Jesus, I would add, not only submits personally to the legal obligations incumbent on a Jew; he more than once expressly urges obedience to the purely ritual and cultic precepts in sayings all the more historically credible in that they are peripheral to the gospel narrative and actually run counter to the essential antinomianism of Gentile Christianity. After curing several lepers, he orders them to report to the priests and to perform the ceremony prescribed by Moses (Mark 1.44 par.; Luke 17.14; cf. Lev. 14.1–32). He approves of sending gifts to the Temple (Matt. 5.33) and of the tithing laws, which will of course have been far from popular among the Galilean rural communities (Matt. 23.23; Luke 11.42). He is even depicted, though I doubt the authenticity of the actual statement, as giving support to the theory, if not the practice, of Pharisee legal teaching.[26]

Where the Law is concerned, the chief distinction of Jesus' piety lies in his extraordinary emphasis on the real inner religious significance of the commandments. Needless to say, he was not the only Jewish teacher to insist on symbolism, inwardness and sincerity. Philo and Josephus did the same.[27] So did many of the rabbis,[28] and the Qumran sectaries.[29] But I believe it is true to say that interiority, purity of intention, played a greater part in Jesus' thought, possibly because of his stress on eschatological finality which we discussed in the previous chapter, but also because of his natural bias towards the invididual and personal rather than the collective.[30] He tends in any case to lay a heavy, and sometimes almost exaggerated, accent on the primary causes and ultimate aim of the religious or irreligious act. Murder has its roots in anger;[31] adultery in the lustful gaze.[32] His followers must therefore avoid the lesser faults as scrupulously as they would shun the greater. Similarly, he clearly regards the ritual impurity contracted through transgressing the dietary laws as insignificant compared with the uncleanness of 'fornication, theft, murder, adultery . . . envy, slander, pride, foolishness' (Mark 7.14–23; Matt. 15.10–20). Jesus' teaching is that it is excretion that defiles, not ingestion, and that nothing defiles more foully than the excretion of the wicked heart with its evil thoughts.

Exactly the same principle underlies Jesus' attitude to almsgiving, prayer and fasting. They stand or fall as religious acts in proportion to the integrity with which they are performed. Charitable gifts must be made in secret, without witnesses. Prayer is to be offered in private, not aloud in the streets or in the synagogue. Fasting is to be undertaken with a smiling face, before God alone.[33] Jesus' religious deed was done, in other words, in accordance with Jewish religious Law and laws, but was invested with an added dimension of effectiveness and power, not through elaboration of casuistical detail, but through his genial perception of the Law's inmost significance, its original purpose: namely, to serve as a vehicle for authentic lived relation with God the Father, God the King.[34]

Before examining the concrete manifestations of this God/man-father/son relation as it is attested in the synoptic gospels, brief mention must be made of a few fragmentary statements somewhat theoretical in their attitude *vis-à-vis* God. They may all ultimately derive from the primitive church, but more probably are in part representative of Jesus' thought, and in part ecclesiastical formulations.

The first is the celebrated thanksgiving recorded in Matthew and Luke: 'All things have been delivered to me by my Father; and no-one knows who the son is except the Father, or who the Father is, except the son, and anyone to whom the son chooses to reveal him' (Matt. 11.27; Luke 10.22).[35] Whether the idea of revelation contained in this text reflects a Hellenistic milieu, as Bultmann has suggested,[36] or an Aramaic wisdom-school,[37] or whether it is akin to the sort of knowledge-speculation found in the Dead Sea Scrolls,[38] is secondary and almost immaterial compared with the fundamental concept, expressed by the evangelists with great perspicuity, of an ideal reciprocity between Father and son. This reciprocity, it must be stressed, is not equality. It is a remarkable fact that the Father's superiority remains impregnable even in face of the church's editorial intervention. The *panta*, all things, revealed to Jesus by the Father do not include that most crucial knowledge, a knowledge of the end-time. Of that day and hour, it is said, 'no one knows, not even the angels in heaven, nor the son, but only the Father' (Mark 13.32; Matt. 24.36).[39]

This passage, despite the dubious authenticity of the eschatological discourse into which it is inserted, is the more likely to be genuine in that it conflicts with later church doctrine that Christ was endowed with perfect wisdom. Similarly, when the two ambitious apostles, James and John, wish to secure for themselves the best places in the kingdom, they are told: 'To sit at my right hand and at my left is not mine to grant, but it is for those for whom it has been prepared by my Father' (Matt. 20.23; Mark 10.40).[40]

As I have said, these apparently dogmatic statements about God must not be allowed to mislead. It was not Jesus' habit to theorize about the divine. His preoccupation was with enacting to perfection, in his own person, the role of son of his Father in heaven, and with teaching his followers to live likewise. 'Ask,' he instructs them, 'and it shall be given you; seek and you shall find; knock and it shall be opened to you.' Would any of them, entreated by their children for bread, give them a stone? Or a snake instead of some fish? 'If you, then, who are evil, know how to give good gifts to your children, how much more will your Father who is in heaven give good things to those who ask him?' (Matt. 7.7–11; Luke 11.9–13).[41] And even this occasional 'asking' is not enough; God's children have to implore their Father daily for the day's needs (Matt. 6.11; Luke 11.3).[42] They must *pester* him like little children until he grants them their desire. Adopting another metaphor, they must be like the man who woke his friend in the middle of the night and importuned him until he arose from his bed and lent him three loaves of bread so that he could feed an unexpected visitor (Luke 11.5–8).[43]

The total simplicity and confidence required of the child of God as Jesus represents him is the biblical *emunah* (faith/trust), the virtue which, according to Martin Buber, Jesus and the prophets possessed in common.[44] It may also point to an inheritance from ancient Hasidism, where the same spirit prevailed. The first-century BC charismatic, Honi (or Onias the Righteous, as Flavius Josephus names him),[45] is famous for his petulant threat that he would not step outside the circle which he had drawn around himself until God showed mercy to his children and ended the long season of drought. Honi's behaviour is said to have provoked Simeon ben Shetah, the leading Pharisee of that time, to comment resentfully: 'If you were not Honi, I would excommunicate you. But what can I do with you, for in spite of your importunity, God does what you want?' (*mTaan*. 3.8).[46] The rabbis were sticklers for correct behaviour and disapproved of temerity such as Honi's; but they were compelled to confess that it sometimes worked. '*Huzpa*', impertinence, 'has its usefulness even towards heaven,' reads the Talmud (*bSanh*. 105a).[47] It is *emunah* that Jesus teaches when he recommends that the child of God should lay aside material and temporal anxieties and commit itself wholly to the care of the Father in heaven. 'Do not be anxious about your life', the Galilean urges; 'what you shall eat . . ., nor about your body, what you shall put on . . . Look at the birds of the air: they neither sow nor reap nor gather into barns, and yet your heavenly Father feeds them. Are you not of more value than they? . . . And why are you anxious about your clothing? Consider the lilies of the field, how they grow; they neither toil, nor spin; yet I tell you, even Solomon in all his glory was not arrayed like one of these . . . Therefore do not be anxious, saying, "What shall we eat?" or "What shall we drink?" or "What shall we wear?" . . . Your heavenly Father knows that you need them all'.[48] And Jesus asks further: 'Are not two small birds sold for an *assarion* (or five for two *assaria*, according to Luke) and not one of them shall fall to the ground without your Father's will . . . Fear not therefore; you are of more value than many sparrows' (Matt. 10.29–31; Luke 12.6–7).

As might be expected, the counterpart of the sort of unconditional surrender to divine providence demanded of his followers by Jesus is a condemnation and rejection of man-made plans and projects, long-term and short. The futility of trying to depend on, and provide for, the future, is illustrated in the parable of the rich landowner who, with a good harvest in view, plans to pull down his barns and replace them with larger ones with the idea of ensuring much food, drink and merriment for years to come. But Jesus exclaims, 'Fool! Tonight your soul is required of you; and the things you have prepared, whose will they be?' (Luke 12.16–20)[49] Even where the immediate future is concerned, his thought extends no further than to the requirements of the day, to the '*daily* bread' (Matt. 6.11; Luke 11.13). Directly and explicitly, his counsel in the Sermon on the Mount is, 'Do not be anxious about tomorrow, for tomorrow will be anxious for itself. Let the day's own trouble be sufficient for the day' (Matt. 6.34).[50] Jesus was a man for whom the present, the here and now, was of unique and infinite importance.

It may be this exclusive concentration on the religious task immediately facing him, inspired by an 'enthusiasm (born) of eschatological presence', to borrow again from Martin Buber,[51] that accounts for Jesus' total lack of interest in the economic and political realities of his age. He was not a social reformer or nationalistic revolutionary, notwithstanding recent claims to the contrary.[52] Nor, provocative though it may appear to say so, did the urgency of his religious vision allow any place for founding, organizing and *extinction of Parousa led to Xianity.*

endowing with permanency an ecclesiastical body of any sort.[53] It was rather the extinction of the *parousia* hope, cultivated in self-contained primitive Christian communities, that conferred durability on a fabric intended by the apostles and the first disciples to last for no longer than a brief span.

In parenthesis, I would once again point out that foresight, far-sightedness, make better sense in the context of an expectation of a second coming, or where the spirit of eschatological presence has died away, than in the thought of Jesus.[54] The parable of the 'wise' virgins – supposedly wise, but to my mind cunning and selfish – reflects an insistence on the part of the church to be constantly ready; it contributes nothing to an active participation in the work for the kingdom of God. The young women, foreseeing that the bridegroom may be late, bring with them a good supply of oil for their lamps. But they refuse to share it with their 'foolish' friends. They send them off to find dealers at midnight. And by the time they return, the gate is closed. When they ask to be admitted, no one complies (Matt. 25.1–13). Did Matthew or his later editor not realize that this parable is a travesty of Jesus' teachings on generosity and confident prayer contained in the same gospel?[55]

Compared with the kingdom and its coming and the affairs of the heavenly Father, everything temporal is of secondary importance. All that matters is action, *now*. There must be no procrastination, no dawdling: 'The kingdom of God is at hand' (Mark 1.15; Matt. 4.17). The disciple must follow the teacher's call, at once. He must not ask for permission to bid farewell to his family; no man 'who puts his hand to the plough and looks back is fit for the kingdom of God' (Luke 9.61–62).[56] He must not return to bury his father (Matt. 8.21–22; Luke 9.59–60). 'Leave the dead to bury their dead', is the paradoxical command.[57] Solemn family ties must take second place to the bond uniting those who do God's will. As Jesus remarks of his waiting relations, 'Who are my mother and my brothers? . . . Whoever does the will of God is my brother, and sister and mother' (Mark 3.33–34).

Two important parables adumbrate the single-minded devotion to the cause of the Father which Jesus promoted and the prompt and decisive action which he required of those who seek to enter the kingdom. In the first, where it is compared to a treasure discovered in a field, the finder covers it over and 'then in joy he goes and sells all he has and buys that field' (Matt. 13.44).[58] In the second, where it is compared to a pearl of great value, a merchant of pearls, noticing it, 'went and sold all that he had and bought it' (Matt. 13.45–46). In both parables, the lesson is identical. When the truth is encountered, a choice has to be made, a decision, and it must be acted on immediately, whole-heartedly. And a price must be paid, one amounting to all that one has.[59]

Now that we know something of the workings of Jesus' mind, of the pressures to which he subjected it, and of the values on which he laid the greatest stress, one fundamental question forms itself: what in the last resort was the principle that he adopted, and himself embodied, in his endeavours to live to perfection as a son of God? The reply must be that it was the principle, well attested in Judaism, biblical and post-biblical, of the *imitatio dei*, the imitation of God. 'You shall be holy, for I the Lord, your God, am holy' (Lev. 19.2).

Rabbinic thought is rich in interpretation of this theme that the lover and worshipper of God models himself on him.[60] Confronted with the verse, 'This is my God, and I will praise him,' *zeh 'eli we'anwehu* (Ex. 15.2), the second-century sage, Abba Shaul, reads instead, *zeh 'eli 'ani wa-hu*, 'This is my God, I and He,' expounding the last clause as, 'O be like Him! As He is merciful and gracious, you also must be merciful and gracious.'[61] Similarly, but entering into more detail, an anonymous exegete comments apropos of the words of Deuteronomy 10.12, 'that you may walk in His ways': 'These are the ways of God, "The Lord, a God merciful and gracious . . ." (Ex. 34.6). "All who are called by the name of the Lord shall be delivered" (Joel 3.5 (ET 2.32)). How can a man be called by the name of God? As God is called merciful, you too must be merciful. The Holy One blessed be He is called gracious, so you too must be gracious . . . and give presents freely. God is called righteous . . . so you too must be righteous. God is called *hasid* (loving, devoted) . . . so you too must be *hasid*' (*Sifre* on Deut. 11.22(49)). But one of the most succinct renderings of this doctrine of the *imitatio dei* is given in an Aramaic paraphrase of Leviticus: 'My people, children of Israel, as your Father is merciful in heaven, so you must be merciful on earth' (*Targum Ps.-Jonathan* on Lev. 22.28).[62]

Jesus proclaims the same basic teachings: 'Be merciful as your Father is merciful' (Luke 6.36). 'Be perfect as your heavenly Father is perfect' (Matt. 5.48), but, as I have indicated earlier, injects them with his own extra dimension of integrity and inwardness. Perfect filial behaviour *vis-à-vis* the Father must show itself not simply in mercy and love towards others, but in a mercy and love that expects no return. 'You received without paying, give without payment', he says (Matt. 10.8; cf. II Cor. 11.7). On another occasion, he speaks more forcefully still. 'When you give a dinner or a banquet, do not invite your friends or your brothers or your kinsmen or rich neighbours, lest they also invite you in return, and you be repaid. But when you give a feast, invite the poor, the maimed, the lame and the blind, and you will be blessed, because they cannot repay you' (Luke 14.12–14).[63]

This is his usual custom: to opt for a maximum of exaggeration in order to underline what he is attempting to convey. No teaching exemplifies this better than the command to his disciples to love their enemies.[64] The saying has been the source of much misunderstanding and misinterpretation for there is no denying that to love persons motivated by hatred of oneself, or who subject one to abuse and persecution, must seem unnatural and humanly impossible. But Jesus' words are no more to be taken literally than in that other text requiring the would-be follower to hate his father, mother, wife, children, brothers and sisters (Luke 14.26),[65] or than his instruction to his disciples, 'To him who strikes you on the cheek, offer the other also' (Luke 6.29; Matt. 5.39).[66] The independent Passion narrative of the Fourth Gospel in no ways bears out this last piece of advice. When an over-zealous policeman slaps his face, Jesus does not turn the other cheek but protests with dignity, 'If I have spoken wrongly, bear witness to the wrong, but if I have spoken rightly, why do you strike me'? (John 18.24). The commandment to love one's enemies is as it were an overstatement intended to impress on his hearers that the perfect manifestation of love is to offer it quite freely, gratis. 'Love your enemies, do good to those who hate you, bless those who curse you, pray for those who abuse you . . . If you love those who love you, what credit is that to you . . .? And if you lend to those from whom you expect to receive, what credit is that to you . . .? But love your enemies, and do good and lend, expecting nothing in return . . . and you shall be sons of the Most High' (Luke 6.27–35; Matt. 5.39–45) – 'sons of your Father who is in heaven' (Matt. 5.45).

Jesus' religiousness, the piety peculiar to Jesus the religious man, is marked by a tendency to give more than is asked for, to probe deeper than expected, to risk more than is safe. The 'neighbours' he is to love as himself often turn out to be the outcasts of society, whose company he does not merely accept (Luke 15.1) but positively seeks. Unlike the pious of his day, and of later times, he enters their houses and eats with them (Mark 2.15 par.). He even – scandal of scandals – allows a woman sinner, a prostitute, to dry his feet with her hair, kiss them and anoint him (Luke 7.37–38). He treats them as friends; hence the sarcastic nickname conferred on him by his critics – 'friend of tax-collectors and sinners' (Matt. 11.19; Luke 7.34).[67] But his behaviour should cause no surprise. He is simply imitating in his personal conduct what he understands to be the conduct of the Father towards those of his children who return to relation with him from a state of irrelation. 'There will be', he maintains, 'more joy in heaven over one sinner who repents than over ninety-nine just' (Luke 15.7).

Turning now to Christian religion and religiousness as distinct from the religiousness and religion of Jesus, I am aware that for the vast majority of Christians – and many Jews for that matter – the very statement that Jesus and Christianity are to be differentiated from one another will come as a shock, a total surprise.[68] Present-day Christians are in the main wholly innocent of the gulf dividing their aims and beliefs from his. Even the learned C. H. Dodd assumed, as is apparent from the title of his last highly influential little book, that Jesus actually established Christianity.[69]

Permit me now to reduce to its essentials my exposition of the gospel of Jesus the Jew and to set alongside it a basic sketch of Christianity almost exclusively with the help of the doctrine on which it rests: the teaching of Paul, the true creator in the opinion of many non-Christian historians of the institutional, ecclesiastical religious body, professing a creed centred on the death and resurrection of the Messiah, known as Christianity.[70]

The first marked dissimilarity lies in the Jewishness of Jesus, his environment, his way of life, his purpose. It is a Jewishness that sometimes amounts to downright chauvinism, as is manifest in the unflattering epithets which the blunt Galilean lets fly against non-Jews. 'Dogs', he observes of them, 'dogs' not fit to eat the bread belonging to the children (Mark 7.27; Matt. 15.26)[71] or to be given a 'holy thing' (Matt. 7.6);[72] 'swine', on which his apostles are not to waste the pearls of their teaching (Matt. 7.6).[73] Do not trouble yourselves with them, he explicitly enjoins on another occasion. 'Go nowhere among the Gentiles . . . but rather to the lost sheep of the house of Israel' (Matt. 10.5–6; 15.24).[74] However did the evangelists manage to record such sayings as these, and at the same time attribute to Jesus the view that the Gentiles were soon to displace

Anti-Gentile bits added later to fit circumstance [handwritten annotation]

'the sons of the kingdom', the Jews, as the elect of God? (Matt. 8.11–12; Luke 13.28–29).[75]

I would suggest that once Paul was acknowledged 'apostle to the Gentiles' (Acts 9.15; Rom. 11.13) and a specifically Gentile mission sanctioned by the church leadership came into being (Acts 15), the original bias of Jesus' ministry suffered a radical transformation. Gentiles in substantial numbers joined the ranks of the church and, following the model of proselytization in Judaism (flourishing in those days), it did its best to comply with the needs of the new situation and to adjust itself to altered circumstances. Moreover, Paul's pronouncement that the Christian communities now formed the 'Israel of God' (Gal. 6.16)[76] will have neutralized the sting of the insults so oddly preserved in the gospel text. The Gentile followers of Jesus, advised to consider themselves henceforth as 'neither Jew nor Greek' (Gal. 3.28), will have been persuaded that it was not they who were the target of their Lord's contempt.

It is possible, incidentally, to argue that an element of universalism is not absent from the inner logic of Jesus' teaching. It may be detected for example in the commandment to love one's enemies, which implies that they are fellow-creatures under the one God to whom charity must be shown, in imitation of the Father of all, who cares for all (Matt. 5.43–48; Luke 6.27–28, 32–36).

Another enormous change arising from the transplantation of the Christian movement into Gentile soil, one that affected its very nature, was that, despite Jesus' injunctions to the contrary, the Torah, the source of his inspiration and the discipline ruling his religious life, was declared by the church to be not merely optional but revoked, abolished, superseded. The Law which he had understood with such simplicity and profundity, and carried out with such integrity in accordance with what he saw to be its inmost truth, was judged by Paul to be in practice an instrument of sin and death. 'Christ', he declared 'is the end of the Law' (Rom. 10.4).[77]

Nevertheless, if Jesus and Christianity seem to stand worlds apart on this issue, neither Paul nor the later church pushed antinomianism so far as to apply it to the ethical sphere. There is no denying that the heart of Jesus' message, with its stress on interiority and supererogation, was heard by the early church and has remained intrinsic to the ideal of individual Christian piety: an ideal on which organized public ecclesiastical piety in its various manifestations has acted as a brake and corrective.

Whereby we arrive at one more radical distinction. The life-blood

Rad distinction was eschatological urgency [handwritten annotation]

of Jesus' mission was, as I have explained, eschatological urgency.[78] He believed and taught that the kingdom of God was actually, at that time, in the process of coming into being, and that it would be fully established in the immediate future. As we know, this did not happen. The eagerness and excitement then transferred itself to hope in a second advent of Christ. But once again, it did not happen. He did not come. The resulting emptiness needing therefore to be made good, a corporate body took shape as a quasi-permanent substitute kingdom which was to serve as a repository of religion until the glorious return of Christ the King at the end of days.

And what happened to Jesus' imitation of God within the frame-work of this institutional church? Primitive Christianity was certainly conscious of it and promulgated it as a rule to be followed. 'Be imitators of God as beloved children', Paul writes to the Ephesians (Eph. 5.1). And yet it was this same Paul who was responsible for giving the unprecedented twist to the *imitatio dei* which opened up a great divide between Judaism and Christianity: 'Be imitators of me as I am of Christ' (I Cor. 11.1). With these words, Paul, deviating from the Jewish imitation of God, introduced intermediaries between the imitator and his ultimate divine model. First of all imitate me: who am an imitator of Jesus: who imitated God. Thus originated the trend, still conspicuous in the more ancient forms of Christianity, to multiply mediators and intercessors between the faithful and God: Jesus, Paul, Mary the mother of Jesus, the martyrs, the saints.

This question of intermediaries brings us in effect to the crux of the problem: that the example of Jesus' *hasiduth*, his *theocentric* devoutness, has been overlaid by the ramifications of Paul's *christo-centric* spirituality. His opinion of human nature, unlike that of Jesus, was deeply pessimistic. In his view, man is sinful, incapable of obeying God, potentially damned, and lost without the saving grace of Christ's atoning death.[79] Christ's sacrificial blood is essential to the cleansing of his sins. Except for the redemption obtained by Christ's passion and resurrection, he can never draw close to God. God 'sent forth his son . . . born under the law, to redeem those who were under the law, so that we might receive adoption as sons' (Gal. 4.4–5).[80] With increasing vehemence, in other words, the religiosity of primitive Christianity became trained on the Mediator in place of God. Prayers continued to be addressed to the Father, but more and more frequently to 'the Father of our Lord Jesus Christ' (Rom. 15.6; II Cor. 1.3; 11.31 etc.). Little by little, the Christ of Pauline theology and his Gentile church took over from the holy man of Galilee. Subject to God, but already enthroned at his side (I Cor. 15.28; Rom. 8.34; Eph. 1.20; Col. 3.1 etc.), he then – no doubt in response to the needs and hopes of non-Jewish Christianity – imperceptibly grew to be the 'image of God' (II Cor. 4.4), the 'effulgence of God's glory and the stamp of his nature' (Heb. 1.3), and finally, the equal of God.[81] 'I bid you', writes Ignatius bishop of Antioch to Polycarp bishop of Smyrna, in the first decade of the second century, 'I bid you farewell always in our God Jesus Christ' (*Epistle to Polycarp*, ch. 8).

And the real Jesus? For there was a real Jesus, without any doubt.

Over the space of months, or perhaps even of two or three years, this Jesus of flesh and blood was seen and heard around the countryside of Galilee and in Jerusalem, an uncompromising, single-minded lover of God and his fellow-beings, convinced that by means of his example and teaching he could infect them with his own passionate sense of relation with the Father in heaven. And he did so. The magnetism of this real Jesus was such that not even the shame and humiliation of the cross, and not even the collapse of his ministry, could extinguish the faith of the men and women of his company. But it is a long time now since he was thought of. Very many ages have passed since the simple Jewish person of the gospels stepped back and gave way to the rich and majestic figure of the church's Christ.

Yet it occurs to the historian, as he reaches the end of his presentation of the gospel of Jesus the Jew, that the world may not have heard the last of the holy Galilean. In this so-called post-Christian era, when Christ as a divine form seems to ever-increasing numbers not to correspond, either to the age's notion of reality, or to the exigencies of the contemporary human predicament, is it not possible that Jesus the healer, teacher and helper may yet be invited to emerge from the shadows of his long exile? And not by Christians alone? If, above all, his lesson on reciprocal, loving and direct relation with the Father in heaven is recalled and found universally valid, may not the sons of God on earth stand a better chance of ensuring that the ideal of human brotherhood becomes something more than a pipe-dream?

5

Jewish Studies and New Testament Interpretation

In the mid-1970s, a biblical expert of international repute described an applicant for a university post as one 'among the few New Testament scholars who can take seriously and walk sure-footedly in the Semitic material to the importance of which we all pay lip-service'. This phrase contains a dreadful admission. Apparently the majority of present-day New Testament specialists are unable to 'take seriously and walk sure-footedly in' the languages and literature which form the Jewish background to the New Testament, even though they concede the usefulness to their subject of 'Semitic material', and 'pay lip-service' to its importance.

This is a strange situation, and to clarify it I will have to devote a good deal of this chapter to a historical survey of the attitude of New Testament interpreters to Jewish religious literature written between 200 BC and AD 400 thought capable of throwing light on the text of the gospels and on other documents of the Christian canon. Today the connection between these two literary corpuses is accepted without demur. It is, I am sure, no surprise to you, as it was to many readers of the great German biblical scholar Julius Wellhausen, at the beginning of this century, to hear that Jesus was not a Christian but a Jew;[1] that with the exception of Luke, all the known New Testament writers, and all the contemporary followers of Jesus, were Jews; and that consequently the exploration of the Jewish world must be relevant, to say the very least, to the study of the New Testament.

In the past, Christian tradition developed a different view. From the conflict recorded in the gospels between Jesus and some of his fellow-countrymen, and from the ultimate failure of the apostles' preaching among Palestinian Jews, it began, from the end of the first century AD onwards, to portray Jesus as an opponent of Judaism.

The Gentile church, already divorced from Israel, saw in all the Jews stood for something fundamentally hostile to Christianity. In such circumstances of heated controversy, it simply never occurred to anyone that familiarity with Judaism could assist the Christian exegete of the New Testament.[2] On the contrary, any recognition of Judaism as not being totally alien to Christianity would have appeared to most church fathers as gross disloyalty to their faith.

This is not to imply that the church in late antiquity was unaware that the Jews were especially expert in biblical matters, but it saw this knowledge as limited to questions pertaining to the Old Testament. In fact, two of the greatest Christian scripture interpreters, Origen of Alexandria in the first half of the third century, and Jerome in the late fourth to early fifth century, are known to have studied with Jews and consulted them on problematic issues.[3] (Jerome even complains that one of his Hebrew masters, a rabbi from Lydda, was charging an exorbitant fee for his lessons on Job![4]) But as far as the New Testament was concerned, the acceptable Jewish contribution seems to have been confined to points of antiquarian interest. Commenting on the mention in Matt. 23.5 that the Pharisees wore broad phylacteries, Jerome explains that these were leather strips attached to the forehead and inscribed with the words of the Ten Commandments, a custom no longer practised in Palestine in his own time, but still prevalent among the Babylonian teachers.[5]

Throughout the whole patristic period, and even more so during the Middle Ages, Jewish–Christian relations in the field of Bible studies continued to be marked by polemics and apologetics. On the one hand, Christian teachers, largely ignorant of the Hebrew language, but helped especially in Spain by educated Jewish converts, insisted in their writings, as well as in public debate, that not only the Old Testament, but even the post-biblical writings of the synagogue, prove the divine truth of the church's teaching. The Jews, they maintained, were simply obdurate. On the other hand, learned mediaeval rabbis found no great difficulty in picking holes in the Christian argument or in demonstrating that Hebrew scriptural proof-texts were wrongly interpreted in the Latin Vulgate used by their opponents, who also misunderstood the sayings of the Talmud or failed to place a particular excerpt into its proper context. Needless to say, the style of the exchanges was neither detached, objective, nor for that matter edifying.[6] Look at the titles. *Pugio fidei*, 'Dagger of Faith'. The work of a thirteenth-century Dominican, this seeks to destroy Judaism.[7] In the opposite camp, Jewish polemicists of the Middle Ages, equally aggressive, set out to defend Judaism through *Milḥamot ha-Shem*, 'The Wars of the Lord', or *Magen wa-Romaḥ*, 'Shield and Spear'.[8] The best known collection of anti-Christian Jewish literature (edited, need I add, by a Christian) bears the title *Tela ignea Satanae*, 'The Fiery Darts of Satan'[9] – and *not*, as a renowned Jewish historian translates it, 'Satan's Fiery Tail'.[10]

A quasi- 'scientific' use of post-biblical Judaica in New Testament interpretation did not appear until the middle of the seventeenth century. Its birthplace was England. One of the earliest publications of this sort came from the pen of a Yorkshire clergyman and Cambridge MA, Christopher Cartwright (1602–58), whose *Mellificium Hebraicum*, 'Hebrew Honey-making', was printed in London in 1660. It consists of five books, the second and third of which contain various New Testament passages followed by copious extracts from post-biblical Jewish documents. But this work was outshone by that of John Lightfoot (1603–75), *Horae Hebraicae et Talmudicae*, published in Leipzig between 1658 and 1674 (with posthumously edited supplements in 1678). Like Cartwright, Lightfoot, who was Master of St Catherine's College, Cambridge, selected New Testament texts and attempted to expound them with the help of rabbinic quotations. This is how he outlines his project in the preface to his section on the Gospel of Matthew:

> . . . I have . . . concluded without the slightest hesitation that the best method to unravel the meaning of the many obscure passages of the New Testament is through research into the significance of the sayings in question in the ordinary dialect and way of thinking of the Jews . . . And this can be investigated only by means of consulting the authors of the Talmud.

These words, written in Latin three hundred and twenty years ago, sound extraordinarily modern and would be largely approved today. Their message is this: Study Rabbinics and you will acquire competence in New Testament exegesis! In a very learned manner, Lightfoot showed how this should be done, producing Talmudic parallels to the four gospels, the Acts of the Apostles, Romans and I Corinthians. But death prevented him in 1675 from completing his task. It was achieved a few decades later by Christian Schoettgen. (Perhaps I should mention that this kind of scholarship left these islands in the eighteenth century and migrated to the continent, to Holland and mainly to Germany.) Schoettgen issued in turn another

Latin volume, *Horae Hebraicae et Talmudicae* (Dresden-Leipzig 1733), the title borrowed from Lightfoot, but offering a commentary to the whole New Testament (*in universum Novum Testamentum*).

By the middle of the eighteenth century, a further step was made towards integrating Judaism into New Testament exegesis on a high scientific level. Johann Jacob Wettstein (1693–1754), a native of Basle and professor in Amsterdam, published in 1751/2 a new critical edition of the Greek New Testament, containing more textual variants than any of the previous editions, but also a commentary from ancient literature, including that of the rabbis.[11] This meant that a student of the Greek Testament now had before him a rich collection of Talmudic illustrations, and was no longer obliged to turn to the separate specialist treatises of Lightfoot and Schoettgen. Throughout the second half of the eighteenth, and most of the nineteenth century, Wettstein exercised a profound influence on New Testament exegesis. Indeed, as recently as 1913, a somewhat naive Oxford divine described the work in the following terms: 'So valuable is the amount of illustrative material . . . that those who know the commentary best would not hesitate to place it first among all that ever one man has produced.'[12] And a witty American expert, George Foot Moore, remarked that the rabbinic quotations printed by Wettstein 'passed into a secondary tradition which in the course of repetition has forgotten its origins'.[13]

The nineteenth century yielded no similar compendia, but that golden age of biblical criticism saw great progress in two other domains. First, the so-called Pseudepigrapha, i.e., Jewish writings produced during the inter-testamental period, influential in their time but not raised to the dignity of Holy Scripture, were ranked with rabbinic literature as auxiliaries for New Testament interpretation. Also, the full text, surviving only in Ethiopic, of two outstanding compositions belonging to this category, the Book of Enoch and the Book of Jubilees, were first published in 1838 and 1859, respectively.[14] But where the nineteenth century excelled above all, was in offering the scholarly world major syntheses in the form of comprehensive handbooks. Let me single out Emil Schürer's *Jewish History* from the age of the Maccabees in the second century BC to the second Jewish war against Rome under Hadrian in AD 132–35.[15] This tremendous undertaking gives a masterly account of the political events, institutions and literature, though only a very limited sketch of the Jewish religion, during the centuries crucial to an understanding of the New Testament. The other significant manual, in my short-list of two, is Ferdinand Weber's *Jewish Theology*, the first modern attempt at an orderly presentation of the rabbis' unsystematic utterances on belief and practice.[16] These works, instead of offering incidental assistance to the New Testament exegete, were intended to serve as constant guides and were warmly welcomed and used with enthusiasm.

The first half of the twentieth century contributed three further reference works to help the New Testament scholars in their occasional forays among the maze of post-biblical Jewish writings. Two appeared in full, and the third in part, before the end of the Second World War. (I consider 1945 as the closing year of that *ancien régime* which started in the first century AD.) The first of these monuments is the collected and annotated edition of the Pseudepigrapha, in German by Emil Kautzsch,[17] and in English by R. H. Charles.[18] The other two indispensable companions of the New Testament interpreter opened to him the contents of *Spätjudentum*, or early post-biblical Judaism. All he needed was familiarity with Greek, a smattering of Hebrew, and a full knowledge of German.[19]

In 1906, the Lutheran pastor, Paul Billerbeck, with the nominal co-operation of the Protestant orientalist and theologian, Hermann Strack, embarked on compiling a large-scale *Commentary to the New Testament from Talmud and Midrash*. It was published in four fat volumes between 1922 and 1928.[20] This *Kommentar* is a modernized and much enlarged Lightfoot, set out in the order of the books of the New Testament, and supplies, wherever Billerbeck judges necessary, illustrative parallels mainly from the Mishnah, Tosefta, Talmud and Midrash – but also from the Pseudepigrapha. Unlike Lightfoot, Billerbeck tries to provide in his presentation of the evidence a semblance of historicity, adding, when possible, supposed dates to the names of the (presumed) rabbinic authors. There are substantial excursuses on special topics, but the literary sources are nowhere subjected to any critical analysis.

Shortly after the completion of Billerbeck's *Commentary*, Gerhard Kittel, heading a German team of contributors, launched the famous *Theological Dictionary of the New Testament*.[21] Here, selected words of doctrinal significance from the Greek New Testament are interpreted in the light of all relevant literatures – biblical, Hellenistic and post-biblical Jewish.

Not surprisingly, perhaps, New Testament scholars of the first half of this century, furnished with Billerbeck and Kittel, happily believed themselves to be fully equipped for a 'scientific-wissenschaftlich' exegesis of the gospels. Indeed their euphoria persisted until fairly recently, a well-known British author not hesitating in 1964 quite seriously to state:

> In this bright post-Strack-Billerbeck epoch, we are all rabbinic experts, though at second hand.[22]

What this writer and his predecessors have failed to realize is not merely the fundamental insufficiency of second-hand knowledge in creative scholarship; they have overlooked a fault intrinsic to most of the studies in Judaica mentioned so far. Religious writings disclose their meaning only to those who approach them in a spirit of sympathy. Such has not normally been the case, apropos of Rabbinic literature, among New Testament specialists.

As I have said, Christian anti-Judaism is age-old. St John Chrysostom compared the Jewish synagogue to a brothel, a *porneion* (*Hom.* I, PG XLVIII, 847). And St Jerome described Jewish prayers as 'grunnitus suis et clamor asinorum' – the grunting of a pig and the braying of donkeys (*In Amos* 5.23 PL XXV, 1054). But even our learned post-Renaissance Hebraists whose purpose was no longer polemical but scholarly, nevertheless still felt obliged to make numerous excuses to their pious readers for the unwholesome rubbish they were being offered. John Lightfoot, that man of admirable insight, hastened to accompany his persuasive statement on the value and necessity of the Talmud to New Testament research with the following warning:

> Intending readers of these volumes may be frightened away by the ill-repute of their authors who are very badly spoken of by all . . . These Jewish writings stink (*foetant Judaica haec scripta*) . . . They suffer from some kind of exceptional bad fate which makes them cause displeasure even unread. They are censured by those who have read them, but even more so by those who have not . . . Their readers are tormented, tortured and tired . . . by the stupendous futility . . . of the topics. They so abound in nonsense as though they wished not to be read . . . (However, although) the Jews give themselves nothing but nonsense, destruction and poison to drink, . . . the Christians with their skill and industry can convert these into useful servants of their studies.

Lightfoot's continuator, Schoettgen, advances an odd justification for his use of 'wicked' Jewish works in interpreting the gospels: they are no more pernicious than heathen classics, yet these are often quoted by Christian Bible experts!

Crude reasoning such as this was to some extent refined, but not altogether eliminated, by nineteenth-century scholarly criticism of scripture. German Liberal Protestantism – represented, say, by Wellhausen – promoted a sort of academic anti-Judaism which, in an oversimplified way, may be summed up thus. Authentic Judaism – i.e., all that a nineteenth-century enlightened Christian found acceptable in the Old Testament – was propounded by the prophets before the Babylonian exile. After the return of the Jews to Palestine, came the law which completely suffocated the free impulses of a living religion.[23] The substance of Wellhausen's historical thesis was taken over by Ferdinand Weber in a very influential manual to which I have alluded earlier, his *Jewish Theology*, first published in 1880. In his preface we read:

> With the return of Ezra . . . the influence of the prophetic word retreated . . . indeed, the Law became the only religious principle. It generated . . . a peculiar Jewish theology, which is distinguished from the teaching of the Old Testament . . .; in fact, it is opposed to it.[24]

Weber's theological 'insight' was borrowed by Schürer in his notorious chapter, 'Life under the Law',[25] and also, be it noted, by Billerbeck, who has passed it on to subsequent generations. Very often the choice of the illustrative material in the famous *Commentary to the New Testament from Talmud and Midrash* is governed by Weber's understanding of Judaism. In fact, there is an all-pervading tendentiousness in this great opus which renders its handling delicate and even dangerous. A recent writer remarks that it

> may retain some usefulness . . . with several provisions; that the user be able to look up the passages and read them in context, that he disregard as much as possible Billerbeck's own summaries and syntheses, and that he be able . . . to find passages on the topic not cited by Billerbeck.[26]

In brief, what this author seems to imply is that Billerbeck's *Commentary to the New Testament*, intended for non-specialists in Judaica, is helpful only to experts in post-biblical Jewish literature – to those who need it the least, that is to say.

And what about Kittel's *Theological Dictionary*, the other sacrosanct work, which together with Billerbeck is considered by critical scholars of the New Testament, who as a rule show limited respect for the integrity, authenticity and historicity of the gospels themselves, as a gospel truth above criticism![27] As far as the use of the Jewish sources is concerned, many of the articles edited by Kittel depend on Billerbeck, and consequently stand, and quite often fall, with the latter. But this is not all. In assessing the *Dictionary*, the personal history of Gerhard Kittel should not be ignored: and it does not inspire confidence. In the same year that the first fascicles of the *Theologisches Wörterbuch* were published – produced by a team chosen by Kittel – the editor-in-chief also issued a little book of his own: *Die Judenfrage*, 'The Jewish Question'. The year was 1933, and it was, as you may have guessed, an anti-Semitic tract.

Perhaps you will allow me to digress slightly at this point in order to make sure that my comments on Kittel will not be misinterpreted. Some civilized German theologians found his behaviour scandalous. Karl Ludwig Schmidt, a renowned New Testament scholar and editor of the monthly, *Theologische Blätter*, was courageous enough to publish in the August 1933 number an open letter to Gerhard Kittel by the great Jewish author, biblical scholar and religious thinker, Martin Buber.[28] This in its turn provoked the following magnificent response to Buber on the part of another leading German New Testament specialist, Ernst Lohmeyer.

> I have just read your open letter to Gerhard Kittel and am impelled to tell you that, for me, every one of your words is as though spoken from my own heart. But what impels me is not only this sentiment of spiritual solidarity . . . but to be frank, something like shame that fellow theologians should think and write as they do, that the Lutheran church should remain silent as she does, and like a ship without captain should herself be blown off course by the political storm of an after all fugitive present. This letter is meant to show you that not all those in the theological faculties, and also not all New Testament scholars, share Kittel's ideas.[29]

Kittel himself, a learned man, split between love and hatred for Judaism (he sent a copy of his odious booklet to Buber as a present), continued both to edit the *Dictionary* and to pursue his political activities. He wrote for the official Nazi publication, *Forschungen zur Judenfrage* (Researches into the Jewish Question)[30] and compromised himself so profoundly that in 1945 he was deprived of his university chair and was subject to a kind of house arrest in the

Benedictine abbey of Beuron. He died in 1948, aged fifty-nine. Some of the other contributors to the *Dictionary* also suffered, I believe, temporary set-backs in the post-war process of de-Nazification in Germany.

What I have said about Kittel does not mean that the early instalments of the *Theologisches Wörterbuch* contain noticeably anti-Semitic utterances, or that they are devoid of valuable articles; nevertheless it is not unreasonable to question whether a work issued by such an editor in Hitler's Third Reich is to be relied on for an unbiased presentation of the Jewish sources.[31]

After this disproportionately long introduction, we may now glance at the post-war scene. The recent developments in our domain are attributable to two main causes. The first is the impact on the Christian world of the horror of the Holocaust. Let me simply quote the words of dedication with which two outstanding books open. Both are devoted to the New Testament and written by Jews. Jules Isaac, the well-known French historian and founder of Amitiés judéo-chrétiennes, or 'Jewish Christian Friendships', published shortly after the end of the Second World War a passionate and powerful criticism of Christian scholarly and ecclesiastical attitudes to Judaism.[32] His dedication runs:

> A ma femme, à ma fille martyres
> tuées par les nazis d'Hitler
> tuées simplement parce qu'elles s'appelaient ISAAC.

And who can remain unmoved by the inscription on the first page of *On the Trial of Jesus*, that splendid work of scholarship composed with loving devotion in the midst of grim poverty in London by the Jewish refugee from Czechoslovakia, Paul Winter?

> To the dead in Auschwitz, Izbica, Majdanek, Treblinka, among whom are those who were dearest to me.[33]

In the shadow of the chimneys of the death-camps, anti-Judaism, even academic anti-Judaism, has become not only unfashionable but obscene. For the moment at least, it has largely disappeared, and we have now a more open, positive and constructive approach by New Testament scholars towards post-biblical Judaism.

A second powerful influence on recent developments has been the discovery of the Dead Sea Scrolls in the vicinity of Qumran in eleven caves between 1947 and 1956. These compositions have not only revived interest in the Jewish background to the New Testament, but in a real, and not journalistic, sense revolutionized it.[34]

The Dead Sea discoveries created much excitement and sensation because they yielded for the first time in history Hebrew and Aramaic manuscripts belonging to the era prior to the destruction of Jerusalem in AD 70. They mark an enormous step forward in our understanding of the history of the biblical text and of Jewish ideas and customs in the inter-testamental era. They were hailed as epoch-making because, among other reasons, deriving as they do from the period between the second century BC and the first century AD, they are potentially able to add to our knowledge of Jesus and the origins of Christianity. Some of the initial views expressed in this respect in the early 1950s were extreme. A French orientalist of international stature claimed to have uncovered in the Scrolls a pre-Christian Christianity, with a suffering and executed Messiah who rose from the dead and returned in glory to take revenge on an ungodly Jerusalem.[35] A Jewish scholar from Cambridge went even further. He identified the Habakkuk Commentary and other Qumran writings as Judaeo-Christian documents in which the leader referred to as the Teacher of Righteousness is none other than Jesus himself.[36] But these were, as I have said, extreme views and their impact was short-lived. The majority of world scholarship, students of every nationality, some of them religious, Christian or Jewish, some agnostic, applied themselves with energy and perseverance to piecing together, deciphering, translating and evaluating the Scrolls. A considerable amount of work aimed also at determining the relationship between them and the books of the New Testament.

The results, which because of the delays in publishing the material are far from complete, are already of major significance.[37] In the field of terminology, Qumran parallels to New Testament phrases prove that the evangelists and the letter-writers used idioms which were current in their time, and that the full meaning of a passing reference to, for example, 'the sons of light' in Luke, John or Paul can be established only when the expression is seen against the rich imagery of a universal struggle between Light and Darkness, between the Prince of Light and the Angel of Darkness, between the Spirits of Light and the Spirits of Darkness, and their earthly allies the Pious and the Wicked.

Certain key New Testament concepts take on new substance. For instance, Messiah as a generic term can apply in the Scrolls to at least two, and possibly three, different persons and functions. The Messiah of Israel, or Branch of David, is the victorious King of the last days. But he is subordinate to the Messiah of Aaron, or the High Priest of the end of time. And both of these are preceded or accompanied by a messianic Prophet or prophetic Messiah who conveys God's final message to the elect.[38]

Moreover, the formation and organization of the Christian community are no longer phenomena *sui generis* but strictly paralleled at Qumran. The Teacher of Righteousness of the Scrolls was, like Jesus, believed to have served as transmitter and interpreter of the divine mysteries, of God's definitive revelation. Like Jesus, he was surrounded by faithful disciples who continued to adhere to, and practise, his doctrines after his death and preached perseverance when the 'final age' and the establishment of the kingdom of heaven were delayed beyond all expectation. Like Jesus' followers, they organized themselves into a separate, self-contained body of the chosen, some of them living like the Jerusalem church out of a common purse and shunning private ownership of property. In fact, it is a comparison of the groups that brings into relief the distinctive marks of each. For example, whilst Jesus addressed himself only to the 'lost sheep of the house of Israel', his disciples decided, not without argument and hesitation, to admit non-Jews into their midst without obliging them to pass through Judaism, and this soon led to a largely, and later exclusively, Gentile church. The Qumran sectaries, by contrast, closed the doors of their community to all except Jews, or possibly also full converts to the religion of Israel.

At this point, a methodological question must be raised. Should the Jewish background to the New Testament be viewed in our post-Qumran era as roughly identical with the Dead Sea Scrolls? Some scholars would answer yes. The Scrolls, they would point out, together with some insignificant inscriptions are the only Jewish writings surviving in their original Hebrew and Aramaic chronologically parallel to the New Testament. In particular, when linguistic aspects are involved, only they can serve as terms of comparison: Jewish traditional literature, the compilation of the rabbis, belongs to the subsequent centuries and its relevance is dubious.[39] There is some truth in this point of view, but on the whole it is a sophism. If we can choose between an evidence that is contemporaneous with the gospels, and another that is more recent, we must obviously prefer the former. But since the Qumran material is tiny compared with Mishnah, Talmud and the rest, and is more often than not fragmentary, many facets of the New Testament would remain deprived of a Jewish background if recourse to rabbinic literature were precluded. But few serious scholars would deny today that rabbinic writings, though compiled between AD 200 and 500, include a large quantity of traditions traceable to the first century AD and that with a minimum amount of critical skill, it is often possible to distinguish among them between the old and the more recent.

Thus instead of restricting the boundaries of the Jewish background to the New Testament, the Dead Sea Scrolls have enlarged them: they are additional to the pre-existing material. As a matter of fact, serious students of the Qumran texts have quickly realized that they cannot be treated as autonomous, but need to be inserted into the larger body of Jewish literature: Bible, Apocrypha, Pseudepigrapha, Dead Sea sectarian writings, the great Hellenistic Jewish authors Philo and Josephus, rabbinic compositions, including the Aramaic paraphrases of the Old Testament. The latter, called Targums, very largely reflect the ordinary understanding of scripture by the ordinary Jew in late antiquity. In fact, apart from the Scrolls, the study of these Targums forms today one of the liveliest branches of Jewish studies.[40] In 1956, the year in which the last of the Dead Sea Scrolls were found, a singularly important copy of the whole Palestinian Aramaic version was also identified, not in an exotic hideout like Qumran, but in Rome, where it had rested unrecognized for centuries because a careless cataloguer of the Vatican Library had recorded it under an erroneous description.[41]

In short, it has become obvious to many – in theory at least! – that expertise in the Jewish background to the New Testament is not an optional extra, but that, on the contrary, no adequate understanding of Christian sources is conceivable without it.

So far the issue of New Testament interpretation has been considered from the viewpoint of its own practitioners. It is now time to ask how it is seen by a historian of first-century Judaism. For him the problem is twofold, and requires a twofold basic reorientation of approach.

First, for theological reasons the New Testament has always been considered by its exegetes as a subject to which all others must be subservient. If the Jewish background – seemingly distinct from the New Testament – is to be studied, it is in the hope that it may throw light on the gospels. It may help to solve New Testament puzzles. It is on this account that the questions are to be asked. The background must speak only when spoken to.

A historian cannot share these attitudes. For him, the New Testament, however marvellous and influential, is but a fraction of the literary legacy of first-century Judaism. In fact, I believe it not improper to suggest that for a *historical* understanding, the age-old distinction between the New Testament and its Jewish background should be abolished and the former looked at deliberately as part of a larger whole. This would mean that the New Testament's monopoly of always formulating the queries would come to an end. Questions should be asked in the light of the total evidence, and answers sought from the various Jewish groups represented by, say, some of the Pseudepigrapha, Josephus and Philo, the Dead Sea Scrolls, the New Testament and rabbinic literature. It is only by comparing these answers with one another, and with Old Testament data, that they can be understood, singly and together, in perspective.

Allow me to illustrate this by means of the problem of divorce in inter-testamental Judaism.[42] The Bible includes no detailed legislation on this important topic: Deuteronomy 24 simply envisages the special case of the remarriage of a man and his former wife, who has in the meantime been married to another man and divorced by him or left a widow. Such a union is forbidden, but in setting out this case, the grounds for divorce are laid down in the vaguest terms by the legislator: a bill of divorce may be given by the husband if the wife 'finds no favour in his eyes because he has found in her (literally) the nakedness of a thing (something indecent)'.

First-century Judaism in general interpreted the divorce rules very elastically. Josephus, describing the Jewish law for Gentile readers speaks of divorce 'for whatever cause', adding that 'with mortals many such may arise (*Ant.* iv, 253). Alluding to his own marital difficulties, he remarks casually that he dismissed his wife because he was 'displeased with her behaviour' (*Vita* 426). The influential Pharisaic school of Hillel likewise argued that even a spoilt dinner was sufficient reason for severing the marriage bond. By contrast, the more demanding rival school of Shammai allowed divorce only if the husband found 'unchastity' in his wife (*mGittin* 9.10). Now let us look at the question put to Jesus in Matt. 19.3. 'Is it lawful to divorce one's wife for any cause?' echoes the current Hillelite view. His answer, 'No, except for fornication', accords with the doctrine of the school of Shammai. But in another New Testament account, in Mark 10, Jesus, when asked in absolute terms whether divorce is permissible, gives a negative reply, allowing for no exception: a man or a woman who initiates divorce and follows it with a second marriage commits adultery. Thus the proper formulation of the conflict between the Jesus of Matthew and the Jesus of Mark, and the possible resolution of the problem of historicity, are more likely to arise from a reconstruction of the entire puzzle in which Matthew and Mark represent two small pieces, rather than the other way round. Incidentally, a woman could not formally divorce her husband in Jewish law; consequently, to be tenable, the Marcan version requires a flexible interpretation, which *ipso facto* weakens its claim for historicity.[43]

In sum, the insertion of the New Testament in a larger canvas provides it with added clarity and fuller meaning. It is a critically sound method, and to my mind the *only* acceptable one.

In addition to realizing that the New Testament is historically part of the greater body of first-century Jewish literature, the exegete must also bear in mind, if he is to comprehend them correctly, that the books of the New Testament belong in a sense to the genre of translation. I do not imply by this that some parts of the New Testament were first composed in Aramaic (or Hebrew), though this may have been the case, and subsequently rendered into Greek, the only surviving form of the text and justifiably designated as original. What I mean is that both Jesus and his immediate disciples were native Semitic speakers. Consequently, if anything genuinely and directly traceable to them remains in the Greek New Testament, apart from *Ephphetha, Talitha kum, Abba, Eloi eloi lamma sabachtani, Maranatha* – the few obvious Aramaic relics – it must have an underlying Aramaic or Hebrew original. Moreover, terminology is not the only area requiring critical analysis: in a broader sense, one must also remember that the religious culture permeating the Greek New Testament is not Greek/Hellenistic but Hebrew/Jewish. Together, these two factors, the terminological and the cultural, prompt a large number of crucial questions in regard to verbal and conceptual equivalents. Let me give you two examples.

The Hebrew word *Torah* (doctrine, instruction) was translated into Greek before the Christian era as *nomos*, law. Hellenistic Jews nevertheless appear to have been aware of the Hebrew connotations of their *nomos*, and Aramaic speakers, perhaps to avoid the pitfalls created by the choice of the Greek term, preferred to render *Torah* as *Orayta*, teaching, enlightenment.[44] It is only by stressing the Greek, without paying attention to the Semitic, significance of the term, that one can with Paul and Hellenistic Christianity construe the law, with its condemnation and death, as the opposite of Christ the Saviour. With *Torah* equated to *nomos*, the Law, Christianity inherited from Hellenistic Judaism an incorrect translation of a key-concept. And by developing its Greek associations alone, the church finished by distorting the Hebrew/Jewish meaning of the Judaeo-Hellenistic *nomos*.

My second example is the phrase, 'son of God'.[45] To a Greek speaker in Alexandria, Antioch or Athens at the turn of the eras, the concept *huios theou*, son of God, would have brought to mind either one of the many offspring of the Olympian deities, or possibly a deified Egyptian-Ptolemaic king, or the divine emperor of Rome, descendant of the apotheosized Julius Caesar. But to a Jew, the corresponding Hebrew or Aramaic phrase would have applied to none of these. For him, son of God could refer, in an ascending order, to any of the children of Israel; or to a good Jew; or to a charismatic holy Jew; or to the king of Israel; or in particular to the royal Messiah; and finally, in a different sense, to an angelic or heavenly being. In other words, 'son of God' was always understood metaphorically in Jewish circles. In Jewish sources, its use never implies participation by the person so-named in the divine nature. It may in consequence safely be assumed that if the medium in which Christian theology developed had been Hebrew and not Greek, it would not have produced an incarnation doctrine as this is traditionally understood.[46]

To conclude, I would like to return to my opening quotation. The candidate recommended by my anonymous referee was said to be 'among the few New Testament scholars who can take seriously, and walk sure-footedly in the Semitic material to the importance of which we all pay lip-service'. If there is truth in what I have tried to convey to you in the foregoing pages, the exceptional knowledge ascribed to our nameless candidate must be downgraded and become the ordinary qualification required of any competent student of the New Testament. In fact, it will be a minimum qualification. A good New Testament scholar will have to endeavour to become a citizen of that larger world to which his discipline belongs (and that means not only the Jewish, but also the Hellenistic world), so that he will be able to understand the arguments advanced by the experts in the various provinces of that world, but also, to think out new and pertinent questions and initiate fresh research likely to be beneficial to New Testament study.

Is this an unattainable reverie? Its fulfilment is admittedly impossible within the framework of our present academic curricula. The New Testament is taught in most British universities as part of an undergraduate programme in theology, a programme in which it occupies an important, but not disproportionately large, part. If we also bear in mind that the classical linguistic instruction in our schools is no longer what it used to be, it is hardly reasonable to expect that at the end of three short years, our theological faculties and departments should turn out New Testament students properly qualified to embark on research. In the circumstances, only graduate training can provide a solution to the problem.

Here it may be claimed with truth that the University of Oxford has taken up an avant-garde position. Since 1977–78, the Faculty of Oriental Studies has been offering a course leading to a Master's degree (MPhil) in Jewish Studies in the Graeco-Roman period. Students admitted to it have to acquire specialized knowledge in the history, literature, religion and culture of the Jews from the second century BC to the fifth century AD, and to familiarize themselves with Jewish literature of that period in Hebrew, Aramaic and Greek.[47] The programme has been devised for graduates of all kinds who wish to become expert in Jewish studies in late antiquity, but those with a particular interest in the New Testament are specifically catered for. If, as we hope, this venture proves a success in Oxford, and if similar courses are established in other centres as well, a new era may open in New Testament research.

One thing is in any case sure. We shall not get the revival of scholarship that we look for until interpreters of the Christian gospels learn to immerse themselves in the native religion of Jesus the *Jew*, and in the general climate of thought of the world and age in which he lived.

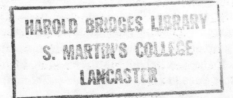

6

Jewish Literature and New Testament Exegesis: Reflections on Methodology

The present study follows an endeavour to lay down a few guiding-lines, within the context of history, for the use of Jewish documents in New Testament interpretation.[1] Here an attempt is made, for the first time as far as I am aware, to provide a methodological outline, incomplete though it may be, of this intricate and complex branch of scholarship.

To start with, two commonplaces have to be taken into account. Firstly, it is accepted that the New Testament is in some way connected, not only with the Hebrew Scriptures (which it often cites), but also with post-biblical Judaism. It is consequently assumed that the literary relics of ancient Israel may from the viewpoint of language and content prove useful to New Testament exegesis. Secondly, the earliest surviving form of the New Testament is Greek. Yet although a good deal of it was actually composed in that language, neither Jesus himself nor his original milieu belonged in any real sense (*pace* Hengel) to Hellenistic Judaism,[2] so any valid approximation of his genuine message must entail a linguistic and religious-cultural 're-translation' from the Greek into Aramaic/Hebrew concepts and thought-forms.[3]

Is such a reconversion possible, and if so by what means?[4]

Apart from the exceptional cases of Origen and Jerome, who applied the expertise acquired from Jewish consultants and teachers in expounding difficult New Testament passages,[5] it was not until the seventeenth century that the technical issue of interpretation with the help of Judaic sources was confronted. In the preface to his section on the Gospel of Matthew, John Lightfoot wrote these remarkable lines in *Horae Hebraicae et Talmudicae* first published in 1658:

I have also concluded without the slightest doubt that the best and most genuine method to unravel the obscure passages of the New Testament (of which there are many) is through research into the significance of the phrases and sayings in question according to the ordinary dialect and way of thinking of that (Jewish) nation, those who uttered them as well as those who listened to the speakers. For it is of no consequence what we can make of those locutions with the help of the anvil of our expressions, but what they meant to them in their common speech. And this can only be investigated by consulting the authors of the Talmud, who both employ the common idiom of the Jews and treat and open up all things Jewish.[6]

Between the seventeenth and the twentieth centuries, however, methodological progress was practically nil. In vain, for instance, does one search the *Kommentar zum Neuen Testament aus Talmud und Midrasch* by Hermann Strack and Paul Billerbeck,[7] or Gerhard Kittel's *Theologisches Wörterbuch zum Neuen Testament*,[8] for a reference to the system they intend to employ. In their *Vorwort* to vol. I of the *Kommentar* dated 1922, Strack and Billerbeck proclaim simply:

> By bodily descent, the Lord belonged to the Jewish people and most of the New Testament writers were Jews . . . So the Judaism of their time must be known if their utterances are to be understood correctly (p. VI).

Some help, they say, may be obtained from the Apocrypha and Pseudepigrapha but the authors themselves concentrate mainly on Talmud and Midrash with a view to presenting objectively the beliefs, outlook and life of the Jews in the first century AD. Their only acknowledgment of the existence of an historical dimension in this enterprise consists in the assertion that whenever possible they give the name and date of the authority quoted (p. VI).

This skeletal manifesto of the *Kommentar* fails to point out one of the major difficulties facing the New Testament interpreter, namely that his recorded comparative material is substantially younger than his documents. On page 1 vol. I of Strack-Billerbeck, citations are borrowed from R. Eleazar (*c.* AD 270), Rav Yehudah (died 299), Samuel (died 254) and R. Pinhas bar Hama (*c.* 360). But not a word is said by way of explaining whether or how these third and fourth century traditions are relevant to the exegesis of Matt.

1.1, which no doubt dates to the end of the first century. The use of the rabbinic data testifies moreover to a kind of historical fundamentalism; every attribution is believed, and every citation is seen to represent the truth. Nowhere is there any sign of awareness that rabbinic ideas themselves evolved. In fact, quite frequently the more developed form of a tradition is preferred to another closer in time to the New Testament!

Kittel has even less to reveal concerning his employment of Jewish texts. *TDNT* being a dictionary and not a commentary, it looks for its relationship to previous works of the same kind rather than for links with the sources of another literary culture attested in a different language. G. Friedrich, editor of the later volumes, reports in 'Prehistory of TDNT', that J. Kögel, the reviser of H. Cremer's *Biblisch-theologisches Wörterbuch der neutestamentlichen Gräzität*,[9] was of the opinion that 'the rabbinic element in his new edition was too brief'.[10] To fill the lacuna, he recruited as a collaborator G. Kittel who, on Kögel's death, inherited the whole project. The preface to vol. I, which appeared in 1933, announces that all the contributions have been sent for annotation from the standpoint of rabbinics to Kittel, and to two other young Judaica specialists of fifty years ago, the late K. G. Kuhn and the still flourishing K. H. Rengstorf. But as far as the use of post-biblical Judaism is concerned, the early volumes of *TDNT*, or rather *TWNT*, chiefly depend on Strack and Billerbeck.

From the 1930s onward, one area of post-biblical Jewish literature largely neglected by Billerbeck, the Aramaic paraphrases of scripture, received fresh attention.[11] Interest in the Palestinian Targums to the Pentateuch was aroused by P. Kahle when he published in 1930 the fragments retrieved from the Cairo Genizah,[12] and was subsequently revived by A. Díez Macho's re-discovery of Codex Neofiti I in the Vatican Library in 1956.[13] The most influential work to result from these finds was the monograph, *An Aramaic Approach to the Gospels and Acts* by M. Black.[14] The Targumic exegesis of the New Testament has the advantage, compared with other branches of rabbinic literature, of being entirely based on Palestinian – i.e. Galilean – Aramaic texts which were probably subjected to a less thorough updating than the Mishnah, Tosefta, Talmud and halakhic Midrashim. It nevertheless suffers from the same methodological weakness as Talmudic-Midrashic New Testament interpretation inasmuch that in its redacted form (even when we discount obviously late additions such as allusions to Byzantium or to Islam), no Palestinian Targum is likely to predate AD 200.

The most revolutionary change in the position of the New Testament exegete concerned with Jewish comparative data occurred in 1947 with the discovery of the Dead Sea Scrolls. Not only did he now find himself equipped with non-biblical Qumran documents written mostly in Hebrew and Aramaic, and in a broad sense contemporaneous with Christian beginnings, but they derive in addition from a sectarian setting more or less similar to that of the early church. Also, practically all of the literature is religious, including a fair amount of Bible interpretation.

In many respects it would be hard to invent a literary corpus more suitable for the study of the New Testament than these scrolls[15] and not surprisingly there is a growing tendency in contemporary New Testament study to restrict comparison exclusively to them. Indeed, apart from the (unacknowledged) advantage of eliminating the arduous work of consulting rabbinic sources, pan-Qumranism has much in its favour: chronology, language, eschatologico-apocalyptic background, similarity in religious aspirations, etc. On the other hand, does recognition of the importance of the Qumran documents (and of epigraphical material of the same period) signify that contributions from Mishnah, Talmud, Midrash and Targum are now to be regarded as negligible, as deprived of any validity? Professor J. A. Fitzmyer seems to think it does.[16]

It should in fairness be stressed that he argues primarily from a linguistic stand, claiming that Qumran Aramaic (and the Aramaic of first-century AD tomb and ossuary inscriptions) – or more abstractly Middle Aramaic evidence – 'must be the latest Aramaic that should be used for philological comparison of the Aramaic substratum of the Gospels and Acts'.[17] Elsewhere, he emphasizes that Qumran Aramaic yields 'privileged data that take precedence over the material derived from the classic targumim and midrashim'.[18] In practice, however, Fitzmyer does not stay with philology. In addition to Aramaic words and phrases preserved in the New Testament and to Aramaisms in, and mistranslations from Aramaic into, New Testament Greek, he deals with literary forms in prose and poetry, Jewish literary traditions in the New Testament and in Aramaic sources, and even with Jewish practices and beliefs emerging from the Qumran Aramaic texts.[19]

In abstracto, Fitzmyer's thesis is defensible. If we could lay hands on comparative material belonging to the appropriate period, in

the appropriate type of language, representing the appropriate
literature, and extant in sufficient quantity, it would be unnecessary
to consult documents of a later age for interpretative purposes of
any description.[20] But we are not so fortunate. An unintentional
and hence particularly significant outcome of Fitzmyer's *Manual of
Palestinian Aramaic Texts*[21] has been, in effect, to highlight the
limitations of the available evidence from the inter-testamental
epoch. Despite inclusion of a substantial number of tiny fragments
producing no meaningful sequences of words, the sample is small,
the literary genres quite limited and the vocabulary meagre. Aramaic
speakers of New Testament times used many more words than those
attested in the extant literary and inscriptional remains. It is with
these facts in mind that we have to judge Fitzmyer's programme:
'Discussions of the language of Jesus in recent decades have been
legion, and much of that discussion has been based on texts that are
of questionable relevance. Our purpose in gathering Palestinian
Aramaic texts of the period . . . is to try to illustrate what should be
the background of that discussion.'[22]

In fact, the policy thus outlined, even if executed blamelessly,
cannot avoid running into serious difficulties because of the scarcity
of comparative material recognized by Professor Fitzmyer as admissible. This basic flaw is compounded by his handling of the evidence
in the few cases where he provides his own illustrations. Examining
Aramaic words preserved in the New Testament, he notes that
korban is still explained by M. Black as 'a form of solemn prohibition
found . . . in the Talmud',[23] and that the overtones of the Talmudic
usage have always embarrassed the New Testament commentator
appealing to them in connection with Mark 7.11 ('any support that
you might have had from me is *korban*', i.e., a gift made to God).
Fitzmyer then reminds the reader of two recently found Aramaic
inscriptions from Palestine, one of which, an ossuary epigraph
published by J. T. Milik, reads: 'All that a man may find to his profit
in this ossuary is a *korban* to God from him who is inside.' Here,
the 'dedicatory sense' of the term is apparent, whereas in the rabbinic
occurrences (as understood by Fitzmyer) it is not. He therefore
concludes that 'such evidence . . . renders unnecessary the references to later Jewish material from sources such as the Talmud'.[24]

Besides stressing the need also to take into consideration Josephus' mention of *qorban* = *dōron theou* as an oath form,[25] I should
also point out that Fitzmyer's statement amounts to a concatenation
of factual errors allied to a possible general misconception. *Ned.*

3.2 quoted by him, refers to the Mishnah and *not* to the Talmud. The text is in Hebrew and *not* in Aramaic. Moreover, the example is not only ill-chosen as far as the substance is concerned; it may also be philologically unsuitable, for the New Testament word, a quasi-liturgical exclamation, can just as well reproduce a Hebrew as an Aramaic original.[26] In this connection it should be noted that Fitzmyer's second so-called Aramaic inscription containing the single word *qrbn* can just as easily be Hebrew.[27] Finally, it can hardly be questioned that the Mishnaic formulae (paralleled in substance though not terminologically in the Damascus Rule 16.14–15, where the notion of *ḥerem* appears) provide a much more apt illustration for Mark 7.11 since they imply that through *qorban* a deprivation was inflicted on the members of a person's family, a nuance missing from the ossuary inscription.

Equally unlucky is the treatment of *mamōnas*. We are informed that what he calls its 'alleged' Aramaic background 'has been illustrated by appeals to the Babylonian Talmud (*bBer.* 61b), a Palestinian Targum (Gen. 34.43) . . ., and to passages in the Palestinian Talmud'.[28] Against these, the American scholar cites the Hebrew Ecclesiasticus 31.8, various Qumran texts also in Hebrew,[29] and the Punic usage mentioned by Augustine (the latter dating to Talmudic times, rather odd *qua* evidence in the circumstances). Fitzmyer then asserts: 'Here is an instance where we may have to cease appealing to Aramaic for the explanation of the Greek *mamōna* and resort merely to a common Semitic background of the word.'[30] This reasoning strikes a sensitive linguist as peculiar. The availability of contemporaneous Hebrew, and more recent Punic, attestations of a term are seen to be sufficient grounds for discarding later Aramaic parallels to interpret a New Testament noun displaying a distinct Aramaic ending! But of course the whole argument is ill-founded for by the time it was published (1975), *(m)am(on)ah* had already been encountered in the Aramaic Job Targum (Job 27.17) from 11Q (1971).[31] Fitzmyer himself lists it in the Glossary of his *Manual* (1978).[32] Yet he still advises us in 1979 to 'cease appealing to Aramaic'.

Among New Testament Aramaisms, Fitzmyer could hardly overlook *ho huios tou anthrōpou*, in his words, 'a Greek phrase that is often said to carry an Aramaic nuance'. He was bound to repeat his by now familiar thesis that the noun *nash/a*, written without the initial aleph, being of late provenience, 'one should . . . be wary of citing texts in which (the shortened) form of the expression occurs as if they were contemporary with the NT material'.[33] Without wishing to launch once more into the 'son of man' debate,[34] I note signs of some *rapprochement* in his position. He now admits (or re-admits) that the case for the circumlocutional use of 'son of man' has been made out at least once, and that Matt. 16.13 ('Who do men say the son of man is?') compared with Mark 8.27 ('Who do men say that I am?') suggests that the substitution of ' "Son of Man" for "I" . . . reflects current Palestinian Aramaic usage'.[35] In the absence of first-century positive evidence supporting my case, he neverthe-less feels entitled to hesitate over 'some of the interpretations' proposed by me.[36] Yet at the same time, he does not flinch from the possibility that the Targumic idiom was influenced by the New Testament![37]

Glancing finally at a conjectural mistranslation from Aramaic into Greek as adduced by Fitzmyer apropos of Matt. 7.6, 'Do not give dogs what is holy // and do not throw pearls before swine', he recalls that it has long since been proposed that the Greek interpreter misread *qᵉdasha*, ring, as *qudsha*, holiness = *to hagion*, and thus spoiled the parallelism between ring and pearls. In the past, the hypothesis was based – Professor Fitzmyer tells us – on 'late Syriac and other texts', but now the 11Q Job Targum (on 42.11) supplies the word in the sense of a ring: 'And each man gave him a sheep and each a gold ring (*qᵉdash had di dᵉhab*)'.[38] I am not sure who it was who appealed to late Syriac texts but am somewhat surprised that Fitzmyer seems to have failed to notice that the reading of 11Qtg Job is almost literally identical with that of the *traditional* Targum of Job, where the second half of 42.11 reads: *we-'ᵉnash qᵉdasha didᵉhaba had*.[39]

In sum, taking into account the patchiness of the new evidence and the imperfections apparent in its application to the study of the New Testament, I believe we may be forgiven for considering the general problem not solved by Fitzmyer but on the contrary still wide open. The one area where Qumran Aramaic could play a decisive role would be the study of first-century literary Aramaic documents, which apart from *Megillath Ta'anith* (not regarded by Fitzmyer as really relevant)[40] and the lost Aramaic draft of Josephus' *War* (*BJ* i. 3, 6), consist only in the Qumran texts themselves, since it is reasonable to suppose that much of the Aramaic reflected in the Greek gospels belongs to the spoken, if not colloquial, form of the language.

Trying now to piece together a methodology, borrowing where appropriate from the theories already outlined, but setting the data into a broader and more refined framework, the first question requiring an answer concerns the purpose of the enterprise. What do we hope to achieve by bringing inter-testamental and Rabbinic Jewish writings to bear on the understanding of the New Testament?

In the case of the gospels and the early chapters of Acts, there is clearly no hope of retrieving their Semitic original beyond transliterated words and phrases and a few obvious Aramaisms in New Testament Greek (e.g., 'to bind and to loose', *'asar* and *sherē*).[41] As for the famous *ipsissima verba*, a quest for these presupposes a degree of reliability in gospel tradition that modern research simply cannot justify. Sayings attributed to Jesus in the New Testament (and to the rabbis in the Mishnah and the Talmud), are often edited and sometimes even freely supplied. But is it possible nevertheless to grasp at the very least something of a master's teaching? I would suggest that we can manage to perceive his ideas, the *ipsissimus sensus*, even without the actual words in which they were formulated. Where the gospels are concerned, the required preliminaries are the various kinds of criticism: form-, source-, tradition- and redaction-criticism. Subsequently, study of the Greek New Testament can be assisted powerfully by means of appropriate Hebrew/Aramaic parallels. Thus if on the basis of internal gospel evidence it is assumed that Jesus' teaching implies not the abolition but the continuity of the Torah (Matt. 5.17; Luke 16.16–17), the Aramaic/Hebrew idiom, *lebattala/lebattēl – leqayyama/leqayyēm*, cannot be without value in interpreting the Greek *katalusai* and *plērosai*.[42]

The sectors likely to benefit most from comparison with Jewish sources are those of religious concepts and motifs such as Messiah, Lord, son of God, holy man/miracle-worker, exorcist/healer, etc. With the proviso that an acceptable method of evaluation is agreed on, the juxtaposition of the New Testament and Jewish parallels is sure to lead to the discovery of how the original audience or readership understood the words, phrases or themes in question. This matter is discussed at length in *Jesus the Jew*, especially in its second half.[43]

Another branch of comparative study is concerned with Aramaic/ Hebrew literary units attested in the New Testament, such as proverbs, Bible interpretation, parables and the like. Here again, if and when the preliminary issue of admissibility is settled, the Semitic material can pinpoint common traits and underline distinctive peculiarities. A certain amount of important work has already been done in this field, to mention only Rudolf Bultmann's analysis of proverbial sayings among the *logia*,[44] or Joachim Jeremias' study of the parables,[45] but it goes without saying that in both domains much remains to be done. In particular, attention should be further concentrated on the special thrust characteristic of common themes. For example, in the parable of the Prodigal Son (Luke 15.18–24), the initiative in the return/*teshuvah* lies with the repentant and trustful son, whereas in the oft-quoted rabbinic parallel attributed to R. Meir (*Dt.R.* 2.3 on Deut. 4.30)[46] the son is too overcome by shame to make such a move and it is the father who prompts the homecoming.

Following this endeavour to outline the purpose of the venture and to offer topics for comparative study, we have now to cope with the thornier task of determining the procedure to be adopted. Here it seems reasonable to argue that if the aim is historical, the method must be similarly historical. In other words, in place of the traditional handling of rabbinic documents, i.e., without regard for the effect on them of evolutionary factors, an eye must constantly be kept on development.

Where, of course, evidence is available from inter-testamental sources such as the Septuagint, Apocrypha and Pseudepigrapha, Qumran, Philo and Josephus, this comparative process can go ahead without further ado. It has to be asserted at this juncture, against occasional ill-conceived criticism,[47] that although Josephus and some of the Pseudepigrapha, e.g., IV Maccabees or Ps.-Philo, may date to decades slightly later than some parts of the New Testament, their use as *inter*-testamental documents remains legitimate inasmuch as they are, in general, not creative works but mostly represent pre-existent religious ideas. Where in any case such straightforward comparative material is at hand, the historico-exegetical work may proceed without glancing backward and forward in time, as Qumran parallels can show. For example, the portrayal of the apostles as princes seated on twelve thrones, and of the church as composed of twelve tribes,[48] echoes the claim encountered in the same form at Qumran. In both, a dissident community models itself on, and identifies itself as, the true Israel.[49] Again, eschatologico-apocalyptic disenchantment (delay of the *parousia*, postponement of the end-time) inspired the leaders of the Essenes and of the Christian church to preach hope and rank perseverance as the most essential virtue of the moment.[50] In a polemical context, the common gospel theme of healing = forgiveness of sins, though depicted as scandalizing lawyers and Pharisees – an attitude manifest in rabbinic tradition, too – finds near perfect support in the Qumran Prayer of Nabonidus in which the Babylonian king speaks of a Jewish exorcist who forgave his sins and thereby cured him of a long illness.[51]

Whilst, as I have already maintained, study of a New Testament passage in the light of inter-testamental parallels leads in many cases to a clarification of its historical significance, it can happen that time after time sources more recent than these contain ideas that improve our understanding of the original sense of a text . . . provided once more that an acceptable methodology is devised to justify the use of such non-contemporaneous material. It is enough to recall rabbinic speculation on the Binding of Isaac and its impact on the explication of the death of Jesus as a sacrifice in the Epistle to the Hebrews and elsewhere;[52] or, as will appear later, the Mishnaic, Talmudic and Midrashic views on divorce in relation to the New Testament, and specifically to the Matthean teaching on that subject.

However, the real crux comes when a New Testament saying, concept or motif figures distinctly in Targum, Midrash or Talmud, but entirely lacks (for the time being at least) pre-rabbinic corroboration. Consider Jesus' quintessential summary of true piety: 'Be merciful as your Father is merciful' (Luke 6.36); 'Be perfect as your heavenly Father is perfect' (Matt. 5.48). The gospel *logion* closely resembles the paraphrase in Targum Ps.-Jonathan of Lev. 22.28: 'My people, children of Israel, as your Father is merciful in heaven, so you must be merciful on earth.' But this Targum is merely part of a much broader rabbinic doctrine on the imitation of God.[53] The second century Tanna, Abba Shaul, bases this teaching on an artifically construed esoterical pun on Exodus 15.2, 'This is my God and I will praise him, which is read as, 'This is my God, I and He, and expounded as, 'Be like Him: as He is merciful and gracious, you also must be merciful and gracious'.[54]

The fullest version of the rabbinic teaching appears in the Babylonian Talmud attributed to the third-century Palestinian sage, Hama bar Hanina, interpreting Deuteronomy 13.5 (*bSot.* 14a), and also in Targum Ps.-Jonathan on Deuteronomy 34.6. The latter runs:

Blessed be the name of the Lord of the World who has taught us his right ways. He has taught us to clothe the naked as he clothed Adam and Eve. He has taught us to join the bridegroom to the

bride as he joined Eve to Adam. He has taught us to visit the
sick as he revealed himself in his Word to Abraham after his
circumcision. He has taught us to comfort the mourners as he
revealed himself to Jacob on his return from Padan in the place
where his mother had died. He has taught us to feed the poor as
he caused bread to descend from heaven for the children of Israel.
He has taught us to bury the dead through Moses to whom
he revealed himself in his Word and with him companies of
ministering angels.

This Talmudic-Targumic form of the doctrine has its Christianized
adaptation in Matthew 25.31–46, where the 'King' in the eschatological judgment commands the 'sheep' on his right hand to 'Come,
enter and possess the kingdom. For when I was hungry you gave me
food; when thirsty, you gave me to drink; when I was a stranger you
took me home; when naked, you clothed me; when I was ill you
came to help; when in prison, you visited me.'

What is the relationship between these two sets of texts? I see four
possibilities that may be represented by the following models (NT =
New Testament: R = Rabbinic literature; JT = Jewish tradition):

1.   The similarities are purely coincidental.

Bearing in mind the amount of overlap and the variety of attestation,
such a diagnosis is highly unlikely.

2.   The rabbinic doctrine is inspired by, or borrowed from, the
New Testament.

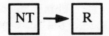

Chronologically, this is obviously possible but to render such a
conjecture viable we must be able to demonstrate that the rabbis of
the Tannaitic and Amoraic age were not only aware of the New
Testament teachings but actually willing to learn from them: which
is asking a lot.

3. The New Testament depends on Targum and Midrash.

That the New Testament should utilize current Jewish themes is both possible and likely, but actual dependence presupposes that R existed in the first century. This too is very problematic; though the Qumran Genesis Apocryphon, with its Midrashic accretions, shows that such material was extant in written form before AD 70.

4. The New Testament and the rabbinic doctrine both derive from a common source, viz., Jewish traditional teaching.

Here we have a theory that is certainly possible and even probable. It could also bring about a much improved understanding of the New Testament. It would nevertheless be difficult to conceal its methodological lameness. It could doubtless be shown that the procedure works and a convincing case could even be made out to demonstrate that the presupposition is reasonable. But the fact remains that such a process would hinge on a presumption, and for the unconverted – e.g., Professor Fitzmyer and his uncritical followers – that would come very close to begging the question.

All the same, it has to be reiterated that the system seems to work. So can it be that we are trying to answer a wrongly formulated question?[55] What if the whole argument were reversed, and instead of interpreting Matthew and Luke with the help of Tannaitic sayings from Mekhilta and Sifre, Amoraic exegesis preserved in the name of a third-century master in the Babylonian Talmud and anonymous and undated Targum excerpts, an attempt were made to trace the Targumic tradition to its origin via the Talmud (say AD 500 in its final redaction, third to fourth century for the formulation of the tradition in question), the Tannaitic Midrash (second to third century) and the New Testament (first century)? Assuming that the basic New Testament divested of its patently Hellenistic accretions is recognized as a witness of first-century Jewish religious thought, a view few serious scholars will contest, does not this suggested procedure seem methodologically sound and valid? And if so, why have we been plagued for so long with a twisted problem?

The answer lies at the heart of the age-old Jewish–Christian conflict. On the one hand, New Testament specialists, as a rule scholars and churchmen in one, almost inevitably attach to the New Testament an image which must appear distorted to the historian. The writings in which the Christian faith originates possess for them centrality, finality and ultimacy. These experts see all else – in historical terms, the whole of Judaism and Hellenism – as gravitating round the New Testament. To adopt another metaphor, for them the New Testament is the mistress, and Jewish documents, especially of the post-biblical variety, mere ancillaries at best. On the Jewish side, by contrast, the New Testament has for religious-polemical reasons been largely ignored and its Jewishness tacitly denied. Even during the last hundred years or so, recourse to it for historico-exegetical purposes has been uncommon, not only because of a lingering subconscious dislike among rabbinic scholars for all things Christian, but also, and perhaps mainly, because of their unfamiliarity with Greek and with the technical issues raised by the academic study of the New Testament.

Divested, however, of its denominational garb, the matter takes on another colour. The New Testament then ceases to be insignificant for Jews or autonomous and in every sense primary for Christians. Jesus and the movement that arose in his wake are recognized as belonging to first-century Jewish history. Furthermore, a good deal of the New Testament appears as reflecting a brief moment in the age-long religious development of Israel that starts with the Bible and continues via the Apocrypha, Pseudepigrapha, Qumran, Philo, the New Testament, Josephus, Pseudo-Philo, the Mishnah, Tosefta, Targum, Midrash, Talmud – and so on and so forth. For Jews, the study of rabbinic literature benefits greatly inasmuch as the New Testament is able to fulfil the exceedingly important function of providing a chronologically well-defined segment of tradition applicable as a yardstick in dealing with undated material.

But what happens to the complex of New Testament interpretation? How does the new perspective affect the scholarly approach to it? Negatively, one outcome is that there is no longer any call for works in which the New Testament occupies the centre of the stage. There is no need for a *Kommentar zum Neuen Testament aus Talmud und Midrasch* or, I regret to say, for *Compendia Rerum Iudaicarum ad Novum Testamentum*.[56] There is no need either for rabbinic theologies where insufficient attention is paid to pre-rabbinic sources, including the New Testament. Positively, what is required is an effort to examine the movement of Jewish religious-theological thought as a whole, and while so doing, to determine the place, significance and distinctiveness of its constituent parts. In other words, instead of looking at the New Testament as an independent unit set against a background of Judaism, we have to see it as part of a larger environment of Jewish religious and cultural history.

Unless I am wholly mistaken, the procedure proposed in this chapter avoids or overcomes the chronological difficulty that has bedevilled until now the utilization of rabbinic literature in the exegesis of the New Testament. If the latter is envisaged, not as standing apart from Judaism and above it, but as organically bound up with it, the stages of religious thought preceding it and following it are not merely relevant but essential to an historical understanding and evaluation of its message, including its originality and peculiarity. This may be illustrated by comparing the two approaches. To interpret the New Testament teaching on divorce,[57] and in particular the Matthean exception clause in Matt. 5.32, *parektos logou porneias* ('except for fornication'), Strack and Billerbeck assemble an impressive array of illuminating rabbinic parallels, starting with *mGittin* 9.10, and follow with citations from Sifre on Deuteronomy, *bGittin*, *yGittin*, etc.[58] Needless to say, all these texts post-date the gospel. In contrast to this, the procedure suggested here examines Jewish attitudes to divorce in the Bible, at Qumran, in Josephus, in the New Testament and in rabbinic literature in such a way that, inserted into a broader canvas, the links between the various units, and also their individuality and bias, stand out in relief and acquire fuller meaning. The effect furthermore is reciprocal in that the New Testament authenticates the second-century echoes in the Mishnah of the alleged first-century controversy between the Houses of Hillel and Shammai. In parenthesis, it should be noted also that in commenting on the *apostasion* (bill of divorce) in Matt. 5.31, the rabbinic data listed by Strack and Billerbeck should not be superseded, as Professor Fitzmyer would no doubt have it, but preceded and supplemented by the well-preserved Aramaic *geṭ* found at Murabba'at.[59]

What in practical terms would be entailed in any serious attempt to substitute a strictly historical treatment of the New Testament for the 'theology' currently in vogue?

Clearly, a critical assessment of the development of Jewish religious ideas from Apocrypha to Talmud would be a long-term

undertaking of monumental proportions. But there is no reason
why two preliminary tasks, and one intermediary operation, should
not be embarked on at once. As a first step, a small group of experts
in inter-testamental, New Testament and rabbinic studies could
initiate a survey with a view to drawing up a list of (*a*) 'Jewish'
problems amenable to explication with the help of the New Testament, and (*b*) New Testament issues needing clarification from
'Jewish' sources. The intermediary project would involve the
composition of a Schürer-type *religious* history of the Jews from the
Maccabees to AD 500[60] that fully incorporates the New Testament
data. Equipped with a detailed index, its aim would be to serve as
a reliable guide to the diverse streams of post-biblical Judaism in all
their manifestations and reciprocal influences.

Who is willing to take up the challenge?

7

The Present State of the 'Son of Man' Debate

A few days after my arrival in Oxford as newly elected Reader in Jewish Studies, the late Dr F. L. Cross was kind enough to accept my last minute offer to read a paper before an international New Testament Congress. The lecture, 'The use of *barnash / bar nasha* in Jewish Aramaic', was delivered in this same hall in September 1965, before appearing in print in 1967.[1] In it, I set out to enquire into the meanings of the Semitic expression underlying the famous gospel phrase, and advanced various conclusions. My task here is to expose the present state of the 'son of man' debate which followed in the wake of 1965 communication.

The issue in a nutshell is this. The expression occurring in the gospels, *ho huios tou anthrōpou*, is not a genuine Greek idiom. In recent years, it has been described as 'unusual in Greek';[2] 'a rather inelegant barbarism';[3] or 'a literal rendering of the determinative [Aramaic] *bar ('e)nasha* which is ambiguous in Greek'.[4] It is in fact generally, though not universally, thought that the Semitic model from which the Greek derives is Aramaic.[5] Hebrew is in disfavour because, with one possible exception, it never uses the definite article with *ben adam*.[6]

Prior to 1965, there had been two waves of philological research. The first, from the turn of the century, comprises the works of Arnold Meyer,[7] Hans Lietzmann,[8] Gustaf Dalman[9] and Paul Fiebig.[10] The next wave, which dates to the years immediately following the end of the Second World War, has as its most important participants J. Y. Campbell,[11] John Bowman,[12] Matthew Black,[13] and Erik Sjöberg.[14] On a number of linguistic points, there was agreement among the protagonists, but on two major matters, the circumlocutional and the titular use of the expression, opinions remained divided.[15]

My own thinking on the subject began with an observation which seemed so self-evident as to constitute a truism: 'Since "the *son of man"* is not a Greek phrase, but Aramaic, if it is to make sense at all, it must be Aramaic sense.'[16] So before we try to determine the meaning of *ho huios tou anthrōpou* in the gospels, it is imperative to find out in what sense, or senses, *bar ('e)nasha* was actually used in real, extant Jewish Aramaic texts. In 1963 and 1964, I therefore completed a survey which, although by no means an exhaustive investigation, was based on a much larger sample than the previous studies. Among its four main results, the first two confirms the theses propounded by Meyer and Lietzmann that (1) *bar nash(a)* is a regular expression for 'man' in general; and (2) that *bar nash* often serves as an indefinite pronoun. The third, and perhaps most novel of the conclusions actually illustrates the circumlocutional use of *bar nasha*, instead of merely postulating it on the basis of a similar Aramaic idiom, *hahu gabra* ('that man'). In fact, I adduced ten examples of direct speech – monologue or dialogue – in which the speaker appears to refer to himself, not as 'I', but as 'the son of man' in the third person, in contexts implying awe, reserve or modesty. The fourth conclusion stresses that in none of the passages scrutinized, not even in the Jewish messianic exegesis of Daniel 7, does the expression *bar nasha* figure as a title.[17] It may even be inferred that Aramaic linguistic usage renders the expression unsuitable to describe an eschatological office because occasionally *bar nash* is employed with the pejorative nuance of a crafty, unscrupulous fellow.[18]

Predictably, the last two theses have aroused mixed reactions, and these form the third wave of the philologically based 'son of man' debate. This may conveniently be outlined with the help of the following three questions:

1. Has a periphrastic use of *bar nash(a)* been convincingly demonstrated, and is the evidence applicable to the New Testament?
2. Is it still tenable that a Jewish 'son of man' concept and title existed during the life-time of Jesus?
3. Can the new linguistic analysis of the Aramaic phrase contribute positively to the interpretation of the New Testament?

I

The first reactions to the new circumlocution theory queried the demonstrative force of the proof-texts marshalled to support it in the 1965 lecture and the 1967 publication. F. H. Borsch[19] and C. Colpe[20] emphasized that my examples are primarily generic statements though they may include the speaker. None of them is a clear-cut substitute for 'I'. Both authors expressed their views as early as 1967, as did also Joachim Jeremias in an argument formulated in greater detail. According to him, whereas the phrase *hahu gabra*, the model on which my theory is constructed, means 'I and no one else', and points exclusively to the speaker, *bar nasha* has a indefinite nuance: 'man, therefore I, too'. It is, consequently, not a circumlocution for the first person personal pronoun.[21]

This objection, I submit, fails on two counts. Firstly, the critics in question do not seem to appreciate that a circumlocution is not just a synonym, but by definition, roundabout and evasive speech. It is expected to entail ambiguity. In genteel English, people speak of 'passing away' rather than of dying, and no one would dream of asking a veterinary surgeon to 'kill' his pet, but to 'put it to sleep'. Aramaic speakers to obtain the same blurred effect, rendered slightly ambiguous, not the predicate, but the subject. They found it easier to say, 'That man' (or 'The son of man') is going to die, than, '*I* am going to die'. Likewise, 'The son of man' will be approved or rewarded by God, sounded in their ears less boastful than if the same assertion were expressed in the first person singular.

As for Jeremias' distinction between the unequivocal *hahu gabra* (standing for 'I and no one else') and the ambiguous *bar nasha* (meaning 'anybody, and that includes me') is forced because *hahu gabra* is not necessarily unequivocal. In the well-known legendary conversation between Yohanan ben Zakkai and Vespasian, the rabbi, who had just escaped from a besieged Jerusalem, salutes the Roman commander, in Latin, with *Vive Domine Imperator*! Vespasian exclaims in Aramaic: 'You have greeted me with a royal greeting although I am no king. When the king (Nero) hears about it, he will kill *hahu gabra*' (*Lam.R.* 1.5(31)). But 'that man' here can refer to *either* speaker. It may apply to Yohanan, as in the parallel Talmud passage where Vespasian tells him that he has brought upon *himself* capital guilt: 'I am no king, and yet you have called me king' (*bGit.* 56a). But *hahu gabra* may equally designate Vespasian, who in another account is reported as expostulating: 'You have killed me! Why have you greeted me with a royal greeting although I am no king? When the king hears of this, he will despatch someone to kill *me*.'[22]

This apparent misunderstanding of the aim of circumlocutional

talk may explain why John Bowker, although in general sympathy
with the Aramaic approach advocated by this writer, is unable to
follow the argument all the way.[23] For him, a circumlocution must be
crystal-clear. 'The case for circumlocution would be immeasurably
stronger', he writes, 'if the text read: "The disciple of *bar nasha* is
as dear to *me* as *my* son" [instead of the extant wording in the third
person: "as dear to him as his son"].'[24] In my view, such a formula
would spoil the original purpose of the idiom. R. Hiyya's wish was
tactfully to appoint his pupil, R. Levi, as his heir. The veiled saying
was obviously understood since Levi is said to have received his
master's valuables.

Though this is a slight digression, it may be worth noting that oral
equivocations of the *hahu gabra/bar nasha* type tend again and again
to be resolved when they reach the written stage. For instance, when
in the Midrash Rabbah Jacob asks Esau: 'Do you want money or a
burial-place?', Esau replies: 'Does *hahu gabra* want a burial place?
Give *me* the money and keep the burial-place for yourself!' (*Gen.R.*
100.5). The same phenomenon – a periphrasis rendered explicit by
a subsequent direct reference to the speaker – appears in Mark 2.10:
'To convince you that *the son of man* has the right on earth to forgive
sins . . . *I* say to you . . .'. Elsewhere we may find the ambiguous
form in one text, and the straight equivalent in a variant, or a
synoptic parallel. 'Not even a bird is caught without the will of
heaven' – comments Simeon ben Yohai – 'how much less the soul
of *bar nasha*'! But another manuscript reads: 'how much less *my*
soul!' (*Gen.R.* 79.6). It is impossible not to be reminded here of
Matt. 16.13, 'Who do men say *the son of man* is?' and compare it
with Jesus' question in the Marcan wording, 'Who do men say that
I am?' (Mark 8.27; cf. Luke 9.18).

Returning to the philological issue, I should mention at this juncture
P. M. Casey's interesting contribution, 'The Son of Man Problem'.[25]
In an attempt to reconcile my thesis and the comments made by
Colpe and Jeremias, Casey suggests that an Aramaic speaker would
choose *bar nasha* as a self-designation when applying a general
statement to himself. Thus in declaring that '*The son of man* is going
the way appointed for him in the scriptures' (Mark 14.22), Jesus
'announces that he is about to die, as all men do, by divine decree'.[26]
Since in the main, Casey argues in what seems to me the right
direction, it would be ungracious to quibble over inessentials.
Nevertheless, his re-formulation would be more impressive if he
were able to provide additional illustrations of how 'general state-

ments are used in Aramaic' – over and above my *bar nasha* quotations – and if he could also justify the need for a special turn of phrase to express the obvious.

In sum, I still venture to maintain that the very nature of the indirect reference to the self requires an element of uncertainty. And if it is correct to apply this linguistic pattern to the New Testament, the thesis advanced by Bultmann and his school, that the 'coming Son of Man' alluded to by Jesus was someone other than himself,[27] provides a nearly perfect example of how sophisticated modern scholars can be taken in by a clever Aramaic *double entendre*.

Joseph A. Fitzmyer's criticism is of a very different kind.[28] For him, it is almost immaterial whether I have made out a case for the circumlocutional use of 'the son of man'. In 1968, he thought the argument 'convincing';[29] six years later he declared that *bar nasha* is 'never found as a circumlocution for "I".'[30] Whatever the merits of my case for the texts examined, it has no relevance to the New Testament because these texts do not belong to works written in the first century AD. Worse still, all my quotations contain the form *bar nash* or *bar nasha*, whereas the noun 'man' in biblical or Qumran Aramaic is spelt with an *aleph: 'enash* or *'enôsh*. Shortening of this sort, he observes, is a sign of lateness, and in 'philological comparisons of the Aramaic substratum of the Gospels . . . it is quite illegitimate to appeal to later texts'.[31]

The methodological principle stated by Fitzmyer is incontestably valid . . . when it is applicable. It would indeed be wrong to rely on sources more recent – or for that matter, older – than the New Testament when the proper kind of contemporaneous documents are available in sufficient quantity. But in the 'son of man' question this is patently not the case. Let us consider then the odd situation that ensues if Fitzmyer is taken as our guide. We all agree that the Greek *ho huios tou anthrōpou* is an Aramaism used in the first century AD. Yet the gospel interpreter is condemned to a stalemate. His first-century comparative material is extremely scarce; moreover, it does not represent the appropriate genre, style, vocabulary and dialect. On the other hand, for mere chronological reasons, he is ordered to forego a wealth of possible clues which appear, indeed are, significant and helpful. Nevertheless, speaking quite objectively, if we accept that the phrase reflected in *ho huios tou anthrōpou* was originally coined in Aramaic by Galileans, is it not sensible, indeed obligatory, to investigate the relics of the Galilean dialect, closest in time to the gospels, the Palestinian Talmud and similar Galilean rabbinic sources, especially when there is good reason to think that their dialectal peculiarities pre-date the period of their codification? Is this plain logic as I will attempt to show, or is it a 'Vermes' flight to *obscurum per obscurius*' as Fitzmyer puts it?[32]

To begin with, is the spelling *nash(a)* with no initial *aleph* (which may have been silent even when written as in Syriac) a definite indication of lateness? Two arguments militate in favour of a negative answer. Firstly, Galileans were notorious for their mis-pronunciation (or non-pronunciation) of gutturals.[33] Secondly, the gospels themselves attest the neglect of the initial *aleph*: they refer to men called *Lazarus*.[34] Now the form *nasha* instead of *'enasha* parallels exactly the change represented by *Lazar* instead of *El'azar*. And the gospel spelling of Lazarus is not a freak occurrence: the Palestinian Talmud regularly substitutes *Lazar* for *El'azar* and *Li'ezer* for *Eli'ezer*.

This observation, expressed lightheartedly in *Jesus the Jew*,[35] provoked the following riposte: 'The difference between the first century Hebrew spellings of the name(s) . . ., and those that he finds in the Palestinian Talmud of several centuries later is just what one would expect! But in all this the real question that he has not faced is whether one can argue from proper names to common nouns; the former are notoriously liable to shortening . . .'.[36]

I believe both halves of Fitzmyer's reply are incorrect. Firstly, is it true that the shortened form of the names *El'azar/Eli'ezer* as *Lazar/Li'ezer* is several centuries more recent than the age of the New Testament? For even if we disregard first-century Greek transcriptions as *Lazar(os)* not only in the gospels, but also in a passage of Josephus[37] and a fragmentary ossuary inscription from Jerusalem,[38] is it exact that the Palestinian Talmud is our oldest source? The truncated spelling of the two names is displayed in some of the best manuscripts of the Mishnah, another Galilean composition preceding the Talmud by a couple of centuries, namely in the manuscripts from Cambridge and Parma and the Kaufmann codex from Budapest.[39] Furthermore, there are several ossuary inscriptions from Jerusalem and its environs which spell both names without the *aleph*. Need I remind you that most of these Jerusalem ossuaries date to the first century or earlier, and that none of them is likely to be post-Hadrianic?[40] We encounter a woman, *Shallon bath Li'ezer*[41] and two men, one called simply *L'azar*[42] and another,

Eli'ezer ben Lazar, the latter figures in a bilingual inscription and is accompanied by the Greek *Eliezros Eleazarou*.[43] So, although the classical spelling with the *aleph* is attested more frequently in first-century documents,[44] there is sufficient evidence to permit us to trace the beginnings of the abbreviating tendency to the age of Jesus.

Secondly, is the dropping of the opening *aleph* in a proper name such a special case that it may not be taken as a model for a common noun of the *'enasha/nasha* type? This question may be disposed of quite promptly. As is evident from Dalman's Grammar,[45] the trend implied was general in the Galilean Aramaic dialect. But examples appear already in the Qumran and Murabba'at documents, where the verb *'amar* (to say) is spelled without the *aleph* on three occasions,[46] and the phrase, 'in the face of', is written once as *banpe* instead of *be'anpe*.[47] The editor of this last text, J. T. Milik, commented in 1961: 'omission de l'aleph comme souvent en judéo-palestinien'.[48]

Here I will rest my case. The arguments in favour of a circumlocutional use of *bar nash/bar nasha qua* indirect reference to the speaker appear able to stand up to all the criticisms formulated until now.

II

The second controversial finding announced in the 1965 lecture, namely the absence of a titular use of *bar nasha* in Aramaic, flatly contradicted the *opinio communis* of that time. Most New Testament interpreters took the opposite view for granted. Some twenty years ago, Oscar Cullmann wrote: 'We come to the following conclusion concerning the Jewish concept of the Son of Man . . . He is a heavenly being, now hidden, who will appear only at the end of time . . . We find this exclusively eschatological figure in Daniel, the Book of Enoch, and IV Ezra.'[49] 'The intimate connexion of the synoptic presentation of the Son of Man with that of Jewish apocalyptic literature can no longer be contested', echoed H. E. Tödt.[50] In a similar vein, Ferdinand Hahn asserted: 'It is . . . overwhelmingly probable that already in pre-Christian Judaism a titular use had established itself which was adopted by Jesus and the primitive community.'[51]

Yet the philologically-based denial of such an eschatologico-messianic title almost immediately found allies among literary critics. In his book, *Rediscovering the Teaching of Jesus*, published in 1967,

the late Norman Perrin discarded in no uncertain terms the so-called
'Son of Man concept',[52] and in March 1968, Ragnar Leivestad read
a paper, which appeared in the same year under the self-explanatory
title, 'Der apokalyptische Menschensohn: ein theologisches
Phantom'.[53] In a revised English version, issued in 1972 with an
equally provocative title, 'Exit the Apocalyptic Son of Man',[54]
Leivestad writes: 'I am quite convinced that the apocalyptic Son of
Man title is a modern invention. A Jewish Son of Man title was
completely unknown to Jesus and the primitive church.'[55] In a style
less blunt, and with gentle irony, my much lamented friend Paul
Winter remarked in, of all places, the *Deutsche Literaturzeitung*: 'If
Perrin's interpretation of the Son of Man sayings in the Synoptic
Gospels is correct . . . then the place of origin of the [Son of Man]
myth is not to be sought in Iran, or in Judea or even in Ugarit, but
in the German universities.'[56]

This wind of change was greatly assisted by the absence of the
Book of Parables, the main alleged source of the 'son of man'
concept, from the Qumran Aramaic manuscripts of Enoch, although
in the late 1960s, reputable scholars admittedly queried the validity
of such a deduction. In 1967, Morna Hooker still preferred to date
the Parables to between 63 BC and AD 70, and declared the Qumran
evidence impressive but indecisive.[57] A year later, J. A. Fitzmyer
expressly attributed to 'sheer chance'[58] the silence of the scrolls.
However, when it emerged from J. T. Milik's publications that Book
II, or the Parables, was not merely lacking in the Enoch material
represented by eleven fragmentary manuscripts from Cave 4, but
was replaced there by the Book of Giants, the chance theory in
regard to the missing Parables became highly improbable.[59] I should
mention in addition Edward Ullendorff's authoritative statement to
the effect that 'the Ethiopic evidence has little or nothing to
contribute [to the "son of man" question] and that it remains
essentially an Aramaic . . . issue.'[60]

My own examination of the relevant sections of Daniel, IV Ezra
and I Enoch, published in *Jesus the Jew*, has persuaded me that no
titular use of the phrase, 'the son of man', can be substantiated in
any of these works.[61] In other words, the date of the Parables is not
an essential ingredient of the thesis. It may be noted in parenthesis
that no argument compels us to adopt Milik's theory that the
Parables were composed by a Christian in Greek, or his extravagant
dating of them to AD 270.[62] This composition belongs most likely to

the last quarter of the first century AD, or perhaps to the first to second century as Matthew Black suggests.[63]

Recent publications of the 1975 to 1977 vintage on this subject seem to adumbrate a new kind of consensus. Barnabas Lindars honestly declares: 'It has now become embarrassingly obvious that the Son of Man was not a current title in Judaism at all.'[64] Maurice Casey's study, 'The Use of the Term "Son of Man" in the Similitudes of Enoch' is just as negative: 'The way is left open to us to deny a special "Son of Man" concept in Judaism.'[65] In the Supplementary Volume to the *Interpreter's Dictionary of the Bible* Norman Perrin re-asserts that the notion presupposed by many New Testament scholars is without support in ancient Judaism,[66] and John Bowker concurs: 'Even if the problem of date (of the Parables) were solved, the apocalyptic use is insufficient to establish that there was a widely known figure in Judaism known as "the son of man".'[67] Even J. P. Brown who at the end of last year appears to have been curiously unaware of the philological debate or of any contribution to the problem after 1972, presupposes, in a paper devoted to the theory that 'son of man' is an ironical self-description, that there was no concept of a coming 'Son of Man' available to Jesus.[68]

The important corollary is this. If the present trend continues and the academic myth of a pre-Christian Jewish 'son of man' concept finishes by being definitively discredited, the bottom will have fallen out of most current exegeses of *ho huios tou anthrōpou*. And this, in turn, will demand a complete re-interpretation of all the New Testament passages.

III

The debate is still in progress and the battle is not yet won. Only New Testament Semitists have reacted so far. As recently as 1975, in a voluminous *Festschrift* of 489 pages entitled *Jesus und der Menschensohn*, the philological issue is bypassed by all its contributors.[69]

Nevertheless, there are also a few hopeful signs. Of course, it is not for me to appraise *Jesus the Jew*, in which, to use our Aramaism, 'the son of man' endeavours to expound the gospel passages in the light of the circumlocutional theory, and claims that the association between *ho huios tou anthrōpou* and Dan. 7.13 constitutes a secondary midrashic stage of development, more understandable in Greek than in Aramaic.[70]

I always remember with emotion and pleasure that admirable octogenarian, C. H. Dodd, who did not hesitate in 1970 to re-adjust a life-time of exegesis so that it accorded with freshly assimilated information concerning the Aramaic usage of 'son of man'.[71] Also in 1970, Jürgen Roloff explicitly appealed to the Aramaic self-reference theory in interpreting the gospel.[72] Barnabas Lindars, although he still entitles his recent paper, 'Re-enter the Apocalyptic Son of Man', bids in fact goodbye to that concept. He whole-heartedly embraces the 'self-reference' theory which enables the speaker 'to make his point with greater delicacy than would be possible otherwise',[73] and notes also its particular relevance to the passion predictions in the gospels.[74] In the end, he proposes to replace the apocalyptic 'son of man' notion by that of an agent of God in the final judgment, and asserts that not only did the New Testament writers identify Jesus as this agent, but he himself was conscious of fulfilling such a function.[75] Be this as it may, it is beyond question that from a philologico-historical viewpoint Lindars' study marks a definite step in the right direction.

John Bowker, though adopting a very different conclusion, strives also to take his inspiration from Semitic data. He sees in the biblical use of 'son of man' a pointer to human subjection to death as well as, in Dan. 7, to divine justification. Acknowledging his dependence, at least partially, on the self-reference theory, he thinks his own formulation suits better the Marcan portrayal of Jesus who 'talked of himself as a man subject (unequivocally) to death, and yet also as one who will be vindicated'.[76]

But this identification of 'the son of man' as a mortal but divinely vindicated individual brings us back to the old 'title-and-concept' situation, with the particular disadvantage that it is derived from the Hebrew where no determined form of the singular *ben adam* is certain to exist. The hypothesis will have, moreover, to face all the classic difficulties: why is 'the son of man' phrase placed only on the lips of Jesus, and why is he never addressed or described as *ho huios tou anthrōpou?*[77]

I have left to the end what seems to be perhaps the most encouraging result of the 'son of man' debate. A few weeks ago in Madrid Luis Alonso Schökel drew my attention to the new Spanish Bible's treatment of the phrase 'the son of man'. 'El Hijo del hombre' has completely disappeared from the *Nueva Biblia Española* of

1975.[78] In Dan. 7.13, *bar'enash* has become 'una figura humana', and in the New Testament *ho huios tou anthrōpou* is rendered as 'hombre' in all the passages where it is thought to be used in a generic sense. But when Jesus employs it as a self-reference, it is translated as 'este Hombre' ('this man').[79] In the Spanish, that is to say, we have the Aramaic underlying the Greek; or as Jerome would have put it, the words of the gospel interpreted 'secundum Chaldaicam veritatem'.[80]

8

The Impact of The Dead Sea Scrolls on Jewish Studies

During the nineteenth century, the 'Jewish science' (*jüdische Wissenschaft*) introduced a new scholarly slant to the study of Judaism. Nevertheless, although the pioneering efforts of Zunz, Fränkel, Graetz and Geiger, followed by the great achievements of the golden generation of the turn of the century – the generation of Bacher and Blau, Büchler and Goldziher, Kaufmann and Krauss, the two Löws and Marmorstein, not forgetting also the occasional non-Hungarians such as Abrahams, Lauterbach and Israel Lévi, and of course Solomon Schechter – resulted in a genuine renewal of Jewish studies, it would be correct however to add that this fell far short of the total upheaval to which the Bible itself was subjected at that time. Jewish scholars of the 1850–1950 period certainly managed, in the main, to free themselves from pure traditionalism, and to apply to rabbinic literature modern methods of research, yet for various reasons, and despite the loud protest of the ultra-conservatives that the contrary was the case, the movement they initiated was in fact not revolutionary.

In part, this is to be attributed to an absence of archaeological finds in the domain of Rabbinica. The acquisition by Western scholars of the contents of the Cairo Genizah came nearest to such a discovery; but although its importance is undeniably great, it never succeeded in firing academic enthusiasm, let alone that of laymen, so much so that at the present time, nearly eight decades after Schechter's visit to Fustat, the main (Cambridge) collection of Genizah fragments still waits to be fully catalogued, evaluated and published.[1]

Another more subtle reason has to do with an unwillingness, by the experts best qualified to do so, to shake the foundations of post-biblical Judaism. This is not the moment to psycho-analyse them, nor am I qualified to perform such a task; suffice it to say that this lack of critical inclination is in keeping with an apathy affecting the *Wissenschaft des Judentums* that is responsible for the failure, after more than a century, to produce a truly critical edition of either the Palestinian or the Babylonian Talmud, or even of the complete Mishnah. Furthermore, I need not remind you that our dictionaries and grammars are antiquated, that concordances are either non existent or incomplete, and mostly based on non-critical texts. Admittedly, the great men of the nineteenth century and those of the pre-Holocaust era in the twentieth, required no such tools since they knew the whole of the rabbinic literature inside out, and by heart. Who, apart from the Kasowskys (pater et filius), would have wasted his time in the pre-computer age in compiling inventories of words and phrases when everything could be quoted from memory? (And what did it matter if now and again the references were within a folio or two from the actual passage?) The various sorts of criticism – Gattungsgeschichte, Formgeschichte, Traditionsgeschichte, Redaktionsgeschichte – had scarcely begun to be applied to biblical studies, and certainly not to Judaica: the masterpieces of that blessed era, Bacher's works on Haggadah and Büchler's attempts at historiography, thoroughly informed and brilliant though they are as far as traditional lore is concerned, intentionally or unconsciously avoid the fundamental questions of historical criticism, particularly those relating to the antecedents and derivation in the Second Temple period of the system often referred to in the past as 'normative Judaism'.

It would of course be unforgivable to ignore the steps taken towards widening the horizon of Jewish studies by drawing on the auxiliary resources of classical philology, Roman law, patristic Bible interpretation and straight New Testament research, as Samuel Krauss,[2] Jean Juster,[3] Louis Ginzberg,[4] and Claude Montefiore[5] endeavoured to do with greater or lesser success. Nonetheless, I venture to suggest that among most spokesmen of the *Wissenschaft des Judentums* – the extreme liberals excepted – it is possible to detect an instinctive apologetical tendency that seeks scientific proof to support traditionally held views.

This was this kind of scholarly world, one unaccustomed to real novelties, that was suddenly faced with the unprecedented phenomenon of Hebrew and Aramaic documents dating to the inter-testamental era. Between 1947 and 1956, eleven caves on the north-western shore of the Dead Sea gave the lie to the axiom that no document written on perishable material could survive in Palestine and disgorged an enormous quantity of leather and papyrus manuscripts and fragments, some large, some tiny, as well as a few ostraca and hoards of coins. The longest of the rolls, the Temple Scroll, did not surface until after the Six-Day-War in 1967. All these, and additional finds, dating to the first and early second centuries AD, made at Murabba'at, Naḥal Ḥever and Naḥal Ẓe'elim, as well as in the fortress of Masada, have altered beyond recognition our documentation regarding the Judaism of that period.

How did the academic world of biblical and post-biblical Jewish research react to this most exciting event?

On the superficial level, there was immediate and almost universal acclaim. The archaeologists and Hebraists who acted as negotiators, advisers and excavators, or as decipherers and editors – Sukenik, de Vaux, Albright and Millar Burrows with his team – used only superlatives in describing the Scrolls as the most ancient and the most important in existence, their discovery as the most significant ever made in biblical archaeology, and everything connected with them as sensational, and indeed epoch-making. Yet the jubilation was more apparent than real. Apart from the scholars already mentioned, who were involved willy-nilly because they happened to be in Jerusalem at the crucial moment – Albright was not, but he was consulted explicitly as the American oracle on all matters pertaining to Palestinian archaeology – most established authorities opted for a wait-and-see attitude. Only a few specialists of international reputation ventured bravely into the Qumran labyrinth: André Dupont-Sommer in France[6] and H. H. Rowley in this country,[7] The already elderly, but still adventurous, Paul Kahle also joined in,[8] without making any noticeable mark on the issue, and the sadly missed Professor G. R., later Sir Godfrey, Driver contributed in 1951 a booklet which is now best forgotten.[9] The one expert in Judaica to throw himself headlong into the argument, that peculiar genius Solomon Zeitlin, declared even before seeing the smallest photograph of the tiniest fragment:

> Although I have not seen these manuscripts and have not the right to pass judgement, I have my doubts about them. I know that during the Second Commonwealth the Jews did not write commentaries on biblical books.[10]

A little later, he became dogmatic:

As to the *Commentary to the Book of Habakkuk* . . . far from being an ancient book, it clearly belongs to the Middle Ages. It is axiomatic that the Jews did not write commentaries on the prophetic book during the period of the Second Commonwealth.[11]

Zeitlin has remained faithful ever since to his original intuition, and has flooded *Jewish Quarterly Review* (edited by him) with ink, if not vitriol, in its defence. His only inconsequential move came in 1950 when, in spite of a formal declaration of intent, 'The Hebrew Scrolls: Once more and finally',[12] he did not stop but continued his anti-Qumran crusade. But of the early well-known protagonists, Dupont-Sommer alone made a lasting impression on the literary and historical study of the Scrolls.[13] Apart from him, the foundations of Qumran research were laid mainly by a new generation of scholars, the young men of twenty-five years ago, untried but eager for adventure.

In 1952, I was preparing for publication my doctoral thesis on 'The Historical Framework of the Dead Sea Scrolls' and travelled to Israel to look at the originals. I was refused access to them by the ailing Sukenik.[14] So, with the connivance of a consul in Jerusalem who furnished me with false papers, I ceased to be a stateless person, and passing through the Mandelbaum Gate (in the consular car) went to spend a month at the Ecole Biblique et Archéologique Française. There I found two scholars (both roughly my contemporaries and famous names today) working on the fragments collected in Cave 1, and studying the new bits and pieces brought by the Beduin to the Palestine Archaeological Museum in cardboard boxes of every size: the Frenchman Jean Dominique Barthélemy, and that most brilliant editor of Qumran material, the Pole, Joseph Milik. Then, in 1953, F. M. Cross – now the leading Scrolls expert in the United States – began his association with the manuscripts from the Judaean Desert; and at the same time a man in his thirties, whose studies had been interrupted by service in the Israeli army, became his father's pupil once again and started his PhD work on, appropriately, the War Scroll. His name was Yigael Yadin.

If I tell this story, it is not only because of the common middle-aged tendency to reminisce, but to point out that the fact that none of us had reputations to risk or lose, or previously advanced theories to defend, turned out to be a distinct advantage. Freedom to move, without the blinkers of prejudice one way or another, and without ties, was absolutely essential if quick progress were to be made in an extremely complex and sensitive area of knowledge.

The first struggle over the authenticity and dating of the Scrolls was soon settled: the discovery of the caves and their contents and the successive stages of the excavation of the Qumran site removed by the mid-50s all reasonable doubt in that respect. It was almost unanimously agreed that the documents were to be assigned to the last couple of centuries of the Second Temple. This conclusion reached chiefly on palaeographical and archaeological grounds, was further indirectly confirmed by the subsequent finds at Masada and in the hiding-places of the Bar Kokhba period.

Transmission of the Text of the Bible

The sudden emergence of a large corpus of Hebrew and Aramaic texts, many centuries older than anything previously known except the Nash Papyrus, had far-reaching implications in most areas of Jewish history and culture. To begin with, it completely revolution-ized – and I am using the term on purpose – our understanding of the history of the biblical text itself. The eleven Qumran caves have revealed scrolls and fragments belonging to all the books of the Hebrew Scriptures, apart from Esther, antedating by over a millenium the earliest Masoretic codices. Clearly, textual criticism will benefit enormously from these documents (especially when Cross and his colleagues release the Cave 4 material), but since our Association is not primarily concerned with the evaluation of the Scrolls from a text-critical viewpoint, I will dwell, instead, on that aspect of the biblical manuscripts which possesses a wider historical significance.

The Qumran Scrolls of the Old Testament represent several textual or recensional traditions and not just a single one. Some biblical books testify to the *textus receptus* of the later Masoretic tradition; others especially the books of Samuel and Jeremiah and the chronology of Kings, echo the Hebrew underlying the Greek Bible; others still correspond to the Samaritan version. To grasp the meaning of this multiplicity, we must bear in mind that it is found in a religious community quick to react in the domain of precision in belief and practice, yet apparently quite happy with a mosaic of textual traditions. It had been the common assumption before Qumran that the canon of the Hebrew Bible was finally established at Yavneh at the very end of the first century. The Scrolls now show that the rabbis assembled there under the leadership of Yohanan ben Zakkai and Gamaliel II had also to decree which single type of text should count henceforward as sacred.

As I have already noted, the text which became the official (proto-) Masoretic text was not a new creation: it was one of the three main types current at Qumran. In other words, when religious authority proceeded to unify the plurality of textual traditions, it canonized one of the existing varieties more or less *in toto* rather than create, as modern biblical scholars often do, a new version with the help of what seems to them to be the best reading found in any of the competing recensions. Whichever method was chosen to achieve a unique canonical text, the basic fact remains that plurality came before an authoritatively imposed unity.

But is there no flaw in this argument? Might not the undeniable plurality at Qumran be attributed to the 'unorthodox' position of a sect? After all, it is possible to surmise – though, no doubt, without hard evidence to back it – that in the 'right' (non-sectarian) circles of Judaism – say among the Pharisees – the sole authority of the (proto-)Masoretic text was never challenged. And the existence of such a text at the time in question is now at least in part vindicated by the Scrolls themselves.

In theory, this would be a perfectly logical attitude. Yet quite apart from whether the notions of orthodoxy and heterodoxy are applicable in the sense implied here during the existence of the Second Temple, the thesis just outlined seems to run against a snag not properly emphasized so far.

Frank Cross, when analysing the variants in the Samuel fragments discovered in Cave 4, noticed that their Hebrew reflects the Semitic substratum of the Greek Samuel, more precisely the so-called Lucianic recension, and that the same type of text recurs again and again in the relevant Greek extracts contained in the *Antiquities* of Josephus. Even more extraordinary, in several passages where Samuel and I Chronicles overlap, the Masoretic version of Chronicles reproduces, not the Masoretic Samuel, but the 4Q-proto-Lucianic variety.[15] In Cross's own words:

> The agreement between the text of Chronicles and 4QSam[a] is most significant. It makes clear now that the text of the Deuteronomic history used by the Chronicler toward 400 BC was by no means identical with the received text.[16]

Set within our frame of reference, this means that when the final compilation of Chronicles was under way, parallel textual traditions were already in existence, and that they were all employed by the ultimate redactor of this biblical work. It would doubtless be inadvisable in the present state of our information to go as far as to suggest that the 4Q type is actually the oldest (and most genuine?) text of the Bible, a text which at a later stage came to be superseded for reasons impossible to guess, by the proto-Masoretic version. Be this as it may, the paradox deserves to be repeated: the Masoretic compiler of I Chronicles quotes, at times, I–II Samuel from a non-Masoretic form of the Hebrew text.

In brief, Qumran has disclosed that even in the field of the transmission of the biblical text itself we have to reckon not with a single chain of tradition, but with a multiplicity of parallel sources. If fully substantiated, this finding will mark a major break-through not only in textual criticism, but also in Jewish intellectual and religious history.

Apocrypha and Pseudepigrapha

Although, in principle, the Apocrypha and Pseudepigrapha are eminently part of the literature of Judaism, before Qumran they were rarely conceived of as properly belonging to the realm of Jewish studies. There were two main reasons for this lack of recognition, one linguistic, the other dogmatic. Concerning the former, none of the compositions classified under the dual heading of Apocrypha and Pseudepigrapha were available in Hebrew or Aramaic until relatively recently. True, a large part of Ecclesiasticus could be read in Hebrew, and a section of the Testament of Levi in Aramaic, thanks to the Cairo Genizah; nevertheless, when we spoke of the Apocrypha, we instinctively associated them wih the Greek language, while the Pseudepigrapha evoked the variegated philological spectrum of Greek, Latin, Syriac and Ethiopic.

The dogmatic reason for keeping this literature in a position apart is that the Tannaim held them to be *sepharim ḥiẓonim*, books beyond the pale of religious influence and not meriting to be preserved. In fact, their survival is due to the interest and respect shown to them, not in Jewish, but in Christian circles.

The Scrolls, needless to say, have fundamentally altered this state of affairs. Not only have they confirmed that the already familiar Hebrew Ben Sira, and Aramaic Testament of Levi, belonged to Jewish antiquity and not to the Middle Ages – as we all know, further

Hebrew remains of Ecclesiasticus were discovered at Masada, too – but they have also provided fragments of the Hebrew and Aramaic originals of Tobit, Jubilees, the Testament of Naphtali and especially of Enoch, not to mention previously unknown works of a similar nature. Thus, Apocrypha and Pseudepigrapha have become demonstrably, and not just hypothetically, Jewish literature, and have had to be accommodated as such. Together with the Qumran Community's own compositions, they have suddenly appeared, not as a secondary and negligible phonomenon, but as clear evidence of Palestinian Jewry's rich intellectual creativity in the multi-party system of the pre-Destruction era. The reduction to unity of religious inspirations which the masters of the Tannaitic age achieved, from Yohanan ben Zakkai to Judah ha-Nasi, was necessitated by the conditions in which Judaism was re-organized, and by the way it responded to the needs and pressures of that period of crisis.

The Aramaic Books of Enoch are likely to form one of the *pièces de résistance* in the pseudepigraphic material from the Dead Sea especially when read in conjunction with M. A. Knibb's new edition of the Ethiopic text, scheduled to appear in 1976.[17] The publication of this work is bound to affect the ideas hitherto in vogue concerning the most important Pseudepigraphon. As you are all aware, the section of the Similitudes (chs 37–72), known also as Book II, is unattested at Qumran, although Book I is represented fragmentarily by five manuscripts, Book III by four, Book IV by five, and even Book V by one manuscript. This means among many other things, that the famous Enochic 'Son of Man' about whom New Testament scholars have speculated so much, appears to be missing from the pre-70 text of the Aramaic Enoch. Milik now advances the theory that the Similitudes were written in the third century, and his arguments will have to be weighed with the greatest care, although on the basis of literary contacts and doctrinal features I myself would be inclined to date it to the last quarter of the first century.

The pseudepigraphic collection from Cave 4 suggests that Aramaic was extensively used during the earliest phase of non-biblical writing activity, and that the revival of Hebrew as normal vehicle came only somewhat later. In a not too distant future it may perhaps be possible to argue that Aramaic was the original language of works such as Tobit and Daniel, surviving bilingually, and that Hebrew is the translation?

At present, the corpus of Pseudepigrapha, so marvellously and competently edited by R. H. Charles some sixty years ago, needs a complete reworking. To my knowledge, three projects are afoot. The first, directed by H. F. D. Sparks, was launched in the fifties, but is still not ready for the printer. The other, a fresh American initiative sponsored by the Society of Biblical Literature and planned as a companion volume to Doubleday's Jerusalem Bible is, as the publishers' jargon goes, 'in active preparation', thanks to the efforts of the energetic secretary of the enterprise, James H. Charlesworth of Duke University. The various works to be included have by now been allocated to an international team of scholars. Meanwhile, a German venture directed by W. G. Kümmel, and planned to consist in five volumes, has taken the lead by starting publication in the form of fascicles.[18] We can await, therefore, a true revival, essentially due to the impetus of Qumran, in this crucial corner of inter-testamental Jewish literature.

Palestinian Jewish History and Culture

Another area in which the Dead Sea Scrolls discoveries are exercising some influence is that of the history and culture of the Jews in Palestine in Late Antiquity. Admittedly none of the Dead Sea Scrolls is a historical document in the strict sense of the word, and the little information we have concerning persons and events and, in general, of the past of the Community, derives from Qumran Bible interpretation. Nonetheless, it must be emphasized that we now possess the literature of a Palestinian group (I try to avoid if I can the term 'sect' which is so misleading), a literature written by its members for internal use (and not for Hellenistic consumption as in the case of Philo and Josephus), in Hebrew and Aramaic. What is more, this literature survives in documents dating to the epoch of the Community's actual existence. These are facts unparalleled in Jewish religious history during those centuries. I hardly need to remind you that no works of the Sadducees have been preserved, and all we know of them derives, with the exception of the brief notices of Josephus and occasional hints in the New Testament, from accounts of controversies reported not by themselves, but by their opponents, the Pharisees. Moreover, neither these accounts, nor those in which the Pharisees describe their own teachings and practices, have reached us in a direct Pharisaic formulation; they are available only in the considerably later rabbinic compilations of Mishnah, Tosephta, Midrash and Talmud. If, to complete the picture, I may be allowed to treat the gospels as Jewish literature of the first century, they can be said to be close in time to the events they relate, but they are extant only in Greek, whereas the language of the chief characters of the story, and even more so their concepts and whole civilization, were Jewish and Aramaic-Hebraic.

An assessment of the Scrolls from the point of view of Jewish history in its broadest sense still largely remains to be done. Some small progress, I hope, has been made in this direction by the revisers of the first volume of Schürer's *History of the Jewish People*,[19] and more is to come in volume II dealing with Jewish institutions.[20] To name only the most obvious topics, Temple, Priests, Levites, worship, biblical exegesis, will bear the noticeable imprint of the Scrolls. It goes without saying that no discussion of the Second War against Rome can now be conducted competently without recourse to the evidence disclosed by the caves of Murabba'at and Naḥal Ḥever.[21] But, I repeat, much is still to be achieved, including a fresh evaluation of the secondary evidence contained in rabbinic literature relating to the period down to Bar Kokhba.[22]

Talmudic experts will be welcomed as partners in a collective task, and as participants in an effort to integrate the sources, *all* the sources, of Jewish culture. Their expertise will complement usefully the specialized knowledge of biblical, inter-testamental and New Testament scholars, and of students of the Graeco-Roman and Parthian-Persian worlds. Perhaps here, too, some optimism is warranted. In the 1950s some of the leading spokesmen of Jewish studies briefly pointed the way. I should like to name Saul Lieberman[23] and Naftali Wieder,[24] and that all-rounder Chaim Rabin.[25] But their example has not always been followed. E. E. Urbach's major work, *The Sages: Their Concepts and Beliefs*,[26] is so construed that in seven-hundred Hebrew pages there is little room for reference to non-rabbinic documents. Enoch and the Testaments obtain three quotations each; the Book of Jubilees four; and the Dead Sea Scrolls, or more precisely the Scrolls of the sect from the Judaean Desert, come on top with nine mentions (of which three are general allusions). S. Safrai has not even Urbach's excuse that the Second Temple period is outside his scope, for it is on the opening page of a volume entitled, *The Jewish People in the First Century*, and in a chapter dealing with 'The Sources' that he writes:

Books . . . belonging to a Jewish sect or sects whose headquarters were at Qumran . . . did not become part of Jewish tradition and . . . will not be discussed directly here.[27]

But there are signs of increasing awareness of the importance of the Dead Sea manuscripts and other non-Talmudic documents among Judaica experts, especially in the writings of the younger generation of practitioners of Jewish studies such as Jacob Neusner[28] in the United States and Bernard Jackson[29] in this country. The new style of scholarship attempts to amalgamate the various sources reflecting Jewish customs, and adopts the sophisticated techniques evolved by biblical and New Testament experts, and by that fine race of proven scholars, the students of classical antiquity. I hope and pray that many more, old and young, will join in in a grand venture of exploration of the entire field of post-biblical Judaism. They will have a special contribution to make to the study of the halakhic literature from the Dead Sea, particularly when the Temple Scroll, the most voluminous source, is published. In the meantime, I would like to stress two issues meriting careful scrutiny. The first concerns the discovery of written religious rules at Qumran. How does this affect the commonly held view that halakhah was, by definition, an oral discipline? Secondly, the Damascus Rule and the Temple Scroll are collections of extra biblical laws arranged according to subject matter. This suggests that the tendency that resulted, after the compilations by Akiba and Meir, in Yehudah ha-Nasi's Mishnah, was already active long before the destruction of the Second Temple.

Haggadah and Religious Thought

I have left to the end the field of haggadic scriptural exegesis in its Qumran connections. The subject has been investigated by many, including myself,[30] so I will restrict my exposition to a few random observations.

1. Haggadah in the Scrolls employs the main techniques of rabbinic haggadah and is directed towards similar ends: clarification, supplementation, and apologetic or polemical argument.

2. Qumran exegesis either precedes Jubilees (as the Genesis Apocryphon may well do), or stands between this second century BC re-writing of the Genesis story and the midrash embedded in rabbinic literature. It displays many similarities to the latter but is at the same time closely connected with the Bible interpretation appearing in Josephus, the Pseudepigrapha and the New Testament.

Consequently the Scrolls constitute a valuable yard-stick for the study of the development of exegesis among Palestinian Jews.

3. In this domain, the Qumran *pesher*, or fulfilment interpretation of real or presumed prophecy, occupies pride of place. In addition to its intrinsic importance, it is as I have already pointed out, our principal source for the Community's history. The Qumran exegetes saw in the words of the prophets predictions referring ultimately to events marking the destiny of their own movement.

4. The close links between the Dead Sea *pesher* and the use of the Hebrew Bible in the New Testament have been noticed since the early days of Qumran research. As is well known, the first generation of Jewish-Christian writers sought to explain and justify or defend their beliefs by appealing, through a special interpretation, to Old Testament oracles. The Scrolls have revealed themselves as a brilliant parallel to this central feature of the gospels. Nevertheless, the eschatological vantage-point suggesting that ancient prediction applies to contemporary event is not exclusively a Qumran and New Testament monopoly: it occurs sporadically in rabbinic literature as well, and is traceable to the most recent book incorporated into the Palestinian canon, that of Daniel.

In chapter 11, verse 30 the author implies that the humiliation of Antiochus Epiphanes (the King of the North) before Alexandria, brought about by the intervention of the Roman navy ('the ships of Kittim'), was simply the fulfilment of a prophecy of Balaam in Numbers 24.24. The words of Numbers 24.17, 'A star shall come forth out of Jacob', were used by Akiba to accredit Simeon ben Kosiba as the royal Messiah. In another context, Yohanan ben Zakkai is said to have announced the imminent rise of Vespasian to the imperial throne by quoting Isaiah 10.34, 'And Lebanon shall fall by a mighty one'. To the contemporaries of the midrashist the sense was crystal clear: when Yohanan surrendered himself to the Roman general, forseeing the futility of any further resistance, he remembered that Lebanon was a symbol of the Sanctuary, and Mighty one, a synonym for a king. So since Vespasian was to destroy the Temple, but first had to be proclaimed king, Yohanan, as we read in the Midrash, greeted him in good Latin, Vive Domine Imperator – Long live my lord, the emperor! The Habakkuk Commentary contains a similar exegesis identifying the Lebanon mentioned by the prophet with the Council of the Community because it tacitly assumes that the Jerusalem Temple has lost its holy status and is superseded by the Community's supreme institution, the Council, until the seventh year of the eschatological war.[31]

The point on which I will end this survey is at first sight of minor importance. One day, some seven or eight years ago, a graduate student of mine came to me and timidly suggested that he'd found something odd in Codex Neofiti. I looked at the passage in question in a photostat copy – this was before the publication by Díez Macho of the volume on Genesis – and immediately realized what he meant. At that point, rather pleased with ourselves, we nearly collided in the corridor of the Oriental Institute with John Barns, our late professor of Egyptology. 'What are you two so jolly about?' – he asked. 'We've discovered a new angel,' I said. Barns laughed. 'You should send him to the Church of England,' he told me. 'She needs all the help she can get.'

Whether or not this angel is available for such onerous additional duties, I don't know, but the passage in which he reveals himself certainly throws a little more light on the intricate bond between Targum, Midrash, Pseudepigrapha and the Scrolls.[32]

The section I have in mind is Genesis 32.25–32, the story of Jacob's struggle with a mysterious and anonymous opponent, a struggle that in spite of the patriarch's injury, finished in a draw, and also in the change of his name to Israel. In Neofiti, the rival is described and named. He is an angel by the name of Sariel, and appears 'in the likeness of a man'. But he is not an ordinary angel; he is a prince in charge of the heavenly choirs.

> Let me go . . . for the time has come for the angels on high to praise and I am the chief of those who praise.

Later on, when Jacob is re-named Israel, Sariel adds the following justification:

> For you have conducted yourself as a prince with angels from before the Lord and with men, and have prevailed against them.

A few interpretative comments may be called for.

Jewish tradition since Hosea 12.5 sees in the heavenly wrestler an angel. Targumic exegesis, moreover, is unanimous in portraying him as a celestial choirmaster. The same view is expressed in the late first-century midrashic composition, Pseudo-Philo's Book of Biblical Antiquities (18.6). However, none of these sources know him as Sariel, and to the best of my knowledge, no angel called by this name ever appears in rabbinic literature.

In the Pseudepigrapha, we find a Sariel among the fallen angels in I Enoch (6.8). In the Greek version of the same book (20.1–8), Michael, Gabriel, Raphael, Uriel, Raguel, Remiel and Sariel are given as the seven chief angels. Yet before claiming this text to be a satisfactory parallel to Neofiti's Sariel, we have to admit that in the Ethiopic text Saraqael is substituted for Sariel.[33]

Instead of these uncertainties, the Scrolls furnish us with a firm pointer. The Qumran War Rule (9.12–15), in its description of the four battle formations called 'towers', each consisting of three hundred men equipped with shields and spears, mentions that they are to be under the protection of the four archangels, and that every soldier is to bear the name of the heavenly protector of his unit inscribed on his shield.

> On all the shields of the towers they shall write: on the first Michael; [on the second Gabriel; on the third] Sariel; on the fourth Raphael.

So at Qumran, Sariel becomes one of the four chief angels, replacing Uriel, the traditional fourth archangel in the Greek Enoch and in midrashic literature (Cf. Num. R. 2.10; Pes. R. 46.3). He also appears in an Aramaic fragment of 4Q Enoch 9.1: 'Michael, Sariel, Raphael and Gabriel'.[34]

Now to find the missing unit in this puzzle, the known elements of which are: Mysterious wrestler (Gen.) = angel (Hos.) = heavenly choirmaster (Palest. Targums) = Sariel (Neof.) = one of the four archangels (Qumran) – I must add the parallel appearing in the Similitudes of Enoch (40.9; 54.6; 71.8; 71.9). Here, the fourth chief angel is neither Uriel, nor Sariel, but Phanuel. But since this name is dependent on the Peniel Penuel of Genesis 32, the designation by Jacob-Israel of the place where he struggled with the angel, it would appear that in the circles represented by the Similitudes of Enoch, Qumran and the Neofiti variety of the Palestinian Targum, the angelic adversary of Jacob was recognized as one of the four celestial princes, and called alternatively as Sariel or Phanuel.

As for the etymology of Israel, Neofiti explains it, not from the root *śrh/* (to struggle) as modern scholars do; nor from *śrr* (to be strong), implied by the Septuagint (*enischuein*) and the Syriac version, but from *śrr* (to rule, to act as a prince). All the other Targumic recensions (*rb, 'trbb*), as well as Aquila and Symmachus (*archein*), represent the same understanding of the title, Israel. It is noteworthy that when the Damascus Rule 6.5–6 seeks to expound the phrase, 'the penitents of Israel', it identifies them as those whom God (*'l*) has called princes (*śrym*).

Is it merely by chance that Qumran and Codex Neofiti go hand in hand in disclosing, and finding an answer to, a Jewish doctrinal issue? I think not. In fact, I am inclined to believe that this conjunction of Scrolls, Pseudepigrapha and rabbinic literature prefigures many more 'happy coincidences'.

I would like to conclude by expressing the hope that the final quarter of this century will be as fortunate as the last one in uncovering new vistas, and in deepening our understanding of inter-testamental and rabbinic Judaism, and that the members of our new-born Association will distinguish themselves in every one of the many branches of Jewish studies.[35]

9

The Impact of the Dead Sea Scrolls on the Study of the New Testament

From the very beginning of Qumran research, the relationship between the Scrolls and the New Testament has been the subject of voluminous, occasionally fanciful, and frequently heated argument. For a correct approach to this problem in the light of a quarter of century of research, a few preliminary remarks may be of use.

Comparison between the two bodies of literature is not only reasonable, but indispensable: they roughly date to the same era and derive from the same milieux. But if we are looking for possible influences of one on the other, it must not be forgotten that the Qumran Community antedates the Christian church, and the Scrolls the New Testament.

Scholars almost without exception would agree that the writings of both religious movements are in some way linked, though they would differ concerning the extent and nature of the connection. At one extreme we find the theory, first propounded by J. L. Teicher[1] and more recently re-stated by Y. Baer,[2] according to which the Scrolls are Christian documents, the Community is the Judaeo-Christian church, and the Teacher of Righteousness is Jesus. An intermediary position is occupied by the thesis claiming that the Community and the church are in straight evolutionary line, i.e. that Christianity is an *off-shoot* of Essenism, and Jesus a *successor* of the Teacher of Righteousness. Its chief spokesman, A. Dupont-Sommer, argues that Qumran confirms Renan's judgment that 'Christianity is an Essenism which has largely succeeded'.[3] But the average academic view conceives of the Dead Sea Sect and Christianity as two separate branches of the same tree, and accounts for the similarities by descent from the common stock of first-century Judaism. There would thus be no need to look for any *direct* impact of the Community on the church.

What are we to think of these theories?

The identification of the Scrolls as Judaeo-Christian documents has so little substance that it can safely be discarded. Essene parentage of Christianity however still remains a distinct possibility and requires further examination. Nevertheless it is not inappropriate to stress in advance that the emphasis laid on the punctilious observance of the Mosaic Law at Qumran contrasts so strongly with the peripheral importance given to it in the New Testament, that a linear descent of one to the other seems extremely unlikely. In the circumstances, therefore, the most sensible way to tackle the question of inter-relationship would be to start with the theory of two independent developments, and subsequently to ask whether *all* the common features can satisfactorily be explained in this manner.

The first major topic to be considered is the prominence given in both corpuses to *eschatological expectation*. Whether in the form of an announcement of the imminent arrival of the kingdom of God, or of the proximity of universal judgment, or of the *parousia* during the life-time of the generation to which the gospels and letters were first addressed, the authors of the New Testament were firmly convinced that they were witnessing the final act of the last age. Similarly, the whole Dead Sea literature is permeated with the idea that the *eschaton* had already begun; that the Teacher of Righteousness had ushered in the ultimate age, and that in the events taking place before their own eyes, the members of the sect could detect the realization of biblical prophecies. However, as the consummation of time was more and more delayed, hope and perseverance became essential virtues, as the Habakkuk Commentary makes plain.

> *If it* (the end) *tarries, wait for it, for it shall surely come and shall not be late* (Hab. 2.3). Interpreted, this concerns the men of truth who keep the Law, whose hands shall not slacken in the service of truth when the final age is prolonged. For all the ages of God reach their appointed end as He determines for them in the mysteries of His wisdom (*1QpHab*. 7.9–14).

The New Testament echoes the same preoccupation.

> You must understand . . . that scoffers will come in the last days with scoffing . . . and saying, 'Where is the promise of his coming? . . .' . . . But do not ignore this one fact, beloved, that with the

Lord one day is as a thousand years, and a thousand years as one day . . . The Lord is not slow about his promise . . . but is forebearing toward you . . . that all should reach repentance. But the day of the Lord will come like a thief . . . (II Peter 3.3–10).

A second parallelism between Qumran and Christianity consists in their respective claims to be the *true Israel*. Each group believed in its own absolute and exclusive election; they alone formed the community of God's chosen. Each group was certain that it was the legitimate heir to all the divine promises made to the historical Israel, and that it, and it alone, was the participant of a new Covenant. The Qumran Community describes itself as a 'house of truth', 'that tried wall, that precious cornerstone, whose foundations shall neither rock, nor sway in their place' (*1QS* 8.7–8). The same metaphor, and a similar use of Isa. 28.16, are prominently displayed in the New Testament (cf. especially Rom. 9.32–33; I Cor. 3.10–13; Eph. 2.20; I Peter 2.6). But the most notable evidence of the conviction of these minority bodies that they truly represented, solely and completely, the 'Chosen People' appears in the symbolical division of their communities into twelve tribes, following the ideal pattern of the biblical Israel. The Qumran sect was led by twelve tribal chiefs (*1QSa* 1.27–2.1) and the supreme council of the sect consisted of twelve laymen and three priests (*1QS* 8.1). By the same token, the twelve apostles of Jesus are promised to 'sit on twelve thrones, judging the twelve tribes of Israel' (Matt. 19.28; Luke 22.30), and the church to which James wrote his letter is defined as 'the twelve tribes in the dispersion' (James 1.1).

The third basic ideological bond between the Scrolls and the New Testament resides in their peculiar *attitude to the Bible*. The prophetic character of the Hebrew Scriptures had acquired paramount importance both for the church and for the Community. The two were convinced that, when correctly interpreted and properly understood, the words of the prophets announcing the final realities refer to the history, doctrines, and beliefs of their own group. Such an attitude towards the Old Testament was conducive to a growing employment of biblical apologetics: the predestined character of the sect or church was proved by the conformity of its history to prophetic prediction. There was of course a certain variation in style in presenting these arguments. The Scrolls, being aimed at initiates, can proceed with less emphasis and even elliptically; whereas the New Testament, addressed to outsiders as well, has to spell out every detail of its demonstration. 'All this took place to fulfil what the Lord had spoken by the prophet' (Matt. 1.22). 'For these things took place that the scripture might be fulfilled' (John 19.36). Another point of obvious difference is that the early church represents Jesus as the subject of prophecies, the person in whom they are realised, whilst the Teacher of Righteousness at Qumran is the final interpreter, the man 'to whom God made known all the mysteries of the words of His servants the Prophets' (*1QpHab.* 7.4–5).

The fourth – partial – overlap between Qumran and primitive Christianity turns on their notions of the significance of the *Jerusalem Temple*. According to biblical tradition, the sanctuary was the chosen dwelling-place of the divine Presence, and sacrificial worship – legitimately performed only in that one place – was the focal point of the religion of Israel. But for the Dead Sea sectaries the Temple had lost its holiness because of the wickedness of the priesthood and they substituted for it under the leadership of the sons of Zadok, the Council of the Community, their supreme institution. Atonement was to be made through the spiritual sacrifice of prayer and suffering.

They shall atone for sin by the practice of justice and by suffering the sorrows of affliction (*1QS* 8.3–4).

They shall atone for guilty rebellion and for sins of unfaithfulness that they may obtain loving kindness for the Land without the flesh of holocausts and the fat of sacrifice. And prayer rightly offered shall be as an acceptable fragrance of righteousness, and perfection of way as a delectable free-will offering (*1QS* 9.4–5).

He (God) has commanded that a sanctuary of men be built for Himself, that there they may send up, like a smoke of incense, the works of the Law (*4QFlor.* 1.6–7).

In this respect, the behaviour of Jesus and the apostles, including that of Paul when he was in Jerusalem, appears to have been conventional. They taught and prayed in the Temple, and in general participated in the cult. At the same time, on the level of doctrine and belief, Paul insists, like the Sect, that the Christian community has replaced the old sanctuary.

(You are) built upon the foundation of the apostles and prophets, Christ Jesus being the chief cornerstone, in whom the whole structure is joined together and grows into a holy temple in the Lord; in whom you also are built into it for a dwelling place of God in the Spirit (Eph. 2.20–22).

Again, as in the Qumran sect, the appeal is for the sanctification of the self to replace sacrifices and offerings.

I appeal to you . . . to present your bodies as a living sacrifice, holy and acceptable to God, which is your spiritual worship (Rom. 12.1).

One important dissimilarity nevertheless exists between the two theologies. At Qumran, withdrawal from the Jerusalem Temple was intended as a temporary measure lasting as long as the rule of the wicked priesthood. In the seventh year of the eschatological war sacrificial worship was expected to be restored. The priestly, levitical and lay leaders of the Community – so the War Rule legislates –

shall attend daily at the gates of the sanctuary . . . These are the men who shall attend at holocausts and sacrifices to prepare sweet-smelling incense for the good pleasure of God, to atone for all His congregation, and to satisfy themselves perpetually before Him at the table of glory (*1QM* 2.3–6).

By contrast, when the visionary of the New Testament Book of Revelation contemplates the new Jerusalem, he perceives it to be without any material place of worship.

And I saw no temple in the city, for its temple is the Lord God the Almighty and the Lamb (Rev. 21.22; cf. John 2.19–21).

Continuing with the issues on which the two movements converge, special attention should finally be given to various aspects of their organization and customs.

The close relationship, both philological and real of the *mebaqer* (overseer/guardian) and the *episkopos* (bishop) has been noticed and emphasized since the publication of the Damascus Rule in 1910, but the reappearance of *mebaqer* in the Qumran Community Rule gives the question renewed actuality.

The economic system characterized by the use of the common purse and partial adoption of common ownership of property is also an obvious point of similarity. Both the Essenes of the classical accounts, and the full initiates of the Scrolls, had to hand over to the authorities their properties and earnings. This regime was so unusual both within and without the boundaries of Jewry that the Essene rejection of money (*sine ulla pecunia* – in Pliny's words)[4] became one of the distinctive marks of the sect.

The New Testament nowhere imposes a similar rule. Yet, the Fourth Gospel at least implies that Jesus and the apostolic community attached to him drew from a common purse, held as at Qumran, by one of their number.

> Some thought that, *because Judas had the money box*, Jesus was telling him, 'Buy what we need for the feast'; or, that he should give something to the poor (John 13.19; cf. 12.6).

More importantly, the description of the original Jerusalem church in Acts strongly suggests that Christian property-owners felt morally obliged to sell their belongings and consign the profits thus acquired to the apostles.

> And all who believed were together and had all things in common; and they sold their possessions and goods and distributed them to all, as any had need (Acts 2.44–45).

> But a man named Ananias with his wife Sapphira sold a piece of property, and with his wife's knowledge, kept back some of the proceeds, and brought only a part and laid it at the apostles' feet (Acts 5.1).

Compared with the drastic punishment that ensued – both of them dropped dead – Qumran was mild towards sectaries dishonest in financial matters:

> If one of them has lied deliberately in matters of property, he shall be excluded from the pure Meal of the Congregation for one year and shall do penance with respect of one quarter of his food (*1QS* 6.24–25).

It is not easy to be positive about the problem of celibacy at Qumran and in the New Testament. The Essenes according to the Greek and Latin sources rejected marriage (*omni venere abdicata*, writes Pliny),[5] but evidence at Qumran in the fields of both literature and archaeology is contradictory. If the sectaries envisaged by the Community Rule were married, one would expect to encounter legislation relating to the married state as in the Damascus Rule for example. But the Community Rule is quite silent on this topic. At the same time, female and child skeletons have been found in the secondary cemeteries at Qumran (though male remains alone in the main one). But be this as it may, the War Rule explicitly envisages the total separation of men and women during the last thirty-three years of the eschatological war (*1QM* 7.3–4; cf. 2.6).

The New Testament does not condemn marriage, but holds celibacy or withdrawal from marital ties, to be preferable (Matt. 19.10–12; Luke 14.26; 18.29; I Cor. 7.1, 7–8, 32–34). One of the reasons given is the practical one that family bonds must be severed by those who wish to accompany Jesus on his journeys (Luke) or to devote themselves fully to 'the affairs of the Lord', i.e. the church (I Cor. 7.32–34). The second is the eschatological requirement that the chosen few, endowed with understanding, should make themselves 'eunuchs for the sake of the kingdom of heaven' (Matt. 19.12). A third is a reason of convenience: the unmarried will have less trouble and worry than the married during the 'impending distress' of the final upheaval (I Cor. 7.26–31; cf. Matt. 24.19).

On the personal level, Paul explicitly declares himself to be wifeless (I Cor. 7.8; cf. 9.5). Inexplicitly, the gospels give the impression that Jesus also was unmarried. As celibacy, or even a lengthy separation of the sexes is alien to the Jewish way of life – Eliezer ben Hyrcanus at the end of the first century AD went as far as to assimilate abstinence from procreation to murder (*bYeb.* 63b) – this could be a domain of some importance to the study of Qumran influence on Christianity.

Another fruitful though perhaps less central subject for consideration is the significance of Pentecost, as developed in the Scrolls and the New Testament. It is generally agreed that Pentecost was the day on which the sect celebrated the annual renewal of the Covenant, enrolled new applicants, and admitted the initiated at the end of their two year training. Can it be a coincidence that chapter 2 of Acts dates the first massive public entry into the new Christian sect to the same feast, during which Peter's sermon was followed by the repentance and baptism of 'about three thousand souls' (Act. 2.41)?

Of the first of these five major areas of contact between Qumran and the New Testament – eschatological expectation, true Israel, attitude to the Old Testament, attitude to the Temple and similar organization and customs – it is undeniable that eschatological ferment was active throughout Palestine in the first century AD. But neither the general picture of Jewish society of that time depicted by Josephus, nor rabbinic traditions traceable with some probability to the pre-70 AD era, would indicate that Palestinian Jewry as such was affected by this fever to the intensity attested in the Scrolls and the New Testament. On the other hand, an all-pervading eschatological expectation is more naturally found in fringe movements or sects than in the more sedate religious mainstream. It is reasonable to infer that the Community and the primitive church belonged to the same socio-religious stratum of Palestinian Jewry. But we would not be justified in seeking to associate them more specifically than this.

General sectarian principles may also explain the claim made by both the Community and the church to be the true Israel, the righteous remnant to which the other Jews must attach themselves if they are to be saved, and their respective convictions that they were fulfilling prophecies. As these claims were of course necessarily contradictory, their separate arguments could have been influenced by controversy. There is, nonetheless, no evidence of any such confrontation in either corpus, and in the circumstances, speculation on the potential effects of polemics between the followers of the Teacher of Righteousness and those of Jesus remain without foundation.

The Temple problem is more complex. For the Qumran sect which was dominated by priests, the sanctuary and the cult were of greater importance than for a group of unsophisticated Galileans who formed the nucleus of Christianity. This could account for the basic difference between the two doctrines regarding the transitory or permanent nature of the Temple's replacement. Yet the likeness of Paul's theology to that of Qumran on this point is too pronounced to be merely accidental, and it is legitimate to surmise that Paul was acquainted, directly or indirectly, with Qumran symbolism and that he adapted it in formulating his own teaching on spiritual worship. The same comment may apply to the genesis of Paul's thought on the 'Israel of God' (Gal. 6.16): in shaping his own doctrine, he imitated, but simultaneously contradicted, the sectarian claims of the Scrolls.

The most probable Qumran influence on the New Testament is associated with organization and religious practice. For the last four decades of the Second Temple the two communities co-existed. But Christianity during that time was no more than a nascent body, whereas the Qumran sect was a well-established institution. It would have been only sensible if in the fields of administration and finance the inexperienced organizers of the church had looked round for inspiration, and had observed existing patterns with a view to taking over and modifying them. As for the dating of the public foundation of the Christian church to the feast of Pentecost, this appears also to disclose polemical self-assertion on the part of Christianity.

The issue of celibacy or discontinuation of marital life is less simple. The New Testament practical argument in favour of the single state, viz. that an itinerant preacher or a person joining such a master needs freedom and mobility is not applicable to Qumran, or to – if they are different – the Essenes of Josephus and Philo: there we deal largely with sedentary communities. On the other hand, the eschatological emphasis manifest in I Corinthians and the War Rule suggests once again that the Scrolls may have had immediate or intermediate effect on Paul's thought. But does it account for Jesus' (apparent) avoidance of marriage? To evaluate the possibility of a Qumran influence on Jesus, we must first examine the Community's justification of sexual abstinence during the eschatological era. It cannot surely lie in the misogynistic tirades of Philo (*Apol.* 14–17) and Josephus (*BJ* ii.121; *Ant.* xviii. 21) that women are selfish, jealous, skilful in seduction, licentious and untrustworthy, and that marriage is harmful to common life and leads to discord. In fact, the only explicit reference to the separation of the sexes in the Scrolls appears in a context of ritual cleanness.

> No boy or woman shall enter their camps, from the time they leave Jerusalem and march out to war until their return. No man . . . smitten with a bodily impurity . . . shall march out to war with them . . . And no man shall go down with them on the day of battle who is impure because of his 'fount', for the holy angels shall be with their hosts (*1QM* 7.3–6).

A ritual motivation of this sort is quite out of place in the case of Jesus, a Galilean charismatic, who never attached much importance to ritual cleanness and uncleanness. Rather is it that the renouncement of marriage imputed to him falls within the pattern of prophetic celibacy attested in Philo and rabbinic literature. The Alexandrian philosopher states that Moses cleansed himself

> . . . of all the calls of mortal nature, food and drink and intercourse with women. This last he had disdained for many a day, almost from the time when, possessed by the spirit, he entered on his work as prophet, since he thought it fitting to hold himself always in readiness to receive the oracular messages (*Vita Mosis II*, 68–69).

In a more colourful style, the midrash places in the mouth of Zipporah, the wife with whom Moses has ceased to cohabit, the following exclamation when she sees the two elders, Eldad and Medad, in a state of prophetic ecstasy:

Woe to the wives of these men![6]

There is in my opinion no better alternative than this to account for Jesus' free embrace of the single state (if indeed he did so). Perhaps John the Baptist's celibate life is also susceptible to a similar explanation. But it should be remembered that before becoming a prophet, John was a hermit.

John the baptizer appeared in the wilderness . . . clothed with camel's hair, and had a leather girdle around his waist, and ate locusts and wild honey (Mark 1.4, 6).

There was no room for women in a life such as his.

One significant conclusion emerges from these considerations. If the Scrolls exerted any influence on the New Testament – and it is reasonable to assume that they did – they will have done so not on Jesus himself, to whom the bulk of Qumran doctrine will have been alien, if not repugnant, but on Paul, John and other leaders of the new church. Their use, that is to say, will reside in throwing light on Christianity of the apostolic age, and in showing, more clearly than every before, negatively what Jesus was not, rather than what he was.

Having dealt with the larger issues, I will be content to leave the details – important though they are – untouched, or refer you instead to the excellent studies which have appeared in the form of learned articles, monographs and collections of essays. May I mention in particular Herbert Braun's two volumes, *Qumran und das Neue Testament* (1966), the first of which lists Qumran parallels arranged in the model of a minor Strack-Billerbeck, according to book, chapter and verse of the New Testament. The second volume summarizes scholarly views inspired by the Qumran Scrolls on various doctrinal subjects selected from the New Testament. You are advised to read also four valuable collective works: *The Scrolls and the New Testament* edited by K. Stendahl (1957); *Paul and Qumran* edited by J. Murphy-O'Connor (1968); *The Scrolls and Christianity* edited by M. Black (1969) and *John and Qumran* edited by J. H. Charlesworth (1972).

Having counselled you on where to turn for reliable further

reading, I must now draw your attention to the less reliable. Firstly, the identification by Jose O'Callaghan, of minute Greek papyrus fragments from Cave 7, with practically nothing legible on them, as belonging to the New Testament (Mark, Acts, Rom., I Tim., James, II Peter) derives exclusively from his fertile imagination. His 'discovery' has been rightly rejected both by Qumran experts and by the British elder statesman of Greek papyrology, C. H. Roberts.[7] Oddly enough, the main following of the Spanish Jesuit appears to come from the American Bible belt.

Secondly, since the publication of Hebrew and Aramaic texts dating to approximately 150 BC–AD 50, a trans-Atlantic New Testament Semitist has stressed that to be valid, comparison, especially philological comparison, between the New Testament and Jewish literature must be based on documents that are contemporaneous.[8] In other words, Qumran manuscripts and first-century AD inscriptions are the only suitable comparative material. Rabbinic writings, including the Palestinian Targums and similar works preserving colloquial Galilean Aramaic, are *a priori* disqualified because they were compiled *after* the first century AD. This is quite wrong, as has been shown earlier.[9] Consequently recourse to rabbinic literature – however tiresome for the insufficiently trained average New Testament scholar – will remain imperative for as long as we can foresee.

In fact, if I may return to the main conclusion of this chapter, if the Qumran Scrolls are invaluable in shedding new light on early Christianity, rabbinic literature skilfully handled, is still the richest source for the interpretation of the original gospel message, and the most precious aid to the quest for the historical Jesus.

10

The Essenes and History

Two aspects of the Qumran discoveries deserve to be characterized as sensational and revolutionary. The first concerns the textual evolution of the Hebrew scriptures. I belong to the generation of scholars who were academically initiated into biblical studies before the emergence of the Dead Sea Scrolls: so the passage from the pre-Qumran to the Qumran era is part of my own experience. When I try to convey to undergraduates of today the true impact of these finds, I keep on reminding them (maybe it is a sign of approaching old age) that in my student days it was accepted as axiomatic that no biblical manuscript dating to antiquity could have survived in Palestine. Or I may formulate my explanation of a problem thus: If someone had put this question to me say in 1946, I would have replied either that I did not know, or that I could produce only a conjectural answer; but now we possess concrete evidence . . . And so on and so forth.

The second domain of learning substantially transformed by the Scrolls is that which deals with the ancient community of the Essenes.[1] As you see, I assume – and my reasons for this assumption will be outlined presently – that there is identity or at least a close relationship between the Qumran sect and the Jewish ascetics described by Philo, Josephus and Pliny the Elder. But, not only did these writers – even Josephus – show no interest in the actual history of Essenism, but for philosophical or propagandistic considerations they appear deliberately to have played down the typically, and in many respects exclusively, Jewish features and the religious, social and political associations of the community. They present the Essenes as models and ideals to the world at large, with emphasis on what is universally human rather than specifically Jewish among them. Not surprisingly, it is the Roman Pliny who manages best to portray the sect as a 'meta-historical phenomenon' in existence since time immemorial.

Ita per saeculorum milia, incredibile dictu, gens aeterna est in qua nemo nascitur.[2]

[Thus, incredible though this may seem, there is an eternal race into which, during thousands of centuries, no one has been born.]

As a result of this general silence, until about 1950 no concrete evidence had been available regarding Essene beginnings so nobody had tried to place the movement within the framework of Jewish history. The old Schürer (as distinct from the Vermes-Millar production) is a perfect mirror image of pre-Qumran scholarly attitudes. For the professor from Göttingen, Essenism 'as a peculiar problem in the *history of religions*'[3] deserved our attention. When he wrote at the turn of the nineteenth and twentieth centuries, the problem was not, and apparently could not be, treated in any other way in spite of the recognized fact that the community 'grew up on Jewish soil' and that 'the origin of the order would have to be placed in the second century BC' . . . 'It is questionable', Schürer wrote, 'whether they proceeded simply from Judaism or whether foreign and especially Hellenistic elements had not also an influence in their organization.'[4]

The effect of the Qumran finds, I believe it is correct to assert, is that the Jewish roots of Essenism are now established and its birth and development linked to some of the salient, and therefore identifiable, events of the history of Israel during the last three centuries of the Second Temple period.

Essenes and Qumran

As soon as the first Dead-Sea-Scroll-extracts appeared in print, the late Professor Eleazar Lipa Sukenik suggested that the sect responsible for them was that of the Essenes,[5] a theory subsequently argued with cogency and enthusiasm by Professor André Dupont-Summer.[6] Other competing theses were also forcefully propounded associating the community with Pharisees,[7] Sadducees,[8] Zealots,[9] Judaeo-Christians[10] and even with medieval Karaites,[11] but the Essene hypothesis quickly gained ground, and after the discovery and exploration of the Qumran ruins became, despite continued opposition from certain quarters, the dominant view among experts, a kind of *opinio communis*.

Comparison of the literary and archaeological data from Qumran, with evidence assembled from the classical sources, supplies the following positive and negative arguments of the basic Essene case.[12]

1. The sectarian establishment at Qumran seems to correspond to the principal Essene settlement located by Pliny between Jericho and Engeddi.

2. Chronologically, the Essenes first mentioned, in Josephus in mid-second century BC, are still flourishing in around 50 CE when Josephus claims to have experimented with their way of life, and continue until the first revolution against Rome. Archaeological evidence seems to date the sectarian occupation of the Qumran site to about the same period (140 BC–AD 68).

3. Within this geographical and chronological context, the common life depicted in the two sets of sources, as well as the community's rites, doctrines and customs, display so numerous and such striking resemblances that the thesis equating the Qumran sectaries and the Essenes possesses a high degree of probability.

Negatively, the major objections raised by some scholars against the Essene theory cannot stand up to criticism. Differences admittedly exist between the portrait contained in the classical accounts and that in the Scrolls. But let us not forget that there are also differences between Philo, Josephus and Pliny, between the various notices of Josephus or Philo and even between the several Qumran descriptions themselves. However, these discrepancies may be resolved if three further points are taken into account.

4. According to the Qumran evidence, the sect consisted of *two* branches with *two* separate economic regimes, one practising common ownership of property, the other not. Similarly, Josephus testifies to a *duality* of Essene discipline in regard to marriage which seems to be confirmed by some of the Dead Sea writings and by Qumran archaeology.[13]

5. Another source of difference is that the Scrolls reflect the ideas of members of the sect and are intended for initiates or for novices undergoing initiation. By contrast, the classical narrators were all outsiders. (Even Josephus, the best informed among them, had only an unfinished Essene apprenticeship to his credit).[14] Moreover, their notices were aimed at a non-Essene and even non-Jewish readership.

6. Finally, no rival identification is, in my judgment, convincing, whereas the Essene theory appears not only to be sound but endowed with a high degree of intrinsic probability. To reject it

would not render any of the other hypotheses more likely but merely lead to the conclusion that the Qumran relics must belong to a hitherto totally unknown Jewish sect almost identical to the Essenes! Which reminds one of the familiar story about the biblical historian who denied that Joshua led the conquest of Canaan and argued that the victorious Israelite general was a cousin who just happened to bear Joshua's name.

The history of the Essenes[15]

While information concerning Essenism can now be gathered from classical and Qumran sources, the placing of the sect within the context of history is, apart from a few data supplied by Josephus and helpful to outline a vague chronological framework, wholly dependent on the Dead Sea discoveries. The literary evidence on which we have to rely is nevertheless of a peculiar kind: it is contained mainly in documents devoted to Bible exegesis proper or to arguments based on scriptural interpretation. I will discuss this phenomenon in the final section of this chapter, but now it is time to turn to the Scrolls and bring together their fragmentary and cryptic historical allusions.

According to the Damascus Rule, the birth of the sect occurred '390 years' after the destruction of the first Temple when a 'root' sprung from 'Israel and Aaron'. This group of priests and laymen 'groped for the way' for twenty years, until they received a guide sent by God, 'the Teacher of Righteousness'. A faction within the congregation designated as 'the seekers of smooth things' rebelled against him and followed 'the Liar', who led them astray in matters of doctrine, morals and liturgical calendar. Violent conflict ensued, and the Teacher together with those remaining faithful to him, was exiled to 'the land of Damascus', where they established the 'new Covenant'. There the Teacher died. The wicked, on the other hand, continued to rule in Jerusalem until they encountered divine vengeance by the hand of 'the chief of the kings of Greece'.

The Habakkuk Commentary also refers to a defection by disciples of the Teacher to the Liar, or 'Wicked Priest'. This man is described in greater detail. He was called by 'the name of truth' before he became Israel's ruler and allowed himself to be corrupted by power and wealth. He re-built and profaned Jerusalem and the sanctuary. He 'chastised' the Teacher and his congregation. He pursued them and confronted them in their refuge on their Day of Atonement.

He was punished by God, who delivered him to enemies who 'took vengeance on his body of flesh'. We hear also of his successors, the 'last priests of Jerusalem', who are accused of plundering the peoples. The riches amassed by them would however be seized by the 'Kittim', the divinely appointed new world conquerors.

A fragmentary Commentary on Psalm 37 further reveals that the Teacher of Righteousness was a priest, and that those who took revenge on the Wicked Priest were not Jews but 'the violent of the nations'.

The Commentary of Nahum, concerned with an epoch later than that of the Teacher of Righteousness, is dominated by the theme of 'the furious young Lion', a Jewish ruler who attacked 'the seekers of smooth things' – a nickname for the sect's opponents – because they had invited 'Demetrius, King of Greece', to come to Jerusalem. His attempt failed – in fact, no foreign prince entered the capital 'from Antiochus until the coming of the rulers of the Kittim' – and Demetrius' Jewish allies were 'hanged alive on the tree' by the 'furious young Lion'. Here as in the Psalm Commentary, 'Ephraim' with their teachers of falsehood, and 'Manasseh' with their mighty dignitaries, are the community's enemies.

It should be noted that in the Commentaries, God's instruments of vengeance are the 'Kittim'. In the War Rule their role changes and they are transformed into Satan's chief support, into the final foe of the elect.

These data, together with a few hints relating to the career of an exiled Teacher in some of the Thanksgiving Hymns and also the archaeological evidence, constitute the Qumran material for Essene history. It is worth pointing out that the vast majority of the literary allusions are cryptic and that, apart from the two Greek kings mentioned in the Nahum Commentary, the only other quasi-straightforward historical references figuring in yet unpublished documents name 'Shelamzion' (Alexandra-Salome), 'Hyrcanus' (John Hyrcanus II) and 'Emilius' (M. Aemilius Scaurus, one of Pompey's generals).[16]

Historical hypotheses

During the 1950s six main types of reconstruction were proposed to explain the references to the Teacher of Righteousness and the Wicked Priest. The allusions were said to concern (1) the pre-Maccabaean stage of the Hellenistic crisis; (2) the age of the

Maccabees (Jonathan and/or Simon); (3) the Hasmonaean era (Alexander Jannaeus or Aristobulus II/Hyrcanus II); (4) the time of Jesus and the origins of Christianity; (5) the period of the first revolution against Rome; or (6) medieval Karaism.

To keep the discussion within manageable proportions, I will be high-handed and eliminate the last three theories without further ado. The Karaite hypothesis, advanced by P. R. Weis and Solomon Zeitlin,[17] is simply untenable in the light of the combined evidence of archaeology, palaeography and literary contents. The Zealot thesis, the brainchild of an oddly matched Oxford couple, the late Sir Godfrey Driver and the late Cecil Roth, cannot account properly for the pre-Christian stage of Qumran archaeology and the pre-Christian date of a good many Dead Sea Scrolls.[18] The same criticism applies also to the Judaeo-Christian theory, first championed by J. L. Teicher.[19] Besides, I cannot see how the Scrolls and the New Testament can possibly speak of the same subject and about the same characters. Indeed, if anyone can persuade me to think otherwise, I am prepared, with the consent of course by the authorities of the Shrine of the Book, to imitate Ezekiel and eat the Scroll containing such a proof.

In regard to the remaining three theories, two preliminary remarks may be useful. First, to interpret a set of cryptograms we can either identify a single notable detail and subsequently use it as a pivot around which the rest must turn. Or we can attempt to fix a framework and piece together a picture within it, trait by trait. Secondly, most historians of Essenism agree that the personality easiest to identify is the Wicked Priest, the persecutor of the Teacher of Righteousness. They assume that any candidate for this role should possess the following characteristics. He should be a ruling pontiff who at an early stage of his public life was acceptable to the sect but lost favour later, and who fell eventually into the hands of the 'violent' among the Gentiles. If we take the last allusion alone and understand it to imply that he was *killed* by them, our choice is reduced to two second-century BCE candidates. If on the other hand the Wicked Priest is thought to have suffered humiliation or maltreatment only, another two names may be added from among the High Priests of the last century of the pre-Christian era.

In 1950, a leading French Orientalist, André Dupont-Sommer, announced that he had found an irrefutable clue to the historical puzzle (then represented by the Habakkuk Commentary only). It had become obvious to him, in reading that the Teacher of

Righteousness had manifested himself to the Wicked Priest and his followers on the Day of Atonement with the aim of destroying them, that this was a sectarian theological description of the conquest of Jerusalem by Pompey on the great fast day of 63 BC (the Kittim being the Romans). The Wicked Priest must therefore be Hyrcanus II (or Aristobulus II). In the end, he opted for Hyrcanus. The other details could all be smoothly arranged once this central point was established. And, in effect, Dupont-Sommer continued throughout the years to use every new piece of information to supplement and strengthen his theory.[20]

Yet in my opinion this is a fundamentally shaky proposition from the literary point of view, and one that is difficult to square with the archaeological evidence. His exegesis of the Habakkuk Commentary passage as hinting at a supernatural self-revelation of the murdered Teacher of Righteousness is without any sound basis in the text, where the obvious subject of the verb 'to appear', *hofia'*, is the Wicked Priest.[21] Besides, it is far from certain that Jerusalem fell to Pompey on the Day of Atonement, since if, as seems likely, Josephus used a Gentile document as his source when he spoke of the 'fast day',[22] then the reference may just as well have been to a sabbath as to Yom Kippur.[23] Finally, for a description of the person responsible for putting Hyrcanus to death, namely Herod the Great, one would expect something more particular and apposite than a 'violent' Gentile.

The Hasmonaean thesis consequently strikes me as unproven. An alternative version postulates Alexander Jannaeus as the Wicked Priest. Supported by, among others, M. Delcor,[24] J. M. Allegro[25] and J. Carmignac,[26] this derives some confirmation from the Nahum Commentary's allusion to a crucifixion echoing that mentioned in Josephus' account of the execution of eight hundred Pharisees by Jannaeus. But neither of the other two characteristic features of the Wicked Priest, an impeccable beginning and a violent death inflicted by pagans, can be verified in the case of Alexander.

The chief exponent of the pre-Maccabaean theory, first elaborated in three lectures delivered in Louvain in the spring of 1952 and published that same year in book form, was the late Professor H. H. Rowley.[27] For Rowley, mention of the 390 years time-span after the capture of Jerusalem by Nebuchadnezzar *ipso facto* settled the matter: the community of the Hasidim was formed in 196 BC. The Teacher of Righteousness, who appeared twenty years later, was the High Priest Onias III. The Wicked Priest responsible for instigating the murder of the Teacher was the Hellenizing High Priest Menelaus, himself subsequently put to death by Antiochus V Eupator.

Even before we examine its compatibility with the archaeological finds – Rowley's thesis was, in fact, worked out before the results of the first season of Qumran excavations were published – it is clear that this reconstruction is confronted by insurmountable obstacles. For one thing, since no ancient Jewish writer seems to have been correctly informed concerning the chronology of the Second Temple era, and especially of the Persian period, it is unlikely that the 390 years of the Damascus Rule are to be accepted at their face value. Moreover, for Rowley the Kittim were Seleucids, an opinion defended today by few – if any. Lastly, it is inconceivable that a sectarian writer should have found Menelaus acceptable at any period of his public life.

The Maccabaean thesis that the Wicked Priest was Jonathan (with possible references to Simon) was first elaborated by me in a 1952 doctoral dissertation, and has since then been reformulated several times wihout any substantial change, most recently in 1977.[28] Although it was at first thought shocking – my own supervisor was firmly unconvinced – it soon attracted powerful allies in the persons of J. T. Milik,[29] F. M. Cross[30] (who preferred Simon to Jonathan) and P. Winter,[31] and further support from the 'converted' R. de Vaux[32] (a former Jannaeus fan), J. Starcky[33] (who in conversation some years earlier expressed total disbelief that a holy Maccabee might be called 'wicked'), G. Jeremias,[34] H. Stegemann,[35] M. Hengel,[36] J. Murphy-O'Connor[37] and others.

In explanation of my reasoning, I should say that I first set out to establish the *terminus a quo* and the *terminus ad quem* of the historical horizon. (For the sake of simplicity, I will outline the most up-to-date version of my exposition.)[38] The probable archaeological time-limits are, as has been noted, the mid-second century BC and 68 CE. The identifiable historical names appearing in the Scrolls also clearly belong to the second and first pre-Christian centuries. The 'age of wrath' that began 390 years after Nebuchadnezzar is a cryptogram for the Hellenistic crisis, also alluded to in similar imagery in Daniel, Enoch, Jubilees, Testament of Levi, Assumption of Moses, etc. The Antiochus of the Nahum Commentary who entered Jerusalem can therefore be only Epiphanes. The *terminus ad quem* is constituted by the appearance of the Kittim on the scene, first as God's instrument for the punishment of the wicked, later as the ultimate satanic force on earth. During the opening stage, their leaders were rulers (*moshelim*); in the end, they were to be commanded by a king (*melekh*). The first Kittim defeated the 'last priests of Jerusalem'; the later Kittim were to present the final threat to truth and justice. The Roman identity of the Kittim having been established by Dupont-Sommer, Qumran history falls neatly into two parts: (1) the period 'from Antiochus to the coming of the Kittim', i.e., the last century of Hellenistic Palestine during which the community came into being and the conflict occurred between the Wicked Priest and the Teacher; and (2) the period of the rule of the Kittim up to the Vespasian-Titus war.

So far, the 'age of wrath' has been identified as the Hellenistic crisis, the Kittim as the Romans, and the 'root' sprung from Israel and Aaron as the Assidaean movement. But who was the principal Jewish enemy of the sect, the Wicked Priest? Bearing in mind the characteristics of this person as they are defined in various documents – a man of good repute before he assumed the high-priestly office, victorious over his adversaries at home and abroad, a rebuilder of Jerusalem, eventually captured and killed by a foreign rival – we are inevitably led to the Maccabee brothers, Jonathan and Simon, preferably Jonathan, the only one to die by the hand of a Gentile, namely Tryphon, appropriately alluded to as 'chief of the kings of Greece' by the Damascus Rule. (Simon, you will remember, was murdered by his son-in-law.)

The phrase 'the last priests of Jerusalem' may well designate various members of the Hasmonaean dynasty, from John Hyrcanus I to Aristobulus II, and in particular Alexander Jannaeus, the 'furious young Lion'. If so, references to the 'seekers of smooth things' of 'Ephraim', and to the influential men of 'Manasseh', may symbolize Pharisees and Sadducees.

In this hypothesis, the Teacher of Righteousness, a priest with Zadokite affiliation though obviously opposed to Onias of Leontopolis, is bound to be a contemporary of Jonathan. Beyond this, however, his historical identity is still unconfirmed and I am not optimistic that this state of affairs will see any improvement. His group supported the Maccabaean cause until Jonathan accepted pontifical office from Alexander Balas. His hostility to the Maccabees caused a split in the ranks of the community and the departure into exile of the Teacher and his adherents. Of his subsequent career we know little, not even how he died.

The Scrolls disclose no further historical details but some additional information may be gleaned with the aid of Josephus and Qumran archaeology. We learn that an Essene, Judas by name, famous for his prophetic gifts, correctly predicted the death of Aristobulus I's brother, Antigonus (*Ant.* xiii. 311–13). Another Essene prophet, Menahem, foretold to Herod that he would rule over Israel, and the latter out of appreciation and gratitude dispensed the sect from the oath of loyalty which he imposed on all his Jewish subjects (*Ant.* xv. 373–8). A third Essene, the dream-interpreter Simon, proclaimed to Archelaus, ethnarch of Judaea, that he would rule for ten years (*Ant.* xvii. 345–8). As for John the Essene, he was appointed *strategos* or military governor of the district of Thamna and the cities of Lydda, Joppa and Emmaus at the start of the first revolution (*BJ* ii. 567), and fell in the battle of Ashkelon (*BJ* iii. 11, 19).

Finally, Josephus speaks of Roman tortures inflicted on Essenes during the first war (*BJ* ii.152–3). This tallies with the archaeologists' claim that the violent end of the Qumran settlement was due to the seizure of the chief Essene establishment by the soldiers of Vespasian in the summer of 68.

Some German scholars, in particular Gert Jeremias and Hartmut Stegemann, have attempted to bridge further gaps in the Maccabaean historical canvas. Subjecting some of the Hymns to a form-critical analysis, and assuming furthermore that the Teacher of Righteousness was their author, they have deduced from vague poetic hints a whole detailed story of an internal struggle among the sectaries.[39] But I am afraid that the matter is far too conjectural for any serious consideration.

In brief, I continue to believe that the identification of the Wicked Priest as Jonathan is, to put it modestly, the least unsatisfactory of the historical reconstructions so far advanced. Nevertheless, when I decided to choose 'The Essenes and History' as the subject of this study, I thought it my duty to draw attention to any discrepant views presented in recent years and to submit them to proper examination. I have come across four such publications, though two of them, whilst they disagree with my thesis on some important details, remain reconcilable with its general tenor.

In a learned paper[40] based on a thorough literary analysis of the Community Rule and the Damascus Rule, Jerome Murphy-O'Connor argues for a Babylonian pre-history to the Essene movement, 'Damascus' being a symbolical name for Babylon. It originated, he suggests, in Mesopotamia in the course of the exile.

The Essenes then returned to Palestine during the leadership of Jonathan (the Wicked Priest), and the prominent Zadokite, who acted as High Priest during the preceding period of 'inter-sacerdotium' but became redundant at the moment of Jonathan's rise to the pontificate, joined them and was recognized as the Teacher of Righteousness. These details, although compatible with the main thesis, strike me as being less than sound. Neither the symbolical value of Damascus = Babylon, nor the idea of a single acting High Priest during the seven years of the inter-sacerdotium (*Ant.* xx. 237), are solid enough to amount to anything more than unsupported speculation.

Equally speculative is Jean Starcky's recent thesis distinguishing two consecutive Teachers of Righteousness, the first appearing under Jonathan, and dying under Jannaeus, and the second manifesting himself after Pompey.[41] With all due respect to the French scholar, I am unable to see how 'l'hypothèse d'au moins deux maîtres de justice rend beaucoup plus aisé l'accord des textes qumrâniens avec les données archéologiques, paléographiques et historiques'.[42] The medieval axiom still commends itself: *entia sine necessitate multiplicanda non sunt.*

A much more substantial disagreement emerges from a paper by Isaac Rabinowitz devoted to the Demetrius passage in the Nahum Commentary.[43] The American professor, one of the early holders of the pre-Maccabaean hypothesis, is convinced that the Demetrius in question is Demetrius I Soter, successor of Antiochus Epiphanes, and that 'the identification establishes a secure temporal frame of reference for the composition not only of this text, but for that of all other Qumran Peshers and related texts'.[44] Rabinowitz reverts to the style of those who believe that one individual point can settle an issue as complex as Qumran history. But until he has shown how it fits into a coherent whole, and also how references to the Kittim can apply to Seleucid Greeks, we are entitled to remain unpersuaded.

The latest revolutionary theory comes from the pen of a woman writer from the Antipodes, B. E. Thiering.[45] Her thesis is highly complex, if not confusing. On the one hand, she tries to refute all the arguments situating the Wicked Priest in the second century BC and to set him instead in the first century CE. On the other, she maintains the longer chronological framework but suggests that the sect underwent a series of mutations, with Essene, Zealot, Judaeo-Christian and once again Zealot phases. To conform to this picture, palaeography has to be completely re-written, and unless I grossly misunderstand Dr Thiering, most of the Qumran documents must be dated to the mid-first century or even to the age of the first Jewish war. If you deduce an absence of enthusiasm on my part, you will be right; but wait, more is to follow. The Teacher of Righteousness is John the Baptist, a not altogether novel view: it was proposed as far back as 1949 by that master of odd ideas, Robert Eisler, in a letter to *The Times*. But when we are told that the Wicked Priest, described in the Scrolls as a lover of wealth, a persecutor of the Poor, master and desecrator of the Temple, is Jesus – this is to overstretch even the elastic standards of Scrolls scholarship.

The Essenes and Jewish historiography

Whichever theory you may adopt – and I trust it will be the right one! – it is beyond dispute that thanks to Qumran, we now have, instead of the '*gens aeterna in qua nemo nascitur*', a community with recognizable roots in the Zadokite priesthood and identifiable aims. We can better comprehend its ideals and form of life and attach a real, rather than speculative, significance to some of its uncommon customs.

It is also possible, as you have seen, to put together a patchy account of the movement's history, from its origins in the earlier part of the second century to the fateful summer of 68. In fact, provided we are not too greedy for *minutiae*, the general picture available to us now is as substantial as many in ancient history.

Such an insertion of Essenism into the Judaism of the inter-testamental era is also bound to have, and to some extent has already had, far-reaching consequences in our understanding of Jewish literary, cultural and religious history, and even in the way Jewish society in the age preceding the destruction of Jerusalem is represented. In the ensuing new epoch in Jewish studies, there will in any case be no room for attitudes such as the one for which an Israeli historian has acquired international notoriety. On the first page of a book sketching the literary sources of first century CE Jewish history, he states:

In recent years, books in Hebrew and Aramaic belonging to a Jewish sect or sects whose headquarters were at Qumran . . . have also been discovered. These . . . did not become part of

Jewish tradition and, like the Apocrypha, will not be discussed directly here.[46]

I hope you will rather agree with the stand adopted by the revisers of the new Schürer, who have not only added a special section on the Dead Sea Scrolls to the chapter devoted to the sources of the late Second Temple period, but have used every opportunity to make the voice of Qumran heard in their discussion of inter-testamental Jewish history, institutions, culture and religion.

To finish on a note of self-congratulation would be un-British. If you are prepared to bear with me a little longer, I will therefore briefly touch on a subject rarely mentioned: the Scrolls in relation to the general problem of ancient Jewish historiography.

I will begin with a question. Why is it so difficult to reconstruct Essene history? The straight answer is that all the written evidence belongs to a peculiar genre: not a single one of the thousands of Qumran fragments detached from hundreds of manuscripts can be classified as historical. Is that accidental? No. Jewish writings composed in Hebrew and Aramaic in the inter-testamental, Mishnaic and Talmudic age show an almost total lack of interest in historiography proper.[47] In an essay entitled, 'La chaîne de la tradition pharisienne' (The chain of the Pharisaic tradition), Elias Bikerman attributes this attitude to the loss by the Jews of *political autonomy* after Herod, and especially after the destruction of Jerusalem. The only historical document kept by the Pharisees was the list of the predecessors of Hillel and Shammai in the first chapter of *Avot*.[48]

More recently, in 1965, Arnaldo Momigliano pertinently commented in his review-article, 'Remarks on Eastern History Writing', that even in biblical times Israelite concern with history was rather special. 'The Jews of the pre-exilic period or of Ezra's time did not do exhaustive historical research in order to understand God's continuous intervention in the world. What the Biblical historian did was to select from tradition those facts which seemed to him relevant to his interpretation of God's Order.' He further argued that the Jews turned their back on history not merely because they had lost their independence, but also because they were busying themselves with a fundamental reconstruction of their religious faith in which relationship between God and the individual Jew mediated by the Torah was substituted for the relationship between God and Israel mediated by 'kings, priests and prophets'.[49]

I think Momigliano is perfecty justified in enlarging the area of enquiry. Biblical history is indeed not history proper. It does not record events for their own sake or for secular purposes, but only on account of their presumed religious significance. According to Josephus, historians are successors to the prophets.[50] And we know from reading their works that it was the prophets' job to demonstrate how victory or defeat in war, peace or social unrest, rich harvest or famine, revealed the nation's virtue or sinfulness.

Qumran historiography – produced at least in part during Hasmonaean autonomy – constitutes a transitional phase from a prophetic presentation of events to a quasi-prophetic *exegesis* of biblical texts in the form of the Dead Sea *pesher* literature. For those 'historians', the true meaning of the occurrences of their time was to be sought in the mysterious significance, revealed by God to the Teacher of Righteousness, of divinely inspired predictions uttered in the past. In fact, by deciphering other biblical prophecies, they could even forecast future happenings. It may consequently be reasonable to add to Bikerman's and Momigliano's diagnoses that the a-historical outlook of the rabbis was the outcome not only of the loss of political independence or of exclusively religious preoccupations, but of the elimination by the sages of the last vestiges of prophecy, probably because prophetic authority and rabbinic tradition appeared to them to be irreconcilable.

But – and I will end on this point – it is also true, is it not, that during the inter-testamental era ancient Judaism produced its *best* historiography, in the works of Josephus . . . written in Greek. And when in the Middle Ages Jews began to show fresh interest in history writing, it was after they had made cultural contact with the Muslim and Christian civilizations. But this is another story, for another occasion.

Abbreviations

Ab.	*Aboth*
Ant.	Flavius Josephus, *Antiquitates*
APOT	R. H. Charles, *The Apocrypha and Pseudepigrapha of the Old Testament* I–II, 1912–13
b	Babylonian Talmud followed by the name of the tractate
BA	*Biblical Archaeologist*, New Haven, Conn.
BB	*Baba Bathra*
Ber.	*Berakhoth*
BJ	Flavius Josephus, *Bellum Judaicum*
BM	*Baba Mezi'a*
CBQ	*Catholic Biblical Quarterly*, Washington
Decal.	Philo, *De Decalogo*
DJD	*Discoveries in the Judaean Desert* I, 1955
DSS	G. Vermes, *The Dead Sea Scrolls: Qumran in Perspective*, 1977, 1981, 1982
DSSE²	G. Vermes, *The Dead Sea Scrolls in English*, ²1975
EH	Eusebius, *Ecclesiastical History*
Enc. Jud.	*Encyclopaedia Judaica* 1–16, Jerusalem 1971
ET	English translation
Flor.	*Florilegium*
GenAp	*Genesis Apocryphon*
History	Emil Schürer, *The History of the Jewish People in the Age of Jesus Christ* I, rev. and ed. G. Vermes and F. Millar, 1973; II, rev. and ed. G. Vermes, F. Millar and M. Black 1979
HTR	*Harvard Theological Review*, Cambridge, Mass.
IDB	*The Interpreter's Dictionary of the Bible* I–IV, New York, Nashville 1962
IDBS	*The Interpreter's Dictionary of the Bible, Supplementary Volume*, Nashville 1976

JAOS	*Journal of the American Oriental Society*, New Haven, Conn.
JBL	*Journal of Biblical Literature*, Philadelphia
JE	*The Jewish Encyclopaedia* I–XII, New York 1901f.
JJS	*Journal of Jewish Studies*, Oxford
JQR	*Jewish Quarterly Review*, London
JSJ	*Journal for the Study of Judaism*, Leiden
JSNT	*Journal for the Study of the New Testament*, Sheffield
JTS	*Journal of Theological Studies*, Oxford
Jub.	*Book of Jubilees*
m	Mishnah followed by the name of the tractate
M	*Milḥamah* (War Rule)
Makk.	*Makkoth*
Meg.	*Megillah*
Mekh.	*Mekhilta*
Ned.	*Nedarim*
NT	*Novum Testamentum*, Leiden
NTS	*New Testament Studies*, Cambridge
p	*Pesher*
PAAJR	*Proceedings of the American Academy for Jewish Research*, New York
PEQ	*Palestine Exploration Quarterly*, London
PG	Patrologia Graeca, ed. J. P. Migne
PL	Patrologia Latina, ed. J. P. Migne
Ps. Jon.	Pseudo-Jonathan
Q	Qumran Cave preceded by its number
R.	Rabbah preceded by the name of the biblical book
RB	*Revue Biblique*, Paris
S	*Serekh* (Community Rule)
Sᵃ	*Serekh*, first annex (Messianic Rule or Rule of the Congregation)
Sᵇ	*Serekh*, second annex (Benedictions)
Sanh.	*Sanhedrin*
Shabb.	*Shabbath*
Sheb.	*Shebi'ith*
Sheq.	*Sheqalim*
Sot.	*Soṭah*
Spec. Leg.	Philo, *De Specialibus Legibus*
Strack-Billerbeck	H. Strack and P. Billerbeck, *Kommentar zum Neuen Testament aus Talmud und Midrasch* I–IV, 1922–28
t	Tasefta followed by the name of the tractate

TDNT	*Theological Dictionary of the New Testament* I–X, ed. G. Kittel and G. Friedrich, 1964–76
TWNT	*Theologisches Wörterbuch zum Neuen Testament* I–X, 1933–76
y	Palestinian Talmud followed by the name of the tractate
Yad.	*Yadayim*
Yom.	*Yoma*
ZDPV	*Zeitschrift des deutschen Palästina-Vereins*, Wiesbaden
ZNW	*Zeitschrift für die neutestamentliche Wissenschaft*, Berlin

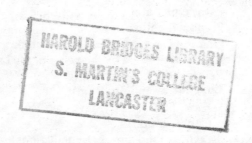

Notes

Preface

1. Josephus, *BJ*, VI, 300–305. The episode is noted by E. Schürer, *Geschichte des jüdischen Volkes im Zeitalter Jesu Christi* II (⁴1907), p. 262, n. 82. In the original English translation (II. i, p. 289, n. 518), the Josephus reference is erroneous. Our revised edition (II, p. 223, n. 93) offers a fuller account of the story. It is discussed by A. E. Harvey (*Jesus and the Constraints of History*, London 1982, pp. 27–28) and briefly mentioned by D. R. Catchpole, *The Trial of Jesus*, Leiden 1971, p. 241.

2. And of John the Baptist as seen by Josephus.

3. Cf. *Jesus the Jew*, London 1973, p. 51.

4. A. E. Harvey, op. cit., p. 28, argues that the transfer of Jesus son of Ananias to the procurator's court resulted from the inability of the Jewish authorities to deal with this recalcitrant man. This is hardly the case. A Jewish offender could be imprisoned; cf. Ezra 7.26; Acts 5.17–18; Damascus Rule (CD) 12.4–6 (seven years for the profanation of the Sabbath), and such a sentence would have excluded further opportunities even for involuntary mischief-making. Harvey does not seem to have paid sufficient attention to Josephus' remark that the officials suspected that God might be involved. This would suggest that the recourse to the Roman jurisdiction was not due to an absence of Jewish legal means to resolve the issue, but rather to the unwillingness of the Jerusalem magistrates to try the case.

It is worth noting in this context that according to the gospel accounts themselves, Jesus was sent from one judicial body to another. He first appeared before the High Priest Caiaphas (after a prior interrogation by Annas, according to John 18.13) and the Sanhedrin. He was then sent to Pilate who, according to Luke, finding no case against him, was glad to hand him over to Herod Antipas, conveniently present in Jerusalem, to whose jurisdiction Jesus as a Galilean belonged (Luke 22.4–7). But Herod declined to become involved and returned him to Pilate (22.11), who finally pronounced the death sentence. While this is not the place to subject these stories to a detailed critical examination, I think it fair to point out that if there is a tendency common to all the authorities in question, it is that each seems to be intent on exonerating themselves from responsibility.

5. I have already explained in *Jesus the Jew* (pp. 127–128) that although

I hold Mark to be more primitive in outlook than Matthew, the latter appears occasionally at least more faithful to the *genre* of Aramaic story-telling.

6. For the question of the *Parousia* expectation, see pp. 24–25, 37–38 below.

1. Jesus the Jew

Delivered as the twenty-first Claude Goldsmid Montefiore Lecture at the Liberal Jewish Synagogue in London on 14 November 1974.

1. Geza Vermes, *Jesus the Jew: A Historian's Reading of the Gospels*, London 1973 and New York 1974, ²1976, 1981, 1983.

2. *The Guardian*, 10 October 1969.

3. Rudolf Bultmann, *Jesus and the Word*, 1962, p. 14. (He died in 1976.)

4. Syme, 'The Titulus Tiburtinus', *Vestigia*, vol. 17, p. 600.

5. *Jewish Antiquities*, viii, 45.

6. *Jewish Antiquities*, viii, 46–47.

7. *Financial Times*, 7 February 1974.

8. It may come as a surprise to many that at the time of the birth of Jesus, the Pharisaic confraternity numbered according to Josephus (*Jewish Antiquities*, xvii, 42), only a little over six thousand members, as against four thousand Essenes (ibid., xviii, 20), whereas the total Jewish population of Palestine is estimated to have amounted to two to two and a half millions.

9. *Jewish Antiquities*, xviii, 117–118.

10. *The Times Literary Supplement*, 7 December 1973.

11. *JJS* 25, 1974, p. 336.

12. *Theology* 77, 1974, p. 277. The same journal carried a rejoinder to Horbury by A. E. Harvey (pp. 376–77).

13. *The Tablet*, 8 December 1974, p. 1179.

14. *The Month*, January 1974.

15. L. E. Keck, *JBL* 95, 1975, p. 509.

16. D(enise) J(udant), *La Pensée catholique*, no. 176, 1978, p. 88.

17. Michel Bouttier, *Etudes théologiques et religieuses* 54, 1979, p. 299.

18. *JTS* 25, 1974, p. 489.

2. The Gospel of Jesus the Jew I: A Historian's Reading of the Gospels

Originally delivered together with chapters 3 and 4 as the Riddell Memorial Lectures in March 1981 and published by the University of Newcastle upon Tyne under the title *The Gospel of Jesus the Jew*, 1981.

1. One of the major problems facing any scholar concerned with Jesus is that the accumulated mass of literature devoted to him not only leaves little room for new insights but positively tends to block the way to a fresh understanding of the gospels. I have therefore decided to re-read the synoptics with my mind on their teaching content and to determine the main lines of my thesis in these chapters on that foundation before looking

into the views of contemporary New Testament scholarship. I have however made use of the latter afterwards, checking and correcting initial conclusions in the light of current theories and debate.

It is important to note that this study of 'The Gospel of Jesus the Jew' cannot include a complete bibliographical survey or discuss all relevant opinions. A detailed account of recent academic work on Jesus is available in the series of review articles published by W. G. Kümmel in *Theologische Rundschau* between 1975 and 1980: 'Ein Jahrzehnt Jesusforschung (1965–1975)', vol. 40, 1975, pp. 289–336; vol. 41, 1976–77, pp. 198–258, 295–363; 'Jesusforschung seit 1965', vol. 43, 1978, pp. 105–161, 232–265; vol. 45, 1980, pp. 48–84, 293–337.

2. Typical of this kind of presentation is one of the introductory objections in Thomas Aquinas's *Summa Theologiae*. The section, 'Utrum Deus sit' (Is there a God), begins as follows: 'Videtur quod Deus non sit' (It would seem that there is no God). See St Thomas Aquinas, *Summa Theologiae. Latin Text and English Translation*, Pars prima, quaestio secunda, articulus tertius, Blackfriars (1964), pp. 12–13.

3. On the history of New Testament exegesis, see *The Cambridge History of the Bible* I–III, 1963–1970; S. C. Neill, *The Interpretation of the New Testament 1861–1961*, 1963; Robert Davidson and A. R. C. Leaney, *Biblical Criticism* 1970; W. G. Kümmel, *The New Testament: The History of the Investigation of its Problems*, [2]1970.

4. The attitude of the so-called quality press to works of sound scholarship on religion, including the study of the New Testament, is distinguished by a shyness oddly at variance with a laudable interest in academic books on archaeology, classics and ancient history. Only such topics as *The Sacred Mushroom and the Cross* and the Turin Shroud seem to attract the large headlines in the national dailies and weeklies nowadays.

5. I hope I shall be forgiven if I reproduce here the opening lines of the original 1973 Preface to *Jesus the Jew*, no longer contained in the current paperback editions: 'During the last few years I have often been asked whether I was writing my book on Jesus from a Jewish point of view. The answer is yes – and no. It is not inspired by traditional Jewish attitudes towards the "Founder of Christianity", and is decidedly not intended to depict a "Jewish" Jesus as a denominational counterpart of the Jesus of the various churches, sects and parties that claim allegiance to him. On the other hand, insofar as it insists that a convincing study of Jesus of Nazareth must take into account that the Gospels containing the story and teaching of this first-century Galilean demand a specialized knowledge of the history, institutions, languages, culture and literature of Israel, both in Palestine and the Diaspora, of the age in which he lived, then it is a very Jewish book indeed.'

An example of the extreme opposite of the historian's approach to the gospels is that of fundamentalist Christians who insist as an absolute condition for the understanding of the gospel message that one shares the evangelist's outlook. See ch. 1, p. 2 above.

6. Up to until the end of the last century, expertise in the Bible, both in the Old and the New Testaments, was regarded as part of the Christian theologians' indispensable appurtenance. It was for such men, familiar as a matter of course not only with Latin and Greek but also with Hebrew and Aramaic, that the highly technical presentation of Jewish history, institutions, doctrine and literature from 175 BC to AD 135 by Emil Schürer was intended. Cf. *Geschichte des jüdischen Volkes im Zeitalter Jesu Christi* I (³⁻⁴1901), p. 1. As the scope of the scriptural field broadened and the need grew for more and wider linguistic, archaeological and historical skills, an autonomous (or quasi autonomous) biblical discipline came into being. To begin with, it embraced the whole of scripture; the giants of those days, say Wellhausen or Lagrange, excelled in both Testaments, not to mention other branches of orientalism and the classics. Later, a growing trend towards specialization resulted in a divorce between Old Testament and New Testament research and the appearance on the scene of two distinct species, 'Alttestamentler' and 'Neutestamentler'. Today the separation seems complete. The run-of-the-mill New Testament specialist rarely possesses more than a rudimentary knowledge of Hebrew: biblical Hebrew, that is, for post-biblical and rabbinic Hebrew is seldom taught in (English and North American) Christian theology courses. As for Aramaic, the spoken language of Jesus, I myself heard a distinguished New Testament professor declare at a professional gathering that the special study of Aramaic is quite unnecessary since it is 'the same as Hebrew'. In 1975, the Oxford Theology Board seriously attempted to make even the Greek text of the gospels optional – biblical Hebrew, as far as I know, has never been compulsory there for theology students – but after lengthy public debate the Board's plan was frustrated through a formal vote by Congregation, the University's parliament. A verbatim report of the speeches may be found in the *Oxford University Gazette*, Supplement (3) to No. 3625, of 11 June 1975, pp. 973–84.

7. P. S. Alexander describes my approach to the gospels as a 'method of moving inwards to the New Testament from a firm control of the surrounding literature'. He considers this method preferable to 'the sorties in search of parallels' adopted by 'many New Testament scholars'. (Review of G. Vermes, *Post-biblical Jewish Studies*, in *JTS* 27, 1976, p. 172.)

8. The interpreter's primary task is to assess the evidence contained in the gospels, detect the basic material, and then form it into a coherent whole. Historical reconstructions based on the (hypothetical) identification of a single trait – a method not uncommon in Dead Sea Scrolls research – are unlikely to provide anything substantial by way of conclusions. See below, pp. 131–32, 136.

9. This same idea is to be found in various guises in the traditional or conservative branches of Judaism (cf. Louis Jacobs, *A Jewish Theology* (1973), pp. 215–18) and in Christianity, Roman Catholic or Protestant. As recently as 18 November 1893, Pope Leo XIII was able to write in his encyclical, *Providentissimus Deus*, that all the canonical books of the Bible

derived directly from the Holy Spirit: 'Spiritu Sancto dictante conscripti sunt'. On the Protestant attitude to the question, see James Barr, *Fundamentalism*, 1977, pp. 286–303. This author notes that in much Calvinist and Lutheran orthodoxy, the Masoretic vowel signs (invented by Jewish scholars between AD 600 and 900) are also held to be part of the inspired content of the Hebrew Bible and that such a doctrine implies a concept of inspiration entailing 'dictation' (ibid., pp. 297–98).

10. For a brief general survey, see G. B. Caird, 'Chronology of the NT', *IDB* I, pp. 601–2.

11. See G. Vermes, 'Bible and Midrash', *The Cambridge History of the Bible* I, 1970, pp. 209–14; *Post-biblical Jewish Studies*, 1975, pp. 69–74.

12. On the *Diatessaron* (literally, 'through four') of Tatian, a second-century Syrian Christian apologist, see Bruce M. Metzger, *The Early Versions of the New Testament*, 1977, pp. 10–36.

13. For a brief sketch of the emergence and development of New Testament criticism in the eighteenth and nineteenth centuries, see A. R. C. Leaney, *Biblical Criticism*, pp. 233–36; W. G. Kümmel, *The New Testament*, ²1970.

14. See ibid., pp. 236–43; W. G. Kümmel, op. cit., pp. 147–55; *Introduction to the New Testament*, ²1975, p. 48.

15. Wrede, *Das Messiasgeheimnis in den Evangelien*, 1910. ET *The Messianic Secret*, 1971. Another highly influential study was Albert Schweitzer's *Von Reimarus zu Wrede*, 1906, better known as *The Quest for the Historical Jesus*, 1910, ³1954.

16. Cf. *Jesus and the Word*, 1958, pp. 17, 48–51; *New Testament Theology* I, 1952. p. 1. 'Bultmann gives the impression that Jesus neither preached nor believed anything specifically Christian. Wellhausen's remark that Jesus was the last of the Jews and Paul the first Christian could be Bultmann's: Jesus belonged to late Judaism, while Christ was first recognized by the primitive church.' (Otto Betz, *What do we know about Jesus?*, 1968, p. 17).

17. Wellhausen, 'Jesus war kein Christ sondern Jude' (Jesus was not a Christian but a Jew), *Einleitung in die drei ersten Evangelien*, 1905, p. 113.

18. Bultmann, *Jesus and the Word*, p. 14.

19. I Cor. 12.28; 14.29, 32; Eph. 2.20; 3.5; 4.11. See G. Friedrich, *Prophētēs TDNT* VI, pp. 848–55; E. E. Ellis, 'Prophecy in the Early Church', *IDBS*, p. 701.

20. Bultmann, *The History of the Synoptic Tradition*, 1963, p. 105. On form criticism, see Leaney, op. cit., pp. 246–65; E. V. McKnight, *What is Form Criticism?*, 1975; C. E. Carlston, 'Form Criticism, NT', *IDBS*, pp. 345–48.

21. Bornkamm, op. cit., p. 13.

22. Manson, *The Teaching of Jesus, Studies of its Form and Content*, 1931, ²1935.

23. The first edition appeared between 1948 and 1955. See also E. Stauffer, *New Testament Theology*, 1955; K. Stendahl, 'Biblical Theology', *IDB* I, pp. 420–22; Rudolf Schnackenburg, *New Testament Theology*

Today, 1963; Hans Conzelmann, *An Outline of the Theology of the New Testament*, 1969; W. G. Kümmel, *The Theology of the New Testament*, 1969; Joachim Jeremias, *New Testament Theology* I, 1971.

24. Bultmann, *Theology of the New Testament* I, p. 1.

25. See Birger Gerhardsson, *Memory and Manuscript: Oral Tradition and Written Transmission in Rabbinic Judaism and Early Christianity*, 1961, ²1964; *Tradition and Transmission in Early Christianity*, 1964; *The Origins of the Gospel Traditions*, 1977.

26. Cf. Norman Perrin, *What is Redaction Criticism?* 1969; R. T. Fortna, 'Redaction Criticism, NT', *IDBS*, pp. 733–35.

27. It is worth pointing out that even a work as exaggerated as Morton Smith's *Jesus the Magician*, 1978 implicitly testifies to the possibility that gospel data confronted with external evidence can lead to historically admissible conclusions.

28. Talmud and Midrash have preserved biographical fragments in the framework of haggadic stories concerning the rabbis of the Tannaitic and Amoraic age, but no connected narration is associated with their sayings. Cf. W. S. Green, 'What's in a Name? – The Problematic of Rabbinic "Biography"', *Approaches to Ancient Judaism: Theory and Practice*, 1978, pp. 77–96; Jacob Neusner, 'The Present State of Rabbinic Biography', *Hommage à Georges Vajda*, ed. G. Nahon and Ch. Touati, 1980, pp. 85–91. The teachings of the sages were memorized, handed down, and no doubt at an early stage recorded in script. But biography as such or autobiography, like Philo's *Life of Moses* or Josephus's *Vita*, is attested only in the Greek language in Jewish literature. It is therefore not unreasonable to conclude that the gospel is essentially a Hellenistic literary form. The question of the non-appearance of historical compositions among the Qumran manuscripts is raised in 'The Essenes and History', see below, pp. 137–39. See also *DSS*, pp. 136–37.

29. See below, p. 54.

30. Cf. *Jesus the Jew*, pp. 145–49.

31. Cf. above n. 18.

32. The book appeared in 1967. Perrin, a British scholar, studied under T. W. Manson and Joachim Jeremias and taught New Testament until his death at the University of Chicago.

33. Cf. Perrin, *Rediscovering the Teaching of Jesus*, pp. 39–47.

34. Perrin, *The New Testament: An Introduction*, 1974, p. 281.

35. I discuss this topic in 'Jewish Studies and New Testament Interpretation', below, pp. 58–73. The two principal sources of danger are Hermann Strack and Paul Billerbeck, *Kommentar zum Neuen Testament aus Talmud und Midrasch* I–IV (1922–28), and G. Kittel – G. Friedrich, *Theological Dictionary of the New Testament* I–X (1964–76). The original German edition, *Theologisches Wörterbuch zum Neuen Testament*, was published between 1933 and 1976.

36. Cf. below, pp. 53–54.

37. *Jesus the Jew*, pp. 83–222.

38. A good case has been made out, I believe, for asserting that the titles 'prophet', 'lord' and 'son of God' possess a definite association with the charismatic of a Hasidic healer and teacher. See *Jesus the Jew*, ibid.

39. Ibid., pp. 160–91. See further 'The Present State of the "son of man" Debate', below, pp. 89, 99. Cf. also J. A. Fitzmyer's rejoinder, 'Another View of the "Son of Man" debate', *JSNT* 4, 1979, pp. 58–68.

40. If, that is, either of them is genuine! It is natural for any New Testament interpretation produced within ecclesiastical circles always to select alternatives serving the long-term interests of the church.

41. This statement does not overlook gospel passages recording real or fictional encounters between Jesus and Gentiles such as the Gerasene demoniac (Mark 5.1ff. par.), the Syro-Phoenician woman (Mark 7.24–30 par.) and the centurion from Capernaum (Matt. 8.5–13 par.). But none of these episodes reveal a deliberate missionary purpose; they are all accidental meetings. In fact, Mark 7.24 explicitly asserts that Jesus wished to remain incognito during his short stay in Tyrian territory. The synoptics never ascribe to Jesus himself proselytizing intentions in Gentile lands. Only in John 7.35 is there such an allusion in the form of a question asked by an unsympathetic audience: 'Where does this man intend to go that we shall not find him? Does he intend to go to the Dispersion among the Greeks and teach the Greeks?' My assessment of the evidence coincides with that of F. C. Grant: 'Jesus never began a ministry among the Gentiles . . . Did Jesus intend (at least eventually) a mission to Gentiles? Luke 4.25–27 may be understood to point that way, and also 13.29; but the evidence as a whole is against the theory' ('Jesus Christ', *IDB* III, pp. 885–86). As for Matt. 28.18–20, it is so patently a church formulation that it requires no direct consideration in the context of Jesus' own thought. Cf. Bultmann, *The History of the Synoptic Tradition*, p. 157.

42. Mark 15.34 par. This Aramaic exclamation, corresponding to the opening verse of Ps. 22, was found disturbing enough by Luke and John for them to substitute for it, 'Father, into thy hands I commit my spirit' (Luke 23.46; cf. Ps. 31.5), and, 'It is finished' (John 19.30). The Marcan/Matthean form of Jesus' last words seems to suggest that although he foresaw resistance and hostility Jesus was convinced that God would at the last moment snatch him out of the hands of his enemies. As will be indicated later (p. 158, n. 71), this is the sole prayer of Jesus in the synoptics in which he does not address God as 'Father'.

43. Paul's 'gospel' preaching salvation through the crucified Christ was 'scandal' to Jews and 'stupidity' to Gentiles (I Cor. 1.23). Among contemporary writers, Michael Grant lays particular emphasis on the failure of Jesus. Cf. *Jesus: An Historian's Review of the Gospels*, 1977, especially chapters 7 and 9.

44. I know of no real evidence prior to the New Testament of belief among Jews in a suffering/dying Messiah. See *Jesus the Jew*, pp. 139–40; *History* II, pp. 547–49.

45. 'This is not a belief that grew up within the church . . . It is the central

belief about which the church itself grew . . . If the resurrection is the dénouement of the whole story and not a "happy ending" tacked on to a tragedy . . .' *The Founder of Christianity*, 1971, pp. 28–29.

46. *Jesus the Jew*, pp. 37–41, 234–35.

47. Luke 24.11. A canon enacted by an eighth-century Irish synod denies validity to any testimony brought by a woman on the grounds that the apostles themselves refused to accept female witnesses. 'Testimonium feminae non accipitur, sicut apostoli testimonium feminarum non acceperint de resurrectione Christi.' (*Capitula selecta ex antiqua canonum collectione facta in Hibernia c. saeculo VIII*, Liber XVI, cap. III in Migne, PL 96, col. 1286). I owe this piece of information to my friend, Bernard S. Jackson.

48. On this see A. Oepke, '*Parousia*', *TDNT* V, pp. 858–71; A. L. Moore, *The Parousia in the New Testament*, 1966; cf. also E. Schlüsser Fiorenza, 'Eschatology of the NT', *IDBS*, pp. 271–77.

49. 'But their eyes were kept from recognizing him' (Luke 24.6). 'Jesus himself stood among them. But they supposed that they saw a spirit' (Luke 24.36–37). In the Fourth Gospel, Mary Magdalene 'saw Jesus standing, but she did not know that it was Jesus' (John 20.14). C. H. Dodd stresses that the 'appearances' are 'centred in a moment of *recognition*' (*The Founder of Christianity*, p. 40). But the important feature, unacknowledged by him, is that this is not a *visual* recognition.

50. 'Now concerning the coming of our Lord Jesus Christ and our assembling to meet him (cf. I Thess. 4.15–17), we beg you, brethren, not to be quickly shaken in mind or excited, either by spirit or by word, or by letter purporting to be from us, to the effect that the day of the Lord has come' (II Thess. 2.1–2).

51. Regarding delay in eschatological fulfilment, see E. Grässer, *Das Problem der Parousieverzögerung in den synoptischen Evangelien und in der Apostelgeschichte*, ²1960; A. Strobel, *Untersuchungen zum eschatologischen Verzögerungsproblem*, 1961.

52. See below pp. 38–39, 50–51.

53. *Habakkuk Commentary* (1*QpHab*) vii. 1–14.

54. Compared with the radical scepticism of much contemporary New Testament scholarship, the stand taken here may be defined as middle-of-the-road. For even such a moderate writer as Norman Perrin, proclaims his overall principle to be, 'When in doubt, discard', and states categorically that 'the burden of proof always lies on the claim of authenticity'; that is to say, whatever is not proved to be genuine is to be presumed inauthentic (*Rediscovering the Teaching of Jesus*, pp. 11–12). Bearing in mind the basic Jewish respect for tradition in general, and attachment to the words of a venerated master in particular, I myself would advocate *a priori* an open mind, and would not tip the balance in favour of inauthenticity.

55. Cf. *Jesus the Jew*, p. 84.

56. Hengel, *Judaism and Hellenism*, 1974, pp. 104–05.

57. 'The Background of the Maccabean Revolution: Reflections on Martin Hengel's "Judaism and Hellenism"', *JJS* 29, 1978, p. 9.

58. In *theory*, this opinion is shared by most New Testament scholars. For example, Rudolf Bultmann writes: 'Critical investigation shows that the whole tradition about Jesus which appears in the three synoptic gospels is composed of a series of layers which can on the whole be clearly distinguished . . . The separating of these layers . . . depends on the knowledge that the gospels were composed in Greek within the Hellenistic Christian community, while Jesus and the oldest Christian group lived in Palestine and spoke Aramaic. Hence everything in the synoptics which for reasons of language or content can have originated only in Hellenistic Christianity must be excluded as a source for the teaching of Jesus.' (*Jesus and the Word*, p. 17).

59. Against those New Testament scholars who, for chronological reasons, consider the Dead Sea manuscripts wholly superior to Mishnah, Tosefta, Talmud, Midrash and Targum, I continue to maintain that 'if the Qumran Scrolls are invaluable in shedding new light on early Christianity, rabbinic literature skilfully handled, is still the richest source for the interpretation of the original message, and the most precious aid to the quest for the historical Jesus' ('The Impact of the Dead Sea Scrolls on the Study of the New Testament', below p. 125).

60. On Judaeo-Christianity and the Ebionites, see Hans Joachim Schoeps, *Theologie und Geschichte des Judenchristentums*, 1949; *Urgemeinde, Judenchristentum, Gnosis*, 1956; Marcel Simon *et al.*, *Aspects du Judéo-Christianisme*, 1965; Marcel Simon and André Benoit, *Le judaïsme et le christianisme antique*, 1968, pp. 258–74; (Jean Daniélou), *Judéo-Christianisme – Recherches historiques et théologiques offertes en hommage au Cardinal Jean Daniélou*, 1972. Marcel Simon, 'Réflexions sur le Judéo-Christianisme', *Christianity, Judaism and other Greco-Roman Cults. Studies for Morton Smith at Sixty* II, ed. J. Neusner, 1975, pp. 53–76.

61. Cf. *Jesus the Jew*, pp. 22–25, 58–82. On the charismatic type, see Rudolf Otto, *Gottesreich und Menschensohn*, [3]1954, pp. 267–309; ET *The Kingdom of God and the Son of Man*, 1943, pp. 333–76.

62. J. B. Segal, 'Popular Religion in Ancient Israel', *JJS* 27, 1976, pp. 1–22; esp. pp. 8–9. Cf. also W. S. Green, 'Palestinian Holy Men: Charismatic Leadership and Rabbinic Tradition', *Aufstieg und Niedergang der römischen Welt*, ed. W. Haase. II *Principat*. 19. 2. *Religion – Judentum: Palästinisches Judentum*, 1979, pp. 619–47.

63. Cf. *Jesus the Jew*, pp. 80–82.

64. On the rabbinic 'man of deed', see my study, 'Hanina ben Dosa', *JJS* 23, 1972, pp. 28–50; 24, 1973, pp. 51–64; *Post-biblical Jewish Studies*, 1975, pp. 178–214.

65. Cf. *Jesus the Jew*, pp. 58–69.

66. Cf. below, pp. 32, 39.

67. *Jewish Antiquities* xviii. 63–64. Cf. *History* I, pp. 428–41.

68. Cf. *Jesus the Jew*, pp. 42–57.

69. Segal, art. cit., p. 20.

70. S. Freyne, *Galilee from Alexander the Great to Hadrian*, 1980, pp.

373, 388, n. 92. 'It is only hypercritical scholarship that ignores or rejects Jesus' teaching as unimportant in locating him within the spectrum of Galilean life of his own day.' The appended note reads: 'This is one of the main criticisms that can be levelled against Vermes's study . . . A subsequent volume is promised that will study the teaching of Jesus . . . but already by focussing on the deeds alone and the suggested parallels with the *hasid* tradition the lines would appear to have been irrevocably drawn.' I remain somewhat perplexed by Seán Freyne's comment for I have never thought or said or written that the teaching of Jesus was 'unimportant' or that the label 'Hasid' could explain all about him. The 'Postscript' to *Jesus the Jew* is scarcely unequivocal in this regard: 'The discovery of resemblances between the work and words of Jesus and those of the Hasidim . . . is however by no means intended to imply that he was simply one of them and nothing more. Although no systematic attempt is made here to distinguish Jesus' authentic teaching – this is an enormous task that will, it is hoped, be undertaken on another occasion – it is nevertheless still possible to say, even in the absence of such an investigation, that no objective and enlightened student of the Gospels can help but be struck by the incomparable superiority of Jesus' (pp. 223–24).

3. The Gospel of Jesus the Jew II: The Father and His Kingdom

1. Cf. *Jesus the Jew*, pp. 26–28.
2. Cf. ibid., p. 115. For a detailed survey, see Gustaf Dalman, *Die Worte Jesu*, [2]1930, pp. 272–80; ET *The Words of Jesus*, 1902, pp. 331–36; E. Lohse, *'Rabbi, Rabbouni'*, *TDNT* VI, pp. 961–65; Ferdinand Hahn, *The Titles of Jesus in Christology*, 1969, pp. 73–81.
3. On the scribes, see *History* II, pp. 322–29; Joachim Jeremias, *'Grammateus'*, *TDNT* I, pp. 740–42; Stephen Westerholm, *Jesus and Scribal Authority* (1978) pp. 26–31. For the Pharisees, see *History* II, pp. 388–403 (cf. the bibliography on pp. 381–82 to which add, Ellis Rivkin, 'Pharisees', *IDBS*, pp. 657–63 and *A Hidden Revolution*, 1978). Cf. in particular Jacob Neusner, *The Rabbinic Traditions about the Pharisees before 70*, I–III, 1971.
4. Bultmann, *Jesus and the Word*, p. 49.
5. *History* II, pp. 325–26.
6. The bulk of the controversies appears in the Marcan tradition. Explicit scriptural argument will be indicated by italics.
Mark 2.5ff. par. / 2.17 par. / 2.19ff. par. / *2.25ff* par. / 3.4 par. / 3.24 par. / 3.33ff. par. / *7.6f.* par. / *10.2ff.* par. / *10.18ff.* par. / 11.27 par. / *11.29* par. / 12.1ff par. / 12.15ff. par. / *12.24ff.* par. / *12.29ff.* par. / *12.35ff.* par. / *12.38ff.* par. / *14.20f.* par. / 14.48f. par.
Matt. 4.4ff. – Luke 4.ff. / Matt. 5.39ff. – Luke 6.27ff. / Matt. 12.27f. – Luke 11.18ff. / Matt. 23.4ff. – Luke 11.39ff.
Matt. 5.21ff. / 5.27f. / 5.33ff. / 11.28f.
Luke 13.12ff.
In Matt. 5.21–48, Jesus' teaching on murder, adultery, divorce, oaths,

revenge and love of one's enemies is presented in the form of controversy, but this is likely to be the responsibility of Matthew. The Lucan parallels lack the formula: 'You have heard that it was said to the men of old . . . But I say to you' and the appropriate biblical quotations.

7. See *Jesus the Jew*, pp. 42–57.

8. In two passages, the Pharisees/scribes met by Jesus in Galilee are expressly said to have been visitors from Jerusalem: Mark 3.22 – Matt. 12.24 and Mark 7.1 – Matt. 15.1. Similarly, Josephus refers to a delegation of four persons, three of whom were Pharisees, despatched from Jerusalem to Galilee to effect his dismissal from the post of regional commander-in-chief. See *Vita* 196–97. As far as I know, this is the only mention of a Pharisee presence in the northern province in the whole of Josephus' work.

It used to be commonly held that during the era of the Second Temple there was no Pharisee influence in Galilee. More recently, Aharon Oppenheimer has advanced a theory denying any basic distinction between Judaean and Galilean Judaism. Expounded in *The 'Am Ha-Aretz*, 1977, and in particular in its chapter VI (pp. 200–17), his thesis appears to have impressed some scholars. Thus John Riches, *Jesus and the Transformation of Judaism*, 1980, believes himself entitled, on the basis of an uncritical acceptance of Oppenheimer's work, to 'treat with considerable caution' views reflecting an alleged Judaean sentiment of superiority towards Galileans (p. 85). Likewise Eric M. Meyers and James F. Strange declare in *Archaeology, the Rabbis and Early Christianity*, 1981, that Oppenheimer's arguments are convincing (p. 36). But these authors do not seem to realize that none of Oppenheimer's proofs actually relate to the pre-Yavneh age. This flaw has been noticed by Seán Freyne (*Galilee from Alexander the Great to Hadrian*, p. 339, n. 48) and fully exposed by Martin D. Goodman in his review of *The 'Am Ha-Aretz*: 'Nothing that O(ppenheimer) presents would preclude the more extreme interests of the Judaean rabbinical academies in purity and tithing being confined in Galilee to those few rabbinic figures . . . of whom the texts tell . . . O. has very few passages to cite of Galilean communities expressing interest before 132 in purity, tithing or sabbatical year and even of those that are given not all are safe . . . What is left? Some Galileans joined Judaean rabbinic schools before 132 . . . and a few issued halakha on return to Galilee to a more or less indifferent populace. Some Judaean rabbis visited Galilee . . . for reasons unspecified . . . Certainly Galileans were Jews, and the Gospels and Josephus confirm their use of synagogues and conformity with the control of the Temple before 70. But O's need to claim any more than that comes from his own apologetic: the assertion that before 132 Palestinian Jews considered the rabbinic Judaism of the sages whose words are recorded in the Mishnah as some sort of "orthodoxy" accepted by all as an essential part of being Jewish' (*JJS* 31, 1980, p. 248–49).

9. The title, 'village scribe' (*kōmogrammateus*) is used sarcastically in Josephus, *Ant.* xvi. 203; *BJ* i. 479.

10. Cf. *Jesus the Jew*, pp. 52, 54.

11. The exegetical arguments appearing in the Gospel of Matthew are most probably the work of this rabbinically trained evangelist. Cf. K. Stendahl, *The School of St Matthew*, 1954, ²1968.

12. On the activity of the scribes and rabbis in the domain of legal development, see *History* II, pp. 330–32. Cf. also my *Post-biblical Jewish Studies*, pp. 80–81.

13. Mark 1.22 par. Cf. *Jesus the Jew*, pp. 28–29. The link between exorcism/healing and the concept of *exousia* is manifest in Mark 3.15; 6.7; Matt. 10.1; Luke 10.19. For a detailed exposition (which is not altogether satisfactory), see W. Foerster, '*Exousia*', *TDNT* II, pp. 562–75, esp. 568–69.

14. Matt. 12.25–28; Luke 11.17–20; Mark 7.14–23; Matt. 15.10–20.

15. Cf. R. Bultmann, *The History of the Synoptic Tradition*, 1963, pp. 39–54 (Controversial Dialogues): 'This means, in my view, that we can firmly conclude that the formation of the material in the tradition took place in the *Palestinian Church*' (p. 48). Apropos of 'scholastic dialogues', Bultmann writes: 'But we must raise the question whether the *Palestinian or the Hellenistic Church* was responsible for formulating the scholastic dialogues. Their form and their relation with both the controversy dialogues, and the Rabbinic scholastic dialogues, show that the former was the case' (p. 55).

16. For an outline of the educational system in Palestine, see *History* II, pp. 417–22. Cf. Also S. Safrai, 'Education and Study of the Torah', *The Jewish People in the First Century*, II, 1977, pp. 945–69; M. Hengel, *Judaism and Hellenism* I, pp. 65–83. On Babylonian Jewish religious education, see D. M. Goodblatt, *Rabbinic Instruction in Sasanian Babylonia*, 1975.

17. Whether a special class of wandering teachers existed is uncertain, but it may be worth noting that the Talmud mentions itinerant Galilean exegetes (*bSanh*. 70a; *bHull*. 27b).

18. It seems to be correct to assert, in fact, that systematization in Judaism reflects foreign cultural influences: Hellenism in the case of Philo, and Islamic and Christian philosophy and theology in medieval or modern Judaism. Even a contemporary author is compelled to write: 'Many Jewish thinkers have written on theological topics since Kohler (*Jewish Theology*, 1918) but there is a real lack of systematic treatment which this book seeks, however inadequately, to fill' (Louis Jacobs, *A Jewish Theology*, 1973, p. vii).

19. This is a kind of litany recited between New Year and the Day of Atonement. Cf. *JE* I, p. 65; *Enc. Jud.* 3, cols. 973–74.

20. Cf. Joseph Heinemann, *Prayer in the Talmud: Forms and Patterns*, 1977, pp. 173–74.

21. A. E. Harvey, 'Christology and the Evidence of the New Testament', in *God Incarnate: Story and Belief*, ed. A. E. Harvey, 1981, p. 50.

22. N. Perrin, *Rediscovering the Teaching of Jesus*, p. 54.

23. Cf. O. E. Evans, 'Kingdom of God, of Heaven', *IDB* II, pp. 17–26; R. H. Hiers, 'Kingdom of God', *IDBS*, p. 516; J. Hering, *Le royaume de Dieu et sa venue*, 1959; Martin Buber, *Kingship of God*, 1967; John Gray,

The Biblical Doctrine of the Reign of God, 1979. For a full survey of the views expressed by New Testament scholars, see N. Perrin, *The Kingdom of God in the Teaching of Jesus*, 1963; id., *Jesus and the Language of the Kingdom*, 1976; J. Schlosser, *Le règne de Dieu dans les dits de Jésus* I–II, 1980.

24. For a comprehensive discussion of the subject, see Sigmund Mowinckel, *He That Cometh*, 1956. The latest study is Joachim Becker's *Messianic Expectation in the Old Testament*, 1980.

25. On the Psalms of Solomon, see Otto Eissfeldt, *The Old Testament. An Introduction*, 1965, pp. 610–13, 773–74. Cf. also Paul Winter, 'Psalms of Solomon', *IDB* III, pp. 958–60; James H. Charlesworth, *The Pseudepigrapha and Modern Research*, 1976, ²1981, pp. 195–97. For the Greek text, see A. Rahlfs, *Septuaginta* II, pp. 471–89. For an English translation, cf. G. Buchanan Gray in *APOT* II, pp. 631–52.

26. *Ps. of Solomon* 17.23–32. Cf. R. H. Charles, *APOT* II, pp. 645–50.

27. *1QS*ᵇ v, 20–25 in D. Barthélemy and J. T. Milik, *Discoveries in the Judaean Desert* I, 1955, pp. 127–28; *DSSE²*, p. 208–09. On the Blessings, see *DSS*, p. 261.

28. On the *Tefillah* or '*Amidah* or *Shemone 'Esre*, see *History* II, pp. 455–63; J. Heinemann, 'Amidah', *Enc. Jud.* 2, cols. 838–46; *Prayer in the Talmud*, 1977, pp. 218–27. The text has been preserved in a Palestinian and a Babylonian recension. Both are translated in *History* II, *loc. cit.*

29. 15th benediction in the Babylonian recension; cf. *History* II, p. 458.

30. On Jewish apocalyptics see Paul Volz, *Eschatologie der jüdischen Gemeinde im neutestamentlichen Zeitalter*, ²1934; D. S. Russell, *The Method and Message of Jewish Apocalyptic*, 1964; P. D. Hanson, *The Dawn of Apolcalyptic*, 1975; 'Apocalypticism', *IDBS*, pp. 28–34.

31. *1QS* iii, 13 – iv, 26; *DSSE²*, pp. 75–78.

32. *1QS* iv, 25; *DSSE²*, p. 78.

33. *1QM* xviii, 1; *DSSE²*, p. 146.

34. *1QM* xvii, 7–8; *DSSE²*, p. 146.

35. Dalman, *Die Worte Jesu*, ²1930, pp. 75–83. ET *The Words of Jesus*, 1902, pp. 96–101.

36. *Sifra* (ed. Weiss) 93d. Cf. Dalman, op. cit., p. 80. (ET p. 97). In interpreting, 'I have separated you from the peoples that you should be mine', in this sense, the midrashist presumes that the Gentiles as a rule are sinners.

37. *Sifre on Num.* (ed. Horovitz), 115 (p. 126).

38. *mBer.* 2.2. Cf. E. E. Urbach, *The Sages. Their Concepts and Beliefs* I, 1975, p. 400.

39. *Tanhuma* (ed. Buber), I, p. 63.

40. I have reached a negative conclusion in my examination of the messianic character of Jesus in the sense that he does not appear to have given much weight to the question of Messianism or to have seen himself as fulfilling such a function. Cf. *Jesus the Jew*, pp. 129–159. Here I am in agreement with Bultmann, who wrote: 'I am personally of the opinion that

Jesus did not believe himself to be the Messiah' (*Jesus and the Word*, p. 15). My own judgment is based on the strict definition of 'Messiah' as a valorous, holy, just and mighty Davidic king of the end of time. Lack of precision in this domain is bound to blur the issue. Yet it is not uncommon among New Testament scholars of today to add to the essential notion of the King Messiah various others arising from diverse circles at different times, some held by many, others by only a few, or even by a single individual. A medley of this sort, proclaimed Jewish Messianism, provides ample scope for detecting features which match up to the 'Christ Jesus' of the New Testament. Some go so far as to recognize all the data relating to Jesus in the gospels as pertaining to christology/messianism without asking whether they are in any way associated with the historical expectation of the Jewish people, let alone with Jesus' self-awareness.

41. 'It is impossible to avoid thinking that Matt. 25. 31–46 derives from Jewish tradition. Perhaps when it was taken up by the Christian Church the name of God was replaced by the title of the Son of Man'. R. Bultmann, *The History of the Synoptic Tradition*, p. 124.

42. *yBer.* ii 5c. Comparison of the two parables yields significant results. In both cases, all the workmen receive the same wage irrespective of the number of hours of actual work, but whereas in the rabbinic story an industrious and skilful person is discharged after two hours' work because, in the king's words, he has achieved more in that short time than the others during the whole day, Jesus' teaching, emphasizes generosity towards the unworthy. According to Joachim Jeremias (*The Parables of Jesus*, [2]1972, p. 138), the Talmudic parable, given in the name of R. Ze'era (*c.* AD 300), is secondary to that of Jesus. But this estimate, described as a 'probability bordering on certainty', depends on the presumption that Ze'era was the actual author of the story. In fact, this type of material is more likely to have circulated as part of popular wisdom for centuries and to have been used and interpreted by preachers according to their lights and varying didactic needs. In connection with the change from king to landowner in the gospels, see also an identical shift in *bSanh.* 91ab from a 'king of flesh and blood' to an 'orchard owner' (*ba'al pardes*).

43. Cf. above, pp. 27–28.

44. Mark 4.3ff. par; Mark 4.26ff; Matt. 13.24ff.

45. Matt. 20.1–16. Apropos of this parable Bultmann writes: 'Matt. 20. 1–16 obviously teaches God's impartial goodness to all his servants; but against whom was the parable directed originally?' (*The History of the Synoptic Tradition*, p. 199). No doubt against conceited and ambitious early disciples?

46. Mark 4.30ff. par. The mustard plant, *brassica nigra* (cf. J. Feliks, 'Mustard', *Enc. Jud.* 12, col. 720), was apparently very successful in Galilee. R. Simeon ben Halafta (*c.* AD 200), praising the fertility of the province, reports that he has one growing in his field which is as tall as a fig tree and which he can actually climb (cf. *yPea* vii 20b).

47. Matt. 5.3; Luke 6.20. – Mark 10.23ff. par. Jesus' saying is only very

slightly less exaggerated than the Talmudic metaphor of passing an elephant through the eye of a needle (*bBer.* 55b; *bBM* 38b).

48. N. Perrin, *The Kingdom of God in the Teaching of Jesus*, 1963, provides a general survey. Cf. also H. Schürmann, 'Eschatologie und Liebesdienst in der Verkündigung Jesu' in *Vom Messias zu Christus*, ed. K. Schubert, 1964, pp. 203–32; A. Strobel, *Kerygma und Apokalyptik*, 1967; G. E. Ladd, *The Presence and the Future*, 1974.

49. See in particular *The Quest for the Historical Jesus*, ³1954.

50. See especially *The Parables of the Kingdom*, 1935, 1978.

51. Cf. *The Parables of Jesus*, ²1972. See also W. G. Kümmel, *Promise and Fulfilment*, 1957.

52. Otto, *The Kingdom of God and the Son of Man*, 1943, pp. 59–63.

53. Albert Schweitzer's thesis that Jesus expected the coming of the kingdom during the first mission of the disciples is based on his interpretation of Matt. 10. When Jesus' hope failed to materialize, he changed his teaching. Cf. *The Quest of the Historical Jesus*, ³1954, p. 358. This exegesis is purely artificial and unsubstantiated: cf. W. G. Kümmel, *Promise and Fulfilment*, pp. 62–63.

54. In the *Testament of Levi* 17, seven periods in the history of the priesthood are to be followed by the new area of the Priest-Messiah (ch. 18). Cf. R. H. Charles, *APOT* II, pp. 313–15. 1 Enoch 93.1–10; 91.12–17 divides world history into ten weeks. Cf. M. A. Knibb, *The Ethiopic Book of Enoch* II, 1978, pp. 219–25. According to J. T. Milik's reconstruction of the 11Q Melchizedek document, the final epoch of history will consist of ten jubilees. Cf. 'Milkîsedeq et Milkî-reša' dans les anciens écrits juifs et chrétiens', *JJS* 23, 1972, pp. 98–99, 124.

55. These are (1) Abraham to David; (2) David to the Babylonian exile; (3) Babylonian exile to the birth of the Messiah. See Matt. 1.17.

56. Cf. B. Rigaux, *Les Epîtres aux Thessaloniciens*, 1956, pp. 653–61, 671–73.

57. Various interpretations of these difficult passages are listed by N. Perrin in *The Kingdom of God in the Teaching of Jesus*, pp. 171–74 and *Rediscovering the Teaching of Jesus*, pp. 74–77. Some exegetes see in the 'violent' the hostile rulers of the world of the spirits or the Jewish opponents of Jesus. Cf. W. G. Kümmel, *Promise and Fulfilment*, p. 123. Others seek to identify them with the Zealots or Sicarii. Cf. S. G. F. Brandon, *Jesus and the Zealots*, 1967, pp. 78, 300. Note however M. Hengel's disagreement in *DieZeloten*, ²1976, p. 345. Perrin adheres to E. Käsemann's conclusion expressed in *Essays on New Testament Themes*, 1964, p. 42: 'The Kingdom of God . . . is hindered by men of violence.' Perrin comments: 'What we have here is the reverse of the situation envisaged in the interpretation of the exorcisms: there the Kingdom of Satan is being plundered, here that of God' (*Rediscovering*, p. 77). I prefer to see in these sayings, and especially in the more original logion of Matthew, one of Jesus' typical exaggerations. The apparent success of John's mission and his own in Galilee, with crowds

elbowing their way forward to reach the teacher, suggests to Jesus the simile of troops storming the kingdom to seize it.

58. Incidentally I agree with Jeremias, *The Prayers of Jesus*, 1977, p. 91, that Jesus may have spoken the 'Our Father' 'on different occasions in slightly differing form', which would imply that the Matthean addition may also have originated with Jesus. For a recent detailed bibliography of the Lord's Prayer, see Jean Carmignac, *Recherches sur le 'Notre Père'*, 1969.

59. Cf. Joseph Heinemann, *Prayer in the Talmud*, 1977, pp. 32–33, 78–80, 93–95, etc.

60. Bultmann (*History of the Synoptic Tradition*, p. 160) attributes the saying to a lost Jewish writing. It does not figure among the logia recognized as authentic by N. Perrin.

61. *Jesus the Jew*, pp. 194–99. For a thorough analysis of the 'Father' concept in the Old Testament and Judaism, see G. Quell and G. Schrenk, '*Patēr*', *TDNT*, V, pp. 959–82; R. Hamerton-Kelly, *God the Father, Theology and Patriarchy in the Teaching of Jesus*, 1979.

62. Cf. Charles, *APOT* II, pp. 12–13.

63. *Mekh. on Ex.* 20:6 (ed. Lauterbach II, p. 247).

64. Cf. J. M. Allegro, *Discoveries in the Judaean Desert* V, 1968, p. 53; *DSSE*[2], p. 246.

65. Heinemann, op. cit., pp. 189–90.

66. *History* II, p. 460.

67. On the Hasidim, see A. Büchler, *Types of Palestinian Jewish Piety from 70 B.C.E. to 70 C.E.*, 1922; S. Safrai, 'The Teaching of Pietists in Mishnaic Literature' *JJS* 16, 1965, pp. 15–33; G. Vermes, 'Hanina ben Dosa', *JJS* 23, 1972, pp. 28–50; 24, 1973, pp. 51–64; *Post-biblical Jewish Studies*, 1975, p. 178–214.

68. Cf. G. Schrenk, '*Patēr*', *TDNT* V, pp. 982–1014; J. Jeremias, *Prayers*, pp. 11–65. For the rabbinic usage, see G. Dalman, *Die Worte Jesu*, pp. 150–59 (ET pp. 184–89).

69. Cf. Jeremias, *Prayers*, p. 32.

70. Cf. G. Dalman, *Worte*, p. 155. (ET p. 189).

71. One departure from the norm is, 'My God, my God, why hast thou forsaken me?' (Mark 15.34 par.), an expression not spontaneous but borrowed from the Aramaic translation of Ps. 22. The other is the Matthean beginning of the Lord's Prayer, '*Our* Father *who art in heaven*' (Matt. 6.9).

72. Cf. Jeremias, *Prayers*; N. Perrin, *Rediscovering*, pp. 40–41.

73. N. Perrin, *Rediscovering*, p. 41.

74. Jeremias, *Prayers*, pp. 57–62.

75. Dan. 5:13; *1QGenAp* ii, 19, 24; iii, 3 (J. A. Fitzmyer, *The Genesis Apocryphon of Qumran Cave 1*, [2]1971, pp. 44, 46); 6Q 8 1.4 (M. Baillet, *Discoveries in the Judaean Desert* III, 1962, p. 117).

76. Jeremias, *Prayers*, p. 59.

77. *Targum Neofiti* to Gen. 44.18.

78. D. Flusser, *Jesus*, 1969, p. 145, n. 159.

79. Among the rabbis of the Tannaitic age, we find Abba Hanin (or

Hanan), Abba Shaul, Abba Yose ben Dostai in addition to the grandsons of Honi. Cf. G. Dalman, *Worte*, pp. 278–79 (ET, p. 339). Jesus disapproves of such a metaphorical use of the title – *patēr* is preceded by 'rabbi' and followed by 'master' – when he instructs his followers not to call any man 'father' (Matt. 23.9). Jeremias (*Prayers*, pp. 41–43) sees this prohibition as an attempt to protect 'the address "Abba" from profanation', but I think Jesus is more likely to have been intending to deflect from religious teachers the veneration due to God alone. Cf. *Jesus the Jew*, p. 211.

80. Cf. *Jesus the Jew*, p. 211.
81. On the *Kaddish*, see *Enc. Jud.* 10, cols 660–62; A. Z. Idelsohn, *Jewish Liturgy and its Development*, 1932, pp. 84–88; J. Heinemann with J. J. Petuchowski, *Literature of the Synagogue*, 1975, pp. 81–84.
82. According to R. Simeon ben Yohai (mid-second century AD), no bird is caught in a fowler's net without a decree from heaven (*ySheb.* ix 38d; *Gen. R.* 79:6, etc. Cf. Vermes, *Post-biblical Jewish Studies*, pp. 162–63)

4. The Gospel of Jesus the Jew III: Jesus and Christianity

1. T. W. Manson, *The Teaching of Jesus*, ²1935, p. 101.
2. The most remarkable feature of this kind of reaction is that the unhistorical nature of belief causes no concern to upholders of a so-called historical religion. Manson did not think it necessary to explain why he could 'rightly' ignore the evidence of the 'earliest records'. The classic justification of such 'apparent' departures from the testimony of the synoptics is sought in a combination of unwritten (supplementary) tradition and in the work of the Holy Spirit in the church (cf. Acts 1.3–5; John 14.26; 16.13). The modern justification consists in denying the reliability of the 'earliest evidence' in connection with the authentic teaching of Jesus, and in asserting that it also mirrors the thought of the church. Cf. p. 20 above, and *Jesus the Jew*, pp. 224–25.
3. On Jewish religion in the inter-testamental era, see *History* II, pp. 464–554; Wilhelm Bousset, *Die Religion des Judentums im spcäthellenistischen Zeitalter*, ²1926; G. F. Moore, *Judaism in the First Centuries of the Christian Era. The Age of the Tannaim* I–III, 1927–30; J. Maier, *Geschichte der jüdischen Religion*, 1972; E. E. Urbach, *The Sages. Their Concepts and Beliefs* I–II, 1975; E. P. Sanders, *Paul and Palestinian Judaism*, 1977; Wolfgang Haase (ed.), *Aufstieg und Neidergang der römischen Welt – Principat – Religion (Judentum: Allgemeines; Palästinisches Judentum)* II 19.1–2, 1979; Jacob Neusner, 'Judaism after Moore: A Programmatic Statement', *JJS* 31, 1980, pp. 141–56; *Judaism: The Evidence of the Mishnah*, 1981.
4. Cf. above, p. 35.
5. Cf. 'Law of God' (Josh. 24.26); 'Law of the Lord' (II Kings 10.31); 'Law of Moses' (Josh. 8.31), etc.
6. *Pace* A. Oppenheimer and his followers (see ch. 3 n.8 above), I still maintain that because of its distance from the Temple and the centres of study in Jerusalem the Galilean practice of Judaism was less sophisticated

and punctilious than that prevailing in general in Judaea in the pre-70 era. Cf. *Jesus the Jew*, pp. 54–55.

7. See Mark 6.56 par. and Num. 15.38–39; Deut. 22.12. Cf. also *History* II, p. 479; J. Schneider, '*Kraspedon*', *TDNT* III, p. 904; Strack-Billerbeck IV, pp. 277–92; Rudolf Schnackenburg, *The Moral Teaching of the New Testament*, 1965, p. 56.

8. It may be asked whether the phrase, 'they make their fringes large' (*megalunousin*), has some midrashic connection with Deut. 22.12, 'You shall make yourselves fringes (*gᵉdilīm*)'. The Hebrew word meaning 'twisted threads', used instead of the familiar *ẓiẓiyoth* of Num. 15.38–39, recalls the root *GDL*. 'to be great, large, to grow'.

9. b*Makk*. 24a.

10. 'The Ten Words, as they are called, the main heads under which are summarized the Special Laws, have been explained in the preceding treatise (*The Decalogue*). We have now . . . to examine the particular ordinances' (*The Special Laws* I, 1, trans. F. H. Colson, *Philo* VII, Loeb Classical Library, 1958, p. 101).

11. It is curious to note that when Philo intends to illustrate a point in the Decalogue, viz. that the 'oracles' are addressed to individuals in the second person singular, he quotes the same three commandments as Jesus. 'Thou shalt not commit adultery, thou shalt not kill, thou shalt not steal' (*Decal*. 36; *Philo* VII (Loeb), p. 25). The main difference is that Philo does not adopt the order of the commandments given in the Hebrew Bible and followed by Jesus, or that of the Septuagint, but quotes freely, no doubt from memory.

12. On the subject of love, see C. Spicq, *Agapè dans le Nouveau Testament* I–III, 1958–59. For the somewhat idiosyncratic view that the dual commandment is a Jewish-Hellenistic creation and has nothing to do with Jesus, see Chr. Burchard, 'Das doppelte Liebesgebot in der frühen christlichen Überlieferung' in *Der Ruf Jesu und Antwort der Gemeinde – Joachim Jeremias Festschrift*, 1970, pp. 39–62.

13. 'What is hateful to you, do not do it to your neighbour. This is the whole Torah; all the rest is only interpretation' (b*Shabb*. 31a). Cf. also Philo, *Hypothetica* 7, 6. For a single principle summarizing perfect moral behaviour even more simply, see the test set by Yohanan ben Zakkai for his five disciples: 'Go forth and see which is the good way to which a man should cleave. R. Eliezer said, A good eye. R. Joshua said, A good companion. R. Jose said, A good neighbour. R. Simeon said, One that sees what will be. R. Eleazar said, A good heart' (m*Ab*. 2.9). Yohanan ben Zakkai is said to have approved of the latter (ibid.).

14. According to Bultmann (*The History of Synoptic Tradition*, p. 103), 'The saying, as an individual utterance, gives moral expression to a naif egoism'. But this view appears totally to misrepresent the thrust of the logion and the underlying concept of religiousness. If one of the chief purposes of the Torah is the creation of a society of brothers, children of the heavenly Father, is it not reasonable to assume that in such a family

each individual member may use his own sensitivity as an instinctive norm for correct fraternal behaviour?

15. 'Christ redeemed us from the curse of the law, having become a curse for us' (Gal. 3.13). On the connection between Paul's thought and Deut. 21.22–23, cf. Max Wilcox, '"Upon the Tree" – Deut. 21.22–23 in the New Testament', *JBL* 96, 1977, pp. 85–99.

16. This is one of the thorniest of gospel passages for Christian exegetes. For recent monographs see H. Hübner, *Das Gesetz in der synoptischen Tradition*, 1973; Robert Banks, *Jesus and the Law in the Synoptic Tradition*, 1975. In both the Lucan and the Matthean versions, Jesus appears to stress the permanency of the whole Torah with its iotas and tittles, i.e. decorative penstrokes. On the latter, see G. F. Moore, *Judaism* III, p. 83. For Bultmann (*The History of the Synoptic Tradition*, p. 138), the saying reflects, not the thought of Jesus, but 'discussions between the more conservative (Palestinian) communities and those that were free from the law (Hellenistic)'. But since Luke, addressing Gentile Christians, depicts Jesus as taking a wholly unconditional stand in favour of the Law, the total unsuitability and embarrassing nature of his version commends itself as genuine. By contrast, Matthew's wording (5.17–18) entails obscure allusions to some kind of fulfilment or accomplishment after which, presumably, changes are expected to occur: 'I have not come to abolish (the Law and the Prophets) but to fulfil them (*plērōsai*). Till heaven and earth pass away, not an iota, not a tittle, will pass from the Law until all is accomplished' (*genētai*). This formulation probably reflects an adaptation of Jesus' saying to the post-70 situation when the destruction of the Temple put an end to the practicability of the sacrificial legislation. As for the concept of fulfilment, it is taken by some scholars in the sense of a realization of prophecy: cf. for example R. Banks, *Jesus and the Law*, pp. 204–13; B. S. Jackson, 'Legalism', *JJS* 30, 1979, pp. 3–4. However, the phraseology, 'to abolish – to fulfil' (Matt. 5.17), clearly mirrors the rabbinic *l^ebattel-l^eqayyem*, i.e. to abolish – that is, to consider cancelled – the Torah in wealth, but fulfil it in poverty (*mAb.* 4.9), and is therefore best interpreted in that sense. For a detailed discussion of this question, see G. Dalman, *Jesus – Jeschua* (1922), pp. 51–62; ET *Jesus–Jeshua: Studies in the Gospels*, 1929, repr. 1971, 56–66. The Matthean addition to the basic logion (Matt. 5.19) may well represent, as Bultmann proposes, 'the attitude of the conservative Palestinian community in contrast to that of the Hellenists' (*The History of the Synoptic Tradition*, p. 138). If Matt. 5.20, proclaiming that the righteousness of Jesus' disciples should exceed that of the scribes and Pharisees, belongs to the present pericopa – as I think it does against Bultmann (ibid.) and others (cf. B. Przybilski, *Righteousness in Matthew and his World of Thought*, 1980, p. 80), then it may be argued that the original saying of Jesus (5.18) is conveyed by Matthew both in an anti-Hellenistic Christian (5.19) and in an anti-Pharisaic (5.20) polemical setting. For Jesus' stress on inwardness in fulfilling the Torah, see p. 47 above. The idea of the perpetuity of the Law is expounded by G. F. Moore, *Judaism* I, p. 269–80.

17. For the Jewish custom, see *mYad.*, Strack-Billerbeck I, pp. 695–704.
18. Mark 2.25ff. par.; 3.1ff. par.; Luke 13.15f.; 14.3ff. Cf. E. Lohse, '*Sabbaton*', *TDNT* VII, pp. 21–26.
19. Cf. among others, G. Bornkamm, *Jesus of Nazareth*, 1960, pp. 97–98; N. Perrin, *Rediscovering the Teaching of Jesus*, p. 150; H. Hübner, *Das Gesetz in der synoptischen Tradition*, 1973, p. 154. See further *Jesus the Jew*, pp. 28–29.
20. See *Jesus the Jew*, p. 29. Cf. M. Black, *An Aramaic Approach to the Gospels and Acts*, ³1967, pp. 217–18. According to W. D. Davies, the Matthean version makes 'the whole discussion turn around the question of the oral tradition rather than the written Law' (*The Setting of the Sermon on the Mount*, 1964, p. 104).
21. Cf. n. 18 above.
22. A highly significant discussion of this issue is preserved in the *Mekhilta* on Ex. 31.13 (ed. Lauterbach III, pp. 197–99): 'Whence do we know that the duty of saving life supersedes the Sabbath laws? . . . R. Eleazar ben Azariah . . . said: If in performing the ceremony of circumcision, which affects only one member of the body, one is to disregard the Sabbath laws, how much more should one do so for the whole body when it is in danger! . . . R. Akiba says: If punishment for murder sets aside even the Temple service, which in turn supersedes the Sabbath (cf. Matt. 12.5: the priests in the Temple profane the Sabbath), how much more should the duty of saving life supersede the Sabbath laws! . . . R. Simeon ben Menasiah says: Behold it is said, "And you shall keep the Sabbath for it is holy for you" (Ex. 31.14). This means: The Sabbath is given you but you are not surrendered to the Sabbath. R. Nathan says: Behold it is said, "Wherefore the people of Israel shall keep the Sabbath, observing the Sabbath throughout their generations' (Ex. 31.16). This implies that we should disregard one Sabbath for the sake of saving the life of a person so that he may be able to observe many Sabbaths' (trans. Lauterbach).
23. *bSanh.* 74a. The general principle is laid down in *b Yom.* 85b: 'Regard for life supersedes the Sabbath'.
24. Cf. J. Klausner, *Jesus of Nazareth*, 1925, p. 279. For a lenient rabbinic ruling, see *mYom.* 8.6, 'If a man has a pain in his throat, they may drop medicine into his mouth on the Sabbath, since there is doubt whether life is in danger, and whenever there is doubt whether life is in danger, this overrides the Sabbath' (trans. H. Danby, *The Mishnah*, 1933, p. 172). On '*Pikkuah nefesh*' (regard for life), see *Enc. Jud.* 13, cols. 509–10.
25. See further Mark 8.36 par.; Matt. 6.25; Luke 12.33, indicating that Jesus bases his teaching on the principle that life is the supreme good (cf. Bultmann, *The History of the Synoptic Tradition*, p. 83). The plucking of grain on the Sabbath is presented as admissible relief from starvation (Mark 2.23–26 par.). It follows naturally from this that to surrender one's life to God is the greatest sacrifice (Mark 8.34–35 par.). This applies also to the poor widow who, by depositing two small coins into the Temple treasury, offers to God 'her whole living' (Mark 12.44 par.).

26. 'The scribes and the Pharisees sit on Moses' seat; so practise and observe whatever they tell you'. The 'chair of Moses' was the seat of the president of the synagogue; cf. *History* II, p. 442.

27. As E. R. Goodenough points out, for Philo 'each law is justified on the basis of its symbolical value' (*An Introduction to Philo Judaeus*, ²1962, p. 42). As an illustration of this principle it may be recalled that for the Alexandrian sage circumcision is 'a symbol of two things most necessary to our well-being. One is the excision of pleasures which bewitch the mind . . . The other reason is that a man should know himself and banish from the soul the grievous malady of conceit' (*Spec. Leg.* I, 8–9). Nevertheless, this emphasis on the allegorical meaning of laws goes hand in hand with an insistence on a simultaneous literal observance of the biblical commandments. Here again Philo and Jesus appear to represent the same religious stand. 'There are some who, regarding the laws in their literal sense in the light of symbols of matters belonging to the intellect, are over punctilious about the latter, while treating the former with easy-going neglect. Such men I for my part should blame for handling the matter in too easy and offhand a manner: they ought to have given careful attention to both aims, to a more full and exact investigation of what is not seen and in what is seen to be stewards without reproach . . . It is quite true that the Seventh Day is meant to teach the power of the Unoriginate and the non-action of created beings. But let us not for this reason abrogate the laws laid down for its observance, and light fires or till the ground or carry loads or institute proceedings in court or act as jurors or demand the restoration of deposits or recover loans, or do all else that we are permitted to do as well on days that are not festival seasons. It is true that the Feast is a symbol of gladness of soul and thankfulness to God, but we should not for this reason turn our backs on the general gatherings of the year's seasons . . . Why, we shall be ignoring the sanctity of the Temple and a thousand other things, if we are going to pay heed to nothing except what is shewn us by the inner meaning of things. Nay, we should look on all these outward observances as resembling the body, and the inner meanings as resembling the soul. It follows that, exactly as we have to take thought for the body, because it is the abode of the soul, so we must pay heed to the letter of the laws.' (*The Migration of Abraham* 89, 91–93; trans. F. H. Colson and G. H. Whitaker, *Philo* IV (Loeb), pp. 183, 185). On Josephus see G. Vermes, 'A Summary of the Law by Flavius Josephus', *NT* 24, 1982, pp. 289–303.

28. Cf. G. F. Moore, *Judaism* II, pp. 6–7. E. E. Urbach, *The Sages* I, pp. 365–99 (passim). The paramount reason for observing the commandments is that they have been decreed by God; hence the performance of every statute, ceremonial or moral, is ultimately an act of obedience. Cf. *Pesiqta de-R. Kahana* (ed. Buber) 40ab; *Tanhuma* (ed. Buber) IV, pp. 118–19, quoted in *Jesus the Jew*, pp. 64–65.

29. *1QS* ii, 25 – iii, 5 (*DSSE²*, p. 74): 'No man shall be in the Community of His truth who refuses to enter the Covenant of God so that he may walk in the stubbornness of his heart . . . He shall not be reckoned among the

perfect; he shall neither be purified by atonement, nor cleansed by purifying waters, nor sanctified by seas and rivers, nor washed clean by any ablution . . .' *1QS* v, 13–14 (*DSSE²*, p. 79): '(The men of falsehood) shall not enter the water to participate in the Purity of the saints, for they shall not be cleansed unless they turn from their wickedness.'

30. Such an emphasis on the individual rather than the community is not difficult to understand in the eschatological context outlined above, pp. 38, 39. Communal legislation can have no meaning where a society is not destined to endure.

31. Homicide and anger are represented as liable to the same punishment. Likewise, seriously to insult a brother is to commit an offence belonging to the same category of crime as murder. At Qumran, words spoken to a priest in wrath (*1QS* vi, 26), short-temper shown towards a superior (vii, 2) and insulting a fellow-sectary (vii, 4) are also singled out as serious infringements of the rule entailing a full year's penance but not permanent expulsion. Cf. *DSSE²*, pp. 82–83. For a highly speculative view of a possible anti-Qumran polemic in Matthew, see W. D. Davies, *The Setting of the Sermon on the Mount*, 1964, pp. 235–239.

A saying similar to Matt. 5.21ff., attributed to a pupil of the fourth-century Amora, R. Nahman b. Isaac, appears in the Babylonian Talmud: 'Whoever causes his companion's face to lose colour (i.e. humiliates him) in public, he is as though he had shed his blood' (*bBM* 58b).

32. *The Mekhilta of R. Simeon ben Yohai* on Ex. 20.14 (ed. Hoffmann, p. 111), advances a point of view similar to that of Jesus: 'Do not commit adultery': he is not to commit adultery . . . either by the eye or by the heart. Whence do we know that the eye and the heart fornicate? As it is written, 'Not to follow after your heart and eyes' (Num. 15.39). Cf. also *Pesiqta Rabbati* 24.2: 'Thou shalt not commit adultery' (Ex. 20.14). R. Simeon ben Laqish said, You are not to say that only he is called adulterer who uses his body in the act. We find scripture saying that even he who visualizes himself in the act of adultery is called an adulterer. And the proof? The verse, 'The eye of the adulterer waits for the twilight' (Job 24.15) (trans. W. G. Braude, *Pesikta Rabbati* I, 1968, pp. 505–6).

33. Whilst the generosity of the rich towards the poor is praiseworthy – 'the assembly will relate his acts of charity' (Ecclus 31.11; 'his renown' according to the Hebrew text) – Jesus warns against the danger of self-aggrandisement. On almsgiving in secret, see the mention in *mSheq*. 5.6 of the 'chamber of secrets' in the Temple where the diffident could help themselves to gifts deposited there by tactful benefactors. Again, the concentration of the ancient Hasidim, whose prayers recited in public places could not be disturbed by greetings addressed to them even by the king himself, was greatly admired (*mBer*. 5.1; *tBer*. 3.20). On the other hand, the *tameion*, or hidden room, is where the patriarch Joseph prays (*Testament of Joseph* 3.3). Similarly, Philo's Therapeutai, or contemplative Essenes, are said to have closeted themselves in consecrated rooms where only scripture was allowed (*The Contemplative Life* 25; F. H. Colson, *Philo* IX

(Loeb), p. 127). The Hasidim, Abba Hilkiah and Hanina ben Dosa, are also depicted as retiring when they intended to pray, either to the flat roof of the house, or to the upper chamber (*bTaan.* 23b; *yBer.* v 9d; *bBer.* 34b). As for fasting, in certain circumstances (e.g. drought or famine) it was a public act, a social duty regulated by Jewish law: 'They are forbidden to wash themselves, to anoint themselves, to wear sandals or to have marital intercourse; and the bath-houses are closed' (*mTaan.* 1.6). Jesus represents fasting as essentially an expression of personal piety.

34. Here again, a code of ethical behaviour composed for a community is replaced by an individual approach to morality. But as soon as Christianity became aware of its social dimensions, church rules came into existence and rapidly grew into a body of complex canon law.

35. On Qumran parallels, see Herbert Braun, *Qumran und das Neue Testament* I, 1966, pp. 23–24.

36. Bultmann, *The History of the Synoptic Tradition*, p. 166. Cf. H. Conzelmann, *An Outline of the Theology of the New Testament*, 1969, pp. 102–04.

37. G. Dalman, *Die Worte Jesu*, pp. 231–33 (ET pp.282–85). On p. 233 (ET pp. 284–85) the saying is rendered into Aramaic.

38. W. D. Davies, *The Setting of the Sermon on the Mount*, pp. 206–7.

39. The embarrassing nature of the saying is revealed by its disappearance from Luke's discourse. Bultmann's hypothesis that the verse is extracted from a Jewish apocalypse and supplemented by a Christian editor (*The History of the Synoptic Tradition*, p. 123) is difficult to reconcile with ecclesiastical aims. 'An assertion of Jesus' ignorance is unlikely to have been created by the Church' (C. E. B. Cranfield, *The Gospel according to St Mark*, 1959, p. 410). Later church fathers (Jerome, Ambrose) declared the verse to be an Arian interpolation. Cf. E. Klostermann, *Das Markusevangelium*, ⁴1950, p. 138.

40. Again Bultmann characterizes the logion as 'a community product' (op. cit., p. 24), but the denial of Jesus' right to allocate seats in 'his' kingdom does not seem to be an invention of the church.

41. The image appears also in rabbinic literature. Mordecai's genealogy is traced to Qish and from this fact it is deduced by means of a pun that he 'knocked (*heqish*) on the gate of mercy' and it was opened to him (*bMeg.* 12b).

Total trust is the key element in the child-father context of the gospel. In the parallel adult setting represented by the parable of the Prodigal son (Luke 15.18–24), the same attitude is linked to repentance-*teshuvah*. It is worth noticing that in an oft-quoted rabbinic parable attributed to the mid-second-century R. Meir, the initiative comes, not from the son, as in Jesus' version, but from the father. The son, though ashamed of his life of wickedness, lacks the confidence to return and confront his father. See *Dt. R.* 2.3 to Deut. 4.30; cf. Strack-Billerbeck II, p. 216; I Abrahams, *Studies in Pharisaism and the Gospels* I, 1917, p. 142; N. Perrin, *Rediscovering*, pp. 91, 95–96.

42. On the meaning of the Greek adjective *epiousios* and its Semitic substratum, see G. Dalman, *Die Worte Jesu*, pp. 321–34; W. Foerster, '*Epiousios*', *TDNT* II, pp. 590–99; M. Black, *An Aramaic Approach to the Gospels and Acts*, ³1967, pp. 203–7. The fundamental teaching is that one prays for a single day's needs.

43. With all respect to J. Jeremias (*The Parables of Jesus*, pp. 157–59) and N. Perrin (*Rediscovering*, pp. 128–29), this is a better exegesis of the parable. According to them, it 'is not concerned with the importunity of the petitioner, but with the certainty that the petition will be granted' (Jeremias, p. 159).

44. Buber, *Two Types of Faith*, 1951, pp. 28–29.

45. 'A righteous man and dear to God' (*J Ant*. xiv. 22).

46. On Honi, see *Jesus the Jew*, pp. 69–72.

47. The saying is based on the Balaam story (Num. 22.12 and 20) where God first refuses the prophet permission to accompany the envoys of Balak, but when he persists, allows him to go.

48. A warning against concern for material possessions is voiced in *Mekh*. on Ex. 13.17 (ed. Lauterbach I, p. 171). The Israelites were not led directly to Canaan so that they would not be immediately absorbed in their fields and vineyards. They were kept by God for forty years in the desert, miraculously provided there with food and drink, and were thus enabled to assimilate the Torah.

49. J. Jeremias's identification of the death mentioned in the parable as 'the approaching eschatological catastrophe' (*The Parables of Jesus*, p. 165) is quite unnecessary. The message has a timeless significance.

50. A similar counsel is given in the Talmud: 'Do not be anxious about the worry of the morrow for you do not know what the day will bring. For one may no longer exist tomorrow and he worries himself over a world (or "a day") that is no more' (*bSanh*. 100b).

51. Buber, *Two Types of Faith*, p. 76.

52. Cf. S. G. F. Brandon, *Jesus and the Zealots*, 1967; J. H. Yoder, *The Politics of Jesus*, 1972; Paul Lehmann, *The Transfiguration of Politics: Jesus Christ and the Question of Revolution*, 1975; Milan Machoveč, *A Marxist looks at Jesus*, 1976; Richard J. Cassidy, *Jesus, Politics and Society*, 1978.

53. I believe it worth mentioning that when I delivered the Riddell Memorial Lectures at the University of Newcastle in March 1981 this was the only remark to provoke audible disagreement in certain quarters of my audience. My questioning of the divinity of Jesus and the reality of his resurrection was received, by contrast, in stoical silence.

54. Wisdom/cunning (*phronēma, phronēsis – phronimos*), the quality of the serpent in the Garden of Eden (Gen. 3.1), scarcely tallies with Jesus' spiritual ideal even when combined with the 'innocence' of a dove (Matt. 10.16). The saying may reflect an old Jewish proverb ascribed to Jesus by the Palestinian church. It has also been inserted into *Cant. R*. 2.14, 'The Holy One blessed be He said to Israel: Towards me they are innocent like doves, but towards the nations of the world they are as crafty as serpents.'

55. It is curious that although J. Jeremias carefully examines details of the parable such as ancient Palestinian wedding customs, he has nothing to say about its moral aspect, maybe because it has no rôle to play in what he believes to be an 'eschatological crisis' story (*The Parables of Jesus*, pp. 171–75).

56. Search for the kingdom overrides family bonds; cf. below.

57. This is a rhetorical exaggeration: the coming of the kingdom of God being imminent, all attention must be centred on it. The dead will be looked after by the dead! To see in this logion a head-on clash between Jesus and the law and pious custom is, I believe, a complete misunderstanding of the gospel message, *pace* A. Schlatter, *Der Evangelist Matthäus*, 1929, p. 288; N. Perrin, *Rediscovering*, p. 144 and M. Hengel, *Nachfolge und Charisma. Eine exegetische-religionsgeschichtliche Studie zu Mt. 8:21f. und Jesu Ruf in die Nachfolge*, 1968, p. 16. Equally mistaken, in my opinion, is the exegesis interpreting 'the dead' metaphorically as 'the wicked' (cf. I Tim. 5.6 and *Gen. R.* 39.7). See Strack-Billerbeck I, p. 489; P. Joüon, *L'Evangile de Jésus-Christ*, 1930, p. 49. For a possible, though not very likely, mistranslation of Aramaic words, see M. Black, *An Aramaic Approach to the Gospels and Acts*, pp. 207–8.

58. The Copper Scroll from Qumran (3Q 15) lists sixty-four locations of hidden treasure. Cf. J. T. Milik, *Discoveries in the Judaean Desert* III, 1962, pp. 284–99. Mishnaic civil law does not envisage the case alluded to in the gospel, but it would be included in the category of a field purchased with 'all that is in it' (*mBB* 4.9).

59. According to J. Jeremias (*The Parables of Jesus*, pp. 200–201) and N. Perrin (*Rediscovering*, p. 89), the main emphasis is on joy, or surprise and joy, rather than on the man's determination to acquire the much-desired object at any price. But not only is such an interpretation contrary to the natural movement of the simile; it overlooks the fact that joy figures only in the story of the hidden treasure and not in that of the pearl. The sole element common to both parables is the sale of everything possessed in order to buy the field or the precious object. The same unreserved devotion inspires the widow to offer to God 'all that she had' (Mark 12.41–44 par.). Similarly, willingness to accept trials and difficulties – the taking up of one's cross (Mark 8.34 par.; Matt. 10.38; Luke 14.27) – is essential to the pursuit of the kingdom. For Jesus, this carrying of the cross symbolizes submission to the Father's will and not self-imposed mortification. He declares fasting at a wedding inappropriate. Indeed, no doubt because of his habit of attending banquets, he was spoken of as 'a glutton and a drunkard' by his opponents (Matt. 11.19; Luke 7.34).

60. Cf. S. Schechter, *Some Aspects of Rabbinic Theology*, 1909, pp. 199–205; A. Marmorstein, 'The Imitation of God (Imitatio Dei) in the Haggadah', *Studies in Jewish Theology*, 1950, pp. 106–21; M. Buber, 'Imitatio Dei', *Israel and the World*, 1963, pp. 66–77; Pamela Vermes, *Buber on God and the Perfect Man*, 1980, pp. 141–44.

61. *Mekh.* on Ex. 15.2 (ed. Lauterbach II, p. 25).

62. The fullest version of the rabbinic doctrine appears in the Talmud and the Palestinian Targum. 'R. Hama son of R. Hanina (third-century Palestinian sage) said: It is written "Follow the Lord, your God" (Deut. 13.5). How can a man follow the Shekhinah? Is it not written, "The Lord, your God, is a devouring fire" (Deut. 4.24)? But follow the attributes of the Holy One blessed be He. As he clothes the naked . . . (Gen. 3.21) so you too must clothe the naked. The Holy One . . . visited the sick . . . (Gen. 18.1), so you too must visit the sick. The Holy One . . . comforted the mourners . . .(Gen. 25.11), so you too must comfort the mourners. The Holy One . . . buried the dead . . . (Deut. 34.6), so you too must bury the dead' (*bSot*. 14a). Cf. also *Ps. Jon.* on Deut. 34.6 on pp. 83–84 below. For a Christianized version of this doctrine, see Matt. 25.31–46. Cf. R. Bultmann, *The History of the Synoptic Tradition*, pp. 123–34.

63. I find Bultmann's assessment of this passage quite incomprehensible: 'This saying is much more akin to the grudging spirit of the last chapter of Eth. Enoch than to the preaching of Jesus' (*The History of the Synoptic Tradition*, p. 103).

64. For a select bibliography, see W. Klassen, 'Love in the NT', *IDBS*, p. 558. See also a recent monograph on the subject by John Piper, '*Love Your Enemies': Jesus' Love Commandment in the Synoptic Gospels and the Early Christian Paraenesis* (1979) with extensive bibliography, pp. 235–48.

65. Luke 14.26. The Matthean parallel reads: 'He who loves father and mother more than me is not worthy of me' (Matt. 10.37).

66. The real meaning seems simply to be: Do not hit back.

67. The contrast between the conduct of John the Baptist and that of Jesus is stressed by the evangelists. Whereas the ascetic John, while ready to exhort tax-collectors to act justly (Luke 3.12), remained socially aloof from them, Jesus took part in their rejoicings. Conventional Jews who criticized both John and Jesus are alluded to in the parable of children who blame their companions for refusing to join in any of their games (Matt. 11.16–19; Luke 7.31–34). The interpretation of the parable proposed by Jeremias (*The Parables of Jesus*, pp. 161–62) and Perrin (*Rediscovering*, pp. 85–86) following F. F. Bishop (*Jesus of Palestine*, 1955, p. 104), appears to be a complete distortion of the obvious meaning of Matt. 11.17; Luke 7.32.

68. Enlightened Jews such as Martin Buber are fully aware of this distinction: 'Christianity – by which I do not mean the teaching of Jesus . . .' (M. Buber, *Israel and the World – Essays in a Time of Crisis*, [2]1963, p. 178).

69. C. H. Dodd, *The Founder of Christianity*, 1970.

70. See for example Martin Buber, *Two Types of Faith*, 1951.

71. For rabbinic association of dogs and Gentiles, see *tYom Tov* 2.6; *bMeg*. 7b. Cf. Strack-Billerbeck I, pp. 724–25.

72. Regarding the hypothesis that 'holy thing' (*to hagion*) is a mistranslation of the Aramaic *qᵉdasha* (ring), confused with *qudsha* (holiness), see

M. Black, *An Aramaic Approach*[3], pp. 200–02; J. A. Fitzmyer, *A Wandering Aramean*, 1979, pp. 14–15 and p. 80 below.

73. For the metaphor, 'swine' = Gentiles, see *Gen. R.* 44.22; *bShab.* 155b. In I Enoch 89.12 the black boar refers to the detested Esau/Edom.

74. For an attempt at conciliation, see W. D. Davies, *The Setting of the Sermon on the Mount*, 1964, pp. 326, 331.

75. This is one of the universalistic features of Matthew. Cf. W. D. Davies, *The Setting of the Sermon on the Mount*, pp. 327–30. Since, as has been suggested earlier (p. 22), the particular and the universal stand can hardly reflect the mind of the same person, it is more likely that the latter derives from editorial activity in a church open to Jews as well as to Gentiles.

76. On the church's representation of itself as the true Israel, see in particular Marcel Simon, *Verus Israel*, [2]1964.

77. See also Rom. 7.5–6: 'While we were living in the flesh our sinful passions, aroused by the Law, were at work in our members to bear fruit of death. But now we are discharged from the Law, dead to that which held us captive, so that we serve not under the old written code but in the new life of the spirit.'

78. Cf. above, pp. 37–38, 50–51.

79. Cf. e.g. Rom. 7.21–25.

80. Thanks to the redemption achieved by the real Son, the believer is granted the title of adopted son.

81. On the few, equivocal, New Testament passages applying the word 'God' to Jesus, see O. Cullmann, *The Christology of the New Testament*, 1959, pp. 306–14. How such an evolution could have occurred in connection with a teacher who not only protested against being called 'good' since 'No one is good but God alone' (Mark 10.18), but for whom the twice-daily recitation of the *Shema'* ('Hear O Israel, the Lord our God is *One* Lord') was the cornerstone of religion (Mark 12.29–30), remains for the historian the most disconcerting feature of all in the formation of Christianity.

5. *Jewish Studies and New Testament Interpretation*

Originally published in *JJS*, vol. XXI, no. 1, 1980, pp. 1–17.

1. Wellhausen, 'Jesus war kein Christ, sondern Jude', *Einleitung in die drei ersten Evangelien*, Berlin 1905, p. 113.

2. The most penetrating study of the Judaeo-Christian conflict is that by Marcel Simon, *Verus Israel*, Paris [2]1964. See also James Parkes, *The Conflict of the Church and the Synagogue*, London 1934, New York 1961.

3. Among the most recent publications see N. R. M. de Lange, *Origen and the Jews*, Cambridge 1976, and J. N. D. Kelly, *Jerome: His Life, Writings and Controversies*, London 1975.

4. '*Memini me . . . Lyddaeum quemdam praeceptorem . . . non parvis redemisse nummis*'; *Praef. in Iob*, PL XXVIII, 1140.

5. Jerome, *Comm. in Ezech.* 24.15, PL XXV, 230; *Comm. in Matth.* 23.5, PL XXVI, 174.

6. Cf. O. S. Rankin, *Jewish Religious Polemic*, Edinburgh 1956; B.

Blumenkranz, *Juifs et chrétiens dans le monde occidental*, Paris 1960; *Les auteurs chrétiens latins du moyen âge sur les juifs et le judaïsme*, Paris 1963; K. H. Rengstorf – S. von Kortzfleisch, *Kirche und Synagoge* I–II, Stuttgart 1968; F. E. Talmage, *Disputation and Dialogue: Readings in Jewish-Christian Encounter*, New York 1975.

7. Raymundus Martini, *Pugio fidei adversus Mauros et Iudaeos*, Leipzig 1687, reprinted 1967.

8. Cf. H. H. Ben-Sasson, 'Disputations and Polemics', *Enc. Jud.* 6, pp. 79–103.

9. Ioh. Christophorus Wagenseilius, *Tela ignea Satanae*, Altdorf 1681, reprinted 1970.

10. Out of respect towards a highly praised senior scholar, I will keep his identity undisclosed. The quotation appears in a book published in 1965.

11. J. J. Wettstein, *Novum Testamentum graece* I–II, Amsterdam 1751–2.

12. A. Souter, *Text and Canon of the New Testament*, Oxford 1913, p. 99.

13. G. F. Moore, 'Christian Writers on Judaism', *HTR* 14, 1921, p. 221.

14. R. Laurence, *Libri Enoch prophetae versio aethiopica*, Oxford 1838; A. Dillmann, *Liber Jubilaeorum aethiopice*, Kiel 1859.

15. This work first appeared in 1874 under the title, *Lehrbuch der neutestamentlichen Zeitgeschichte*; a second edition, renamed *Geschichte des jüdischen Volkes im Zeitalter Jesu Christi*, was published between 1886 and 1890, and a third/fourth edition followed (1901–1909). Two volumes of a fully revised and modernized English edition have been issued by Geza Vermes, Fergus Millar and Matthew Black, with Pamela Vermes as literary editor, under the title *The History of the Jewish People in the Age of Jesus Christ*, Edinburgh 1973, 1979 (*History*). A third volume with an index is in preparation.

16. Ferdinand Weber, *System der altsynagogalen palästinischen Theologie aus Targum, Midrasch und Talmud dargestellt*, Leipzig 1880. A second edition appeared under the title, *Jüdische Theologie auf Grund des Talmud und verwandter Schriften gemeinfasslich dargestellt*, Leipzig 1897.

17. E. Kautzsch, *Die Apokryphen und Pseudepigraphen des Alten Testaments* I–II, Tübingen 1900.

18. R. H. Charles, *The Apocrypha and Pseudepigrapha of the Old Testament* I–II, Oxford 1912–13.

19. The latter requirement no longer applies to one of the works as it has since been translated into bad English.

20. H. L. Strack – P. Billerbeck, *Kommentar zum Neuen Testament aus Talmud und Midrasch* I–IV, München 1922–28. Two further volumes of indices were compiled and published in 1956 and 1960 by Joachim Jeremias and Kurt Adolph.

21. Gerhard Kittel, *Theologisches Wörterbuch zum Neuen Testament* I–X, Stuttgart 1933–76; ET by G. W. Bromiley, *Theological Dictionary of the New Testament* I–X, Grand Rapids 1964–76.

22. Stephen Neill, *The Interpretation of the New Testament 1861–1961*, London 1964, p. 292.

23. Julius Wellhausen, *Israelitische und jüdische Geschichte*, Berlin ⁸1958, p. 193.

24. Cf. note 16 above. The quotation is taken from the 1897 edition p. XIII.

25. In the English revised version vol. II, § 27 is restyled as 'Life and the Law', and the contents are thoroughly cleansed.

26. E. P. Sanders, *Paul and Palestinian Judaism*, London 1976, pp. 234–5.

27. For a severe criticism of the linguistic misconceptions in this Dictionary, see J. Barr, *The Semantics of Biblical Language*, London 1961, pp. 206–62.

28. Martin Buber, *Der Jude und sein Judentum*, Köln 1963, pp. 621–4. For an English version see Talmage, *Disputation and Dialogue*, pp. 49–54.

29. Martin Buber, *Briefwechsel aus sieben Jahrzehnten. II (1918–1938)*, Heidelberg 1972, p. 499.

30. G. Kittel, 'Die Entstehung des Judentums und die Entstehung der Judenfrage', *Forschungen sur Judenfrage* 1, 1937; 'Das Konnubium mit den Nicht-Juden im antiken Judentum', ibid., 2, 1937; 'Die ältesten Judenkarikaturen', ibid., 4, 1940; 'Die Ausbreitung des Judentums bis zum Beginn des Mittelalters', ibid., 5, 1941; 8, 1944; 'Das antike Weltjudentum', ibid., 7, 1943. See also 'Die historische Voraussetzung der jüdischen Rassenmischung', *Schriften des Reichsinstituts für Geschichte des neuen Deutschland*, Hamburg 1939.

31. On anti-Jewish utterances in modern theological literature see Charlotte Klein, *Theologie und Anti-Judaismus*, München 1975 = *Anti-Judaism in Christian Theology*, London 1978.

32. Jules Isaac, *Jésus et Israël*, Paris 1946.

33. Paul Winter, *On the Trial of Jesus*, Berlin 1961. A second (posthumous) edition was issued by T. A. Burkill and G. Vermes, Berlin 1974.

34. For the latest general introduction to the Scrolls see G. Vermes, *The Dead Sea Scrolls: Qumran in Perspective*, London 1977, 1982; Philadelphia. A handy translation of the non-biblical texts may be found in G. Vermes, *The Dead Sea Scrolls in English* 1981, Harmondsworth ²1975.

35. A. Dupont-Sommer, *Aperçus préliminaires sur les manuscrits de la Mer Morte*, Paris 1950 = *The Dead Sea Scrolls. A Preliminary Survey*, Oxford 1952; *Nouveaux aperçus sur les manuscrits de la Mer Morte*, Paris 1953 = *The Jewish Sect of Qumran and the Essenes*, London 1954.

36. J. L. Teicher in a series of articles published in *JJS*, vol. 2, 1951 onwards.

37. For detailed bibliographical information see the relevant sections in B. Jongeling, *A Classified Bibliography of the Finds in the Desert of Judah: 1958–1969*, Leiden 1971, or J. A. Fitzmyer, *The Dead Sea Scrolls. Major Publications and Tools for Study*, Missoula ²1977. Readers may consult in particular K. Stendahl (ed.), *The Scrolls and the New Testament*, London

1957; J. van der Ploeg (ed.), *La secte de Qumrân et les origines du christianisme*, Bruges 1959; M. Black, *The Scrolls and Christian Origins*, London 1961; H. Braun, *Qumran und das Neue Testament* I–II, Tübingen 1966; J. Murphy-O'Connor (ed.), *Paul and Qumran*, London 1968; M. Black (ed.), *The Scrolls and Christianity*, London 1969; J. H. Charlesworth (ed.), *John and Qumran*, London 1972; G. Vermes, 'The Impact of the Dead Sea Scrolls on the Study of the New Testament' see below pp. 115–25; J. Coppens, 'Où en est le problème des analogies qumrâniennes avec le Nouveau Testament?', *Qumrân. Sa piété, sa théologie et son milieu*, ed. M. Delcor, Paris-Gembloux 1978, pp. 373–83; J. Schmitt, 'Qumrân et la première génération judéo-chrétienne', ibid., pp. 385–402.

38. On Qumran messianic doctrine see *History* II, pp. 489–92, 550–54.

39. See in particular J. A. Fitzmyer. 'The Contribution of Qumran Aramaic to the Study of the New Testament', *NTS* 20, 1974, pp. 382–407; 'Methodology in the Study of Jesus' Sayings in the New Testament', *Jésus aux origines de la christologie*, ed. J. Dupont, Gembloux 1975, pp. 73–102.

40. For a reasonably up-to-date introduction to the Rabbinic literature including the Targums see *History* I, pp. 68–118. B. Grossfeld, *A Bibliography of Targum Literature* I–II, 1972–77.

41. The Aramaic text with Spanish, French and English translations has now been edited in full by A. Díez Macho, *Neophyti I. Targum Palestinense MS de la Biblioteca Vaticana* I–VI, Madrid 1968–79. For a French translation with introduction and notes of Targum Neofiti and Targum Ps-Jonathan see R. Le Déaut and J. Robert, *Targum du Pentateuque* I, Paris 1978–79.

42. For a full exposition see Z. W. Falk, *Introduction to Jewish Law in the Second Commonwealth* II, Leiden 1978, pp. 307–16. A brief discussion may be found in G. Vermes, *Post-Biblical Jewish Studies*, Leiden 1975, pp. 65–67. Cf. also J. A. Fitzmyer, 'The Matthean Divorce Texts and some new Palestinian Evidence', *Theological Studies* 37, 1976, pp. 197–226.

43. See D. Daube, *The New Testament and Rabbinic Judaism*, London 1956, pp. 365–68; for an argument in the opposite direction cf. J. D. M. Derrett, *Law in the New Testament*, London 1979, pp. 362–88. According to Josephus, when Herod's sister, Salome, despatched a document (*grammateion*) to her husband to dissolve their marriage, she acted against the law of the Jews. 'For only a man is allowed among us to do this' (*Ant.* xv, 259).

44. Cf. *History* II, p. 321.

45. See Vermes, *Jesus the Jew*, pp. 192–222.

46. J. Barr puts forcefully the same ideas in his criticism of Kittel's Dictionary: 'It could be argued that this emphasis upon the Hebraic background of ideas may indeed have been present in the minds of instructed Jews like St Paul, but that the words which had this series of associations for him could for the most part be *understood* by Gentile Christian hearers especially by the less instructed among them, in the normal Hellenistic sense of the words.' *Semantics of Biblical Language*, p. 250.

47. This is a two-year course entailing a written examination which

consists of a general paper (Jewish literature, history, and institutions from 200 BC to AD 425) and three further papers chosen from the following topics: Jewish historiography, Jewish law, Jewish Bible interpretation, Jewish eschatology, Jewish liturgy, Jewish wisdom literature. The topics are studied from prescribed texts in Hebrew, Aramaic and Greek. Candidates must also submit a short thesis (30,000 words) on an approved subject. (Since 1983, a simplified one-year course, qualifying for a Master of Studies (MSt) degree, is also available.)

6. *Jewish Literature and New Testament Exegesis*

Delivered as the Presidential address at the first Congress of the European Association for Jewish Studies at Hertford College, Oxford on 19 July 1982. Published in *JJS*, vol. XXXIII, no. 2, 1982, pp. 361–76.

1. See above pp. 58, 73.
2. Cf. Martin Hengel, *Judaism and Hellenism*, London 1974, pp. 104–5; see above p. 26.
3. Cf. above p. 71.
4. The subsequent outline partly relies on evidence adduced in the previous chapter.
5. Cf. above p. 59.
6. Atque hinc aeque indubitanter a me conclusum est etiam secundo, quod in locis istius Testamenti obscurioribus (quae sunt quamplurima) optimus & summe genuinus sensum eruendi modus est inquirendo, quomodo & quonam sensu intellectae sunt istae phraseologiae & locutiones, secundum vulgarem & communem gentis istius dialectum et sententiam, et ab iis quae eas protulerunt, & ab auditoribus. Non enim valet, quid nos de istiusmodi locutionibus a conceptus nostri incude fingere possimus; sed quid illae apud eos sonuerint vulgari sermone. Quod cum nullo alio modo perquiri possit, quam auctores Talmudicos consulendo; qui et vulgari loquuntur Judaeorum dialecto; atque omnia Judaica tractant & patefaciunt. Johannis Lightfooti, *Horae Hebraicae et Talmudicae in Quatuor Evangelistas*, Lipsiae MDCLXXV (*In Evangelium Matthaei*) 173–74.
7. Strack-Billerbeck, vols I-IV, München 1922–28.
8. Kittel, vols I–X, Stuttgart 1933–76; ET vols I–X, Grand Rapids 1964–76.
9. First published in 1883 and revised in 1915.
10. *TDNT*, vol. X, p. 649.
11. On the Targums see *History* I, pp. 99–114.
12. P. Kahle, *Masoreten des Westens* II, Stuttgart 1930.
13. *Neophyti 1. Targum Palestinense MS de la Biblioteca Vaticana* I–VI, Madrid 1968–79.
14. First issued in Oxford in 1946 and subsequently revised and re-edited in 1954 and 1967.
15. For a recent introduction see G. Vermes, *The Dead Sea Scrolls: Qumran in Perspective*, London 1977, rev. ed. Philadelphia 1981, London 1982.

16. His most important papers have been assembled in *A Wandering Aramean: Collected Aramaic Essays*, Missoula 1979. See also 'The Aramaic Language and the Study of the New Testament', *JBL* 99, 1980, pp. 5–21.

17. Fitzmyer, *A Wandering Aramean*, p. 8.

18. Ibid., p. 86.

19. Ibid., p. 96.

20. See my comments in *JTS* 31, 1980, pp. 581–82.

21. Joseph A. Fitzmyer and Daniel J. Harrington, *A Manual of Palestinian Aramaic Texts*, Rome 1978. For my review see *JTS* 31, 1980, pp. 580–82.

22. *Manual*, p. xii.

23. M. Black, *An Aramaic Approach to the Gospels and Acts*, Oxford ³1967, p. 139.

24. Fitzmyer, *A Wandering Aramean*, p. 11.

25. Josephus, *Contra Apionem* i, 167.

26. Of course this remark does not apply to the Greek transliteration *korbanas* or *korbōnas* used in the sense of Temple treasury in Matt. 27.6 and expressly interpreted as *hieros thēsauros* by Josephus (*Ant.* ii, 175).

27. Cf. B. Mazar, *Eretz-Israel* 9, Albright Volume, 1969, pp. 168–70.

28. Black, *Aramaic Approach*, pp. 139–40.

29. *1QS* 6.2; *1Q*27 ii, 5 (*DJD* I.105); CD 14.20.

30. Fitzmyer, *A Wandering Aramean*, p. 12, reproducing 'Methodology in the Study of the Aramaic Substratum of Jesus' Sayings in the New Testament' from *Jésus aux origines de la christologie*, ed. J. Dupont, Gembloux 1975.

31. J. P. M. van der Ploeg et al., *Le Targum de Job de la grotte XI de Qumrân*, Leiden 1971, col. XI, 8, p. 32. Reproduced in *Manual*, p. 20.

32. See *Manual*, p. 327.

33. *A Wandering Aramean*, p. 13.

34. See below pp. 89, 99.

35. Fitzmyer, 'Another View of the Son of Man Debate', *JSNT*, 1979, pp. 58–68. Cf. also 'The Aramaic Language and the Study of the New Testament', *JBL* 99, 1980, pp. 5–21.

36. 'Another View', p. 65.

37. Ibid., p. 59.

38. *A Wandering Aramean*, p. 15.

39. A similar criticism applies to Professor Fitzmyer's comments on *ma'ᵃmara – memra*, ibid., pp. 94–95.

40. See *Manual*, p. xii.

41. See Vermes, *Post-Biblical Jewish Studies*, pp. 121–24.

42. Cf. above p. 162, n. 16.

43. See also above p. 165, n. 41.

44. Bultmann, *The History of the Synoptic Tradition*, Oxford 1963, pp. 69–108.

45. Jeremias, *The Parables of Jesus*, London ³1972.

46. Cf. above Chapter 4, n. 41, pp. 165–66.

47. See for instance, P. R. Davies and B. D. Chilton, 'The Aqedah: A Revised Tradition History', *CBQ* 40, 1978, pp. 515, 517.

48. Cf. Matt. 19.28; Luke 22.30; James 1.1.

49. See e.g., *1QS* 8; *1QM* 2 etc.

50. Cf. *1QpHab* 7; II Peter 3 etc.

51. See Mark 2.5–7 par.; *4QPrNab* fr. 1–4. Cf. above p.10.

52. For the latest discussions, see Robert Hayward, 'The Present State of Research into the Targumic Account of the Sacrifice of Isaac', *JJS* 32, 1981, pp. 127–50; James Swetnam, *Jesus and Isaac: A Study of the Epistle to the Hebrews in the Light of the Aqedah*, Rome 1981.

53. Cf. above pp. 52 and 168, notes 60–62.

54. *Mekh.* in loc. (ed. Lauterbach II, 25). Abba Shaul sees in 'I (man) and He (God)' a mystical correspondence demanding that man should model his actions on the conduct of his Creator.

55. This is an illustrated reworking of the problem first raised in *JTS* 31, 1981, p. 582.

56. S. Safrai et al. (eds), *Compendia Rerum Iudaicarum ad Novum Testamentum. Section One. The Jewish People in the First Century* I–II, Assen 1974, 1976.

57. Cf. above pp. 70, 71.

58. Strack-Billerbeck, I, pp. 513–14.

59. *DJD* II, 1961, no. 19, pp. 104–9.

60. As is well known, the original Schürer – and the revised English version does not differ from it in this respect – devotes only two chapters to religious ideas: 'Life and the Law' and 'Messianism'; cf, *History* II, pp. 464–554.

7. The Present State of the 'Son of Man' Debate

An expanded version of a paper read at the Sixth International Congress of Biblical Studies in the Examination Schools at Oxford on 6 April 1978. Published in *JJS* vol. XXIX, no. 2, 1978, pp. 123–34.

1. See 'Appendix E' in Matthew Black, *An Aramaic Approach to the Gospels and Acts*, pp. 310–28, reprinted with an additional footnote in my *Post-biblical Jewish Studies*, pp. 147–65. For an abridged presentation of the evidence, see *Jesus the Jew* pp. 163–68, 188–91.

2. F. Hahn, *The Titles of Jesus in Christology*, London 1969, p. 15.

3. F. H. Borsch, *The Son of Man in Myth and History*, London 1967, p. 22.

4. Carsten Colpe, article on *huios tou anthrōpou*, *TWNT* VIII, p. 406, *TDNT* VIII, p. 404.

5. This view is reiterated by C. F. D. Moule, *The Origin of Christology*, London 1977, p. 13, with special reference to Dan. 7.13, a matter to be considered presently. Cf. note 17 below.

6. Cf. *Jesus the Jew*, pp. 162, 256 n. 8.

7. Meyer, *Jesu Muttersprache*, Freiburg i.B. 1896.

8. Lietzmann, *Der Menschensohn*, Freiburg i.B. 1896.

9. Dalman, *Die Worte Jesu*, Leipzig 1898, ²1930. ET *The Words of Jesus*, Edinburgh 1909.

10. Fiebig, *Der Menschensohn*, Tübingen 1901.

11. Campbell, 'The Origin and Meaning of the Term Son of Man', *JTS* 48, 1947, pp. 145–55.

12. Bowman, 'The Background of the Term "Son of Man"', *Expository Times* 59, 1947/48, pp. 283–88.

13. Black, '"The Son of Man" in the Teaching of Jesus', *Expository Times* 60, 1948/49, pp. 32–36.

14. Sjöberg, '*Ben 'adam* und *bar 'enash* im Hebräischen und Aramäischen', *Acta Orientalia* 21, 1950/51, pp. 57–65, 91–107.

15. Rejected by Lietzmann and Sjöberg, the circumlocutional use has been advocated by Meyer, Campbell and Black among the authors cited, and also by P. Joüon, *L'évangile de Notre-Seigneur Jésus-Christ*, Paris 1930, p. 604, and more recently by R. E. C. Formesyn, 'Was there a Pronominal Connection for the Bar Nasha Selfdesignation?', *NT* 8, 1966, pp. 1–35. However, apart from M. Black, none of these writers have felt it necessary to look for Aramaic instances. Since the self-reference theory has never ceased to have its partisans, it seems odd that Simon Légasse should be 'un peu surpris' by my attempt at 'reviving' it. Cf. 'Jésus historique et le Fils de l'Homme: Aperçus sur les opinions contemporaines', *Apocalypse et théologie de l'espérance*, Paris 1977, pp. 273–4. The titular use has been maintained by Dalman, Bowman, Black and Sjöberg, but denied by Lietzmann and Campbell.

16. *Jesus the Jew*, p. 177.

17. *An Aramaic Approach*, pp. 327–28; *Post-biblical Jewish Studies*, p. 164; *Jesus the Jew*, pp. 171–72. It is on this point that the philologists and theologians appear unable to find a common language. For example, in his highly praised book, *The Origin of Christology*, C. F. D. Moule argues that the definite article used in the New Testament indicates that the phrase is 'demonstrative' because it expressly refers to 'Daniel's Son of Man' (p. 13). He is aware that his statement is contrary to the findings of Aramaic scholars who, in Professor Moule's words, claim it to be 'a mistake to assume that the Greek phrase with the definite article, *ho huios tou anthrōpou*, could have reflected a distinctively demonstrative form in the original language of Jesus'. 'This', he adds, '(though I am not an Aramaist) I would venture to challenge. I cannot believe that it was impossible to find a phrase that would unequivocally mean "the Son of Man" or "*the* Son of Man"' (p. 15). For a fuller exposition of his theory, see 'Neglected Features in the Problem of "the Son of Man"', *Neues Testament und Kirche* (für Rudolf Schnackenburg), ed. J. Gnilka, Freiburg 1974, pp. 413–28.

18. E.g., 'Whoever says, "Here are five (pieces of money), give me something worth three" is a fool. But he who speaks thus, "Here are three (pieces of money), give me something worth five" is a *bar nash*' (*ySanh*. 26b).

19. Borsch, *The Son of Man in Myth and History*, p. 23, n. 4.

20. Colpe, article on *huios tou anthrōpou*, *TWNT* VIII, p. 406, *TDNT*, VIII, pp. 403–04. Cf. also A. Polag, *Die Christologie der Logienquelle*, Neukirchen 1977, pp. 104–5.

21. Jeremias, 'Die älteste Schicht der Menschensohn-Logien', *ZNW* 58, 1967, p. 165 and n. 9. These early reactions to a study which appeared at the end of 1967 are attributable to the fact that already in 1966 a large number of advance off-prints were despatched to interested scholars, a matter explicitly mentioned by Jeremias.

22. *Ekhah Rabbati* 1.5 (ed. Buber, p. 67).

23. Bowker, 'The Son of Man', *JTS* ns 28, 1977, pp. 19–48.

24. Ibid., pp. 31–32. The text quoted is *yBer.* 5b. See *An Aramaic Approach*, p. 323; *Post-biblical Jewish Studies*, p. 160.

25. Casey, 'The Son of Man Problem', *ZNW* 67, 1976, pp. 147–54.

26. Ibid., p. 149.

27. R. Bultmann, *Theologie des Neuen Testaments*, Tübingen ⁵1965, pp. 30–32; H. Conzelmann, *An Outline of the Theology of the New Testament*, London 1969, p. 135, etc.

28. Review of *An Aramaic Approach* in *CBQ* 30, 1968, pp. 417–28; esp. pp. 424–28; 'The Contribution of Qumran Aramaic to the Study of the New Testament', *NTS* 20, 1974, pp. 382–407; 'Methodology in the Study of Jesus' Sayings in the New Testament', *Jésus aux origines de la christologie*, ed. J. Dupont, 1975, pp. 73–102.

29. Fitzmyer, art cit., *CBQ*, p. 427.

30. Fitzmyer, art cit., *NTS*, p. 397, n. 1. For his latest opinion see above p. 80.

31. Fitzmyer, art cit., *CBQ*, p. 420.

32. Fitzmyer, 'Methodology', p. 85, n. 44.

33. Cf. G. Dalman, *Grammatik des jüdisch-palästinischen Aramäisch*, Leipzig ²1905, pp. 57–58, 96–99.

34. Luke 16.20 etc.; John 11.1 etc.

35. *Jesus the Jew*, pp. 190–91, 261.

36. Fitzmyer, 'Methodology', p. 93, n. 69.

37. *BJ* v. 567: *Mannaios ho Lazarou*.

38. P. Thomsen, 'Die lateinischen und griechischen Inschriften der Stadt Jerusalem und ihrer nächsten Umgebung', *ZDPV* 44, 1921, no. 199, p. 118: *Lazarou*.

39. See for instance, the *Textkritischer Anhang* compiled by E. Güting in his edition of the tractate *Terumot (Priesterheben)* in *Die Mischna*, ed. K. H. Rengstorf and L. Rost, Berlin 1969, pp. 192–220.

40. Cf. P. Thomsen, art. cit., p. 113. The legitimacy of the use of these inscriptions is admitted by Fitzmyer, art. cit., *CBQ*, p. 420.

41. J.-B. Frey, *Corpus Inscriptionum Iudaicarum* (=*CII*) II no. 1296, Rome 1952, p. 283.

42. *CII*, no. 1309, p. 290. The patronym is missing.

43. *CII*, no. 1337, p. 298. It is worth observing that not only the *aleph*,

but even the *'ayin*, is omitted. Nevertheless the shortening is not reflected in Greek.

44. This was already noted in *Jesus the Jew*, pp. 190–91, 261.

45. Dalman, op. cit., p. 97. For instance, *na* for *'ana*, *nan* for *'anan*, *tun* for *'attun*, *mar* for *'amar*, *nash* for *'enash*, *ta* for *'etha*. Apropos of the last example it should be remarked that if Fitzmyer's methodological principle were applied to I Cor. 16.14, the reading *Marana tha* (Come, our lord!) would not be permissible because of the missing *aleph*, for the imperative of the verb is spelt as *'etho* in Dan. 3.26. Yet cf. Fitzmyer, *Jerome Bible*, London 1977, pp. 275, 812.

46. See 6Q8 8, line 1 in *DJD*, III, 1962, p. 118; Mur 19, lines 10, 24 in *DJD*, II, 1961, p. 105.

47. See Mur 18, line 3 (*DJD* II, p. 101).

48. Ibid., p. 103.

49. Cullmann, *The Christology of the New Testament*, London 1959, p. 150. The original German edition appeared in 1957.

50. Tödt, *The Son of Man in the Synoptic Tradition*, London 1965, p. 22. The German original was published in 1959.

51. Hahn, *The Titles of Jesus in Christology*, p. 20. The German text was issued in 1963.

52. Perrin, *Rediscovering the Teaching of Jesus*, pp. 164–73.

53. Leivestad in *Annual of the Swedish Theological Institute* 6, 1968, pp. 49–105.

54. Leivestad, 'Exit the Apocalyptic Son of Man', *NTS* 18, 1972, pp. 243–67.

55. Ibid., p. 244.

56. Winter, *Deutsche Literaturzeitung* 89, 1968, col. 784.

57. Hooker, *The Son of Man in Mark*, London 1967, p. 48.

58. Fitzmyer, art. cit., *CBQ*, p. 428.

59. See in particular his paper, 'Problèmes de la littérature hénochique à la lumière des fragments araméens de Qumrân', *HTR* 64, 1971, pp. 333–78, and above all, his edition of *The Books of Enoch. Aramaic Fragments of Qumran Cave 4*, Oxford 1976. Note in this respect Fitzmyer's changing opinions. 'If Milik's latest theory . . . proves to be acceptable . . . then the whole question of the conflated titles in the second part of I Enoch, including the "Son of Man", must be re-worked in the discussions of the material regarding the title as used by Jesus' *NTS*, 1974, p. 397. 'If . . . Milik is correct . . . we can no longer look to the second part of Enoch . . . the so-called Similitudes, for the titular use of "Son of Man"', 'Methodology', 1975, p. 94.

60. Ullendorff, *Ethiopia and the Bible*, London 1968, p. 61.

61. *Jesus the Jew*, pp. 169, 257–60.

62. Milik, *The Books of Enoch*, pp. 91–96.

63. Cf. *Jesus the Jew*, p. 176 and my recent volume, *The Dead Sea Scrolls: Qumran in Perspective*, pp. 210–11, 223–24. M. Black, 'The Throne-Theophany, Prophetic Commission and the "Son of Man"', *Jews, Greeks*

and Christians, Religious Cultures in Late Antiquity. Essays in Honor of W. D. Davies, ed. R. Hammerton-Kelly and R. Scroggs. Leiden 1975, p. 68.

64. Lindars, 'Re-enter the Apocalyptic Son of Man', *NTS* 22, 1975, p. 52.

65. Casey, in *JSJ* 7, 1976, p. 29.

66. Perrin, 'Son of Man', *IDBS*, 1976, p. 883.

67. Bowker, art. cit., *JTS*, p. 26.

68. Brown, 'The Son of Man: "This Fellow"', *Biblica* 58, 1977, p. 367.

69. *Jesus und der Menschensohn* (Anton Vögtle Festschrift), ed. R. Pesch and R. Schnackenburg, Freiburg 1975. Another tendency to evade the problem begins to show itself. 'It cannot be our purpose', writes J. D. Kingsbury, 'to ascertain what *bar nasha* may have meant to the historical Jesus. But as for Matthew, we believe that he does indeed construe the term *ho huios tou anthrōpou* as a christological title and not merely as a circumlocution for the personal pronoun.' *Matthew: Structure, Christology, Kingdom*, London 1976, p. 118. Cf. also Fitzmyer, 'Methodology', pp. 93–94.

70. *Jesus the Jew*, pp. 177–86, 260–61.

71. C. H. Dodd, *The Founder of Christianity*, 1970, pp. 119–21, 184.

72. Roloff, *Das Kerygma und der irdische Jesus*, Göttingen 1970, pp. 61–62 and n. 38. Cf. also Richard N. Longenecker, *The Christology of Early Jewish Christianity*, London 1970, pp. 85–86.

73. Lindars, art. cit., *NTS*, p. 53.

74. Ibid., p. 54.

75. Ibid.

76. Bowker, art. cit., p. 44.

77. The interpretation put forward by C. F. D. Moule is in some ways akin to that of Bowker. Its literary Achilles heel, in addition to the philological weakness mentioned in n. 17 above, is exposed by Professor Moule himself: 'No doubt the position I have presented would stand more securely if, in each several strand of the Gospel traditions . . . "the Son of Man" carried all the associations of suffering, vindication and judgement simultaneously, and if Dan. 7 were more specifically cited in the Son of Man sayings.' *The Origin of Christology*, p. 19.

78. This translation has been directed by Luis Alonso Schökel and Juan Mateos and issued under the imprint of the Madrid publishing house, Cristianidad.

79. Attached to Matt. 8.20, we find a footnote indicating the translators' point of view but keeping other options open: '"este Hombre", lit. "el Hijo del hombre", locución aramea para designar a un individuo; a veces, alusión a la "figura humana" de Dn 7.13' (p. 1505).

80. The text of the original lecture was published under the title, 'The "son of man" Debate' in *JSNT* 1, 1978, pp. 19–32 and a rejoinder from J. A. Fitzmyer appeared in the following year: 'Another View of the "Son of Man" Debate', *JSNT* 4, 1979, pp. 58–68. See above p. 80.

The argument continues and the following studies have been published since 1978: J. A. Fitzmyer, *A Wandering Aramean: Collected Aramaic Essays*, Missoula 1979; M. D. Hooker, 'Is the Son of Man Problem really insoluble?', *Text and Interpretation*, ed. E. Best and R. McL. Wilson, Cambridge 1979, pp. 155–68; Maurice Casey, *Son of Man: The Interpretation and Influence of Daniel 7*, London 1979; Barnabas Lindars, 'Jesus as Advocate: A Contribution to the Christology Debate', *Bulletin of the John Rylands Library* 62, 1979–80, pp. 476–97; A. J. B. Higgins, *The Son of Man in the Teaching of Jesus*, Cambridge 1980; James D. G. Dunn, *Christology in the Making: A New Testament Inquiry into the Origins of the Doctrine of the Incarnation*, London 1980, pp. 65–97; Francis J. Moloney, 'The Reinterpretation of Psalm VIII and the Son of Man Debate', *NTS* 27, 1981, pp. 656–72; Barnabas Lindars, 'The New Look on the Son of Man', *Bulletin of the John Rylands Library* 63, 1980–81, pp. 437–62; Joseph Coppens, *Le Fils de l'Homme néotestamentaire*, Leuven 1981; F. F. Bruce, 'The Background of the Son of Man Sayings', *Christ the Lord: Studies in Christology presented to Donald Guthrie*, Leicester 1982, pp. 50–70; Ragnar Leivestad, 'Jesus – Messias – Menschensohn', *Aufstieg und Niedergang der römischen Welt* II, 25/1, 1982, pp. 221–64; Hans Bietenhard, 'Der Menschensohn', ibid., pp. 265–350; Joseph Coppens, *Le Fils de l'Homme vetéro-et intertestamentaire*, Leuven 1983; Barnabas Lindars, *Jesus, Son of Man*, London 1983.

8. The Impact of the Dead Sea Scrolls on Jewish Studies during the Last Twenty-five Years

Delivered as the first Presidential Address at the foundation meeting of the British Association for Jewish Studies in London on 1 January 1975. Published in *JJS*, vol. XXVI, no. 1, 1975, pp. 1–14.

1. In 1978 the Cambridge University Library Genizah Series began to appear, and so far three volumes of a new catalogue have been published.

2. Krauss, *Griechische und lateinische Lehnwörter in Talmud, Midrasch und Targum* I–II, 1898–99.

3. Juster, *Les Juifs dans l'empire romain* I–II, 1914.

4. Ginzberg, *Die Haggada bei den Kirchenvätern* I–II, 1899–1900.

5. Montefiore, *The Synoptic Gospels* I–II, 1909, ²1927.

6. Dupont-Sommer, *Aperçus préliminaires sur les manuscrits de la Mer Morte*, 1950; *Nouveaux aperçus sur les manuscrits de la Mer Morte*, 1953.

7. Rowley, *The Zadokite Fragments and the Dead Sea Scrolls*, 1952.

8. Kahle, *Die hebräischen Handschriften aus der Höhle*, 1951.

9. Driver, *The Hebrew Scrolls from the Neighbourhood of Jericho and the Dead Sea*, 1951.

10. Zeitlin, 'The Hoax of the Slavonic Josephus', *JQR* 39, 1948, p. 180.

11. Zeitlin, 'A Commentary on the Book of Habakkuk. Important Discovery or Hoax?', *JQR* 39, 1949, pp. 236–37.

12. Zeitlin, 'The Hebrew Scrolls: Once more and finally', *JQR* 41, 1950, p. 1.

13. See in particular, *The Essene Writings from Qumran*, 1961.

14. I took my scholarly revenge by deciphering, translating and publishing a Hodayoth photograph which he mistakenly allowed the London society journal, *The Sphere*, to print on 18 February 1950. See Vermes, *Les manuscrits du désert de Juda*, ²1954, pp. 193–94.

15. F. M. Cross, 'The History of the Biblical Text in the Light of the Discoveries in the Judaean Desert', *HTR* 57, 1964, pp. 292–97.

16. Ibid., p. 294.

17. J. T. Milik, *The Book of Enoch: Aramaic Fragments of Qumran Cave 4*, 1976; M. A. Knibb with the assistance of Edward Ullendorf, *The Ethiopic Book of Enoch* I-II, 1978.

18. The general title is *Judische Schriften aus hellenistisch-romischer Zeit*, the first fascicle of which appeared in 1973.

19. Emil Schürer, *The History of the Jewish People in the Age of Jesus Christ* I, revised and edited by Geza Vermes and Fergus Millar; literary editor Pamela Vermes; organizing editor Matthew Black, 1973.

20. Schürer volume II appeared in 1979.

21. See e.g., ibid., pp. 534–57.

22. Cf. how Peter Schäfer, *Der Bar Kokhba-Aufstand*, 1981.

23. Lieberman, 'Light on the Cave Scrolls from Rabbinic Sources', *PAAJR* 20, 1951, pp. 395–404.

24. Wieder, 'The Habakkuk Scroll and the Targum', *JJS* 4, 1953, pp. 14–18; 'The "Law-Interpreter" of the Sect of the Dead Sea Scrolls: the Second Moses', ibid., pp. 158–75.

25. Rabin, *The Zadokite Documents*, 1954; *Qumran Studies*, 1957.

26. The Hebrew edition appeared in 1969. A two-volume English translation was published in 1975.

27. S. Safrai, *The Jewish People in the First Century*, 1974, p. 1.

28. Among his numerous publications, I would single out *The Rabbinic Traditions about the Pharisees before 70*, I–III, 1971, and *The Idea of Purity in Ancient Judaism*, 1973.

29. Jackson, *Theft in Early Jewish Law*, 1972, and *Essays in Jewish and Comparative Legal History*, 1975.

30. Cf. *Scripture and Tradition in Judaism. Haggadic Studies*, 1961, ²1973; *Post-biblical Jewish Studies*, 1975.

31. See *Scripture and Tradition*, pp. 32–35, 165–66.

32. Cf. G. Vermes, 'The Archangel Sariel. A Targumic Parallel to the Dead Sea Scrolls', *Christianity, Judaism and other Greco-Roman Cults: Studies for Morton Smith at Sixty*, ed. J. Neusner, III, 1975, pp. 159–66.

33. Suriel, prince of the Presence in *bBer*. 51a is probably a conflation of Uriel and Sariel. The latter is mentioned twice as overseer of the camps in the sixth heaven in *Sefer ha-Razim*, ed. M. Margolioth, 1966, pp. 104–105. (Information supplied by Dr P. S. Alexander.)

34. Cf. J. T. Milik, 'Problèmes de la littérature hénochique à la lumière des fragments araméens de Qumrân', *HTR* 64, 1971, p. 346. (See *The Book of Enoch*, pp. 170–74.)

35. During the discussion which followed the paper, a number of valuable suggestions were made, some of which have been introduced into the present text. I am particularly indebted to Professor Edward Ullendorf of the School of Oriental and African Studies, London, Dr M. A. Knibb of King's College, London, Dr Emanuel Tov of the Hebrew University, Jerusalem and Dr Philip Alexander of the Department of Near Eastern Studies, Manchester for their helpful criticism and comments.

9. The Impact of the Dead Sea Scrolls on the Study of the New Testament

A lecture delivered at the University College of North Wales, Bangor on 15 October 1975. Published in *JJS* vol. XXVII, no. 2, 1976, pp. 107–116.

1. In the numerous articles of Dr Teicher, the first editor of *JJS* appeared in *JJS* 2–5, 1950–54.
2. '*Serekh ha-Yaḥad* – The Manual of Discipline. A Jewish-Christian Document from the Beginning of the Second Century CE', *Zion* 29, 1964, pp. 1–60 (in Hebrew).
3. Dupont-Sommer, *The Essene Writings from Qumran*, 1961, pp. 13, 368–78.
4. *Natural History* v. 17, 4.
5. Ibid.
6. *Sifre* on Num. 12.1 (99), ed. H. S. Horovitz, 1971, p. 98.
7. See in particular, J. O'Callaghan, *Los papiros griegos de la cueva 7 de Qumrân*, 1974. C. H. Roberts, 'On some presumed Papyrus Fragments of the New Testament from Qumran', *JTS* 23, 1972, pp. 446–47. For a detailed bibliography, cf. J. A. Fitzmyer, *The Dead Sea Scrolls. Major Publications and Tools for Study*, 1975, pp. 119–23. For a selected bibliography on 'The Qumran Scrolls and the New Testament', see ibid., pp. 124–30.
8. Cf. J. A. Fitzmyer, 'The Contribution of Qumran Aramaic to the Study of the New Testament', *NTS* 20, 1974, pp. 382–407; 'Methodology in the Study of the Aramaic Substratum of Jesus Sayings in the New Testament', in J. Dupont (ed.), *Jésus aux origines de la christologie*, 1975, pp. 73–102. Cf. further his collected papers, *A Wandering Aramean*, 1979.
9. See above pp. 77–80.

10. The Essenes and History

The edited version of a lecture delivered on 11 December 1979 at the Department of History of the University of Tel Aviv under the chairmanship of Professor Z. Yavetz. Published in *JJS* vol. XXXII, no. 1, 1981, pp. 18–31.

1. For a full discussion of the present state of knowledge concerning the Essenes see *History* II, pp. 555–90.
2. *Natural History* v. 15, 73.
3. Schürer, *A History of the Jewish People in the Time of Jesus Christ* II/2, 1885, p. 190.
4. Ibid., p. 191.

5. Sukenik, *Megillôt genuzôt mim-Midbar Yehûdah* I, 1948, p. 16.

6. Dupont-Sommer, *Aperçus préliminaires sur les manuscrits de la Mer Morte*, 1950, pp. 105–17. For a more detailed argument, see *The Essene Writings from Qumran*, 1961, pp. 39–67.

7. Cf. C. Rabin, *Qumran Studies*, 1957.

8. Cf. R. North, The Qumran Sadducees', *CBQ* 17, 1955, pp. 164–88.

9. Cf. C. Roth, *The Historical Background of the Dead Sea Scrolls*, 1958; G. R. Driver, *The Judean Scrolls: the Problem and a Solution*, 1965.

10. J. L. Teicher, *JJS* 2–5, 1950–54, passim; Y. Baer, '*Serekh ha-Yaḥad* – The Manual of Discipline. A Jewish-Christian Document from the Beginning of the Second Century CE', *Zion* 29, 1960, pp. 1–60 (in Hebrew).

11. S. Zeitlin, *The Zadokite Fragments*, 1952; P. R. Weis, 'The Date of the Habakkuk Scroll', *JQR* 41, 1950, pp. 125–54.

12. Cf. *History* II, pp. 583–85.

13. See *DSS*, pp. 87–115.

14. Cf. *Vita* ii (9–12).

15. See *DSS*, pp. 142–62; *History* II, pp. 585–90.

16. Cf. J. T. Milik, *Ten Years of Discovery in the Wilderness of Judaea*, 1959, p. 73.

17. See n. 11 above.

18. See n. 9 above.

19. See n. 10 above.

20. Cf. Dupont-Sommer, *Observations sur le Commentaire d'Habacuc découvert près de la Mer Morte*, 1950; *Aperçus préliminaires sur les manuscrits de la Mer Morte*, pp. 38–39; *Essene Writings*, pp. 266, n. 4, 338–57; 'Observations sur le Commentaire de Nahum découvert près de la Mer Morte', *Journal des Savants*, 1963, pp. 201–27.

21. Cf. *History* I, p. 242.

22. *Ant.* xiv. 66.

23. Cassius Dio xxxvii 16.4; Strabo xvi 2. 40/762–3. Cf. *History* I, pp. 239–40.

24. Delcor, *Le Midrash d'Habacuc*, 1951.

25. Allegro, *The Dead Sea Scrolls and the Christian Myth*, 1979, p. 196.

26. Carmignac, *Les textes de Qumrân* II, 1963, pp. 48–55.

27. Rowley, *The Zadokite Fragments and the Dead Sea Scrolls*, 1952, esp. pp. 62–88. Cf., id., 'The History of the Qumran Sect', *Bulletin of the John Rylands Library* 49, 1963, pp. 203–32.

28. *Les manuscrits du désert de Juda*, 1953, pp. 92–100; *Discovery in the Judean Desert*, 1956, pp. 89–97; *DSSE²*, pp. 63–64; *DSS*, pp. 150–54.

29. Milik, *Ten Years of Discovery*, pp. 84–87.

30. Cross, *The Ancient Library of Qumran and Modern Biblical Studies*, 1958, pp. 135–53; *Canaanite Myth and Hebrew Epic*, 1973, pp. 626–42.

31. P. Winter, 'Two Non-Allegorical Expressions in the Dead Sea Scrolls', *PEQ* 91, 1959, pp. 38–46.

32. R. de Vaux, *Archaeology and the Dead Sea Scrolls*, 1973, pp. 116–17.

33. F. M. Abel and J. Starcky, *Les livres des Maccabées*, 1961, p. 58.

34. G. Jeremias, *Der Lehrer der Gerechtigkeit*, 1963, pp. 36–78.

35. Stegemann, *Die Entstehung der Qumrangemeinde*, 1971.

36. Hengel, *Judaism and Hellenism* I, 1974, pp. 224–27.

37. Murphy-O'Connor, 'The Essenes and the History', *RB* 81, 1974, pp. 215–44; 'Demetrius and the Teacher of Righteousness', *RB* 83, 1976, pp. 400–20; 'The Essenes in Palestine', *BA* 40, 1977, pp. 100–24.

38. *DSS*, pp. 142–62.

39. Cf. notes 34–35 above.

40. 'The Essenes and their History', *RB* 81, 1974, pp. 215–44.

41. Starcky, 'Le Maître Justice et la chronologie de Qumrân', *Qumrân*, ed. M. Delcor, 1978, pp. 249–56.

42. Ibid., p. 256.

43. Rabinowitz, 'The Meaning of the Key ("Demetrius") Passage of the Qumran Nahum Commentary', *JAOS* 98, 1978, pp. 394–99.

44. Ibid., p. 394.

45. Thiering, *Redating the Teacher of Righteousness*, 1979. See now her more recent book, *The Gospels and Qumran: A New Hypothesis*, 1981.

46. S. Safrai in *The Jewish People in the First Century* I, 1974, p. 1.

47. We have two specific references to historical works written in a Semitic language (Aramaic or Hebrew) by Palestinian Jews during this period: I Maccabees according to Origen (in Eusebius, *EH* vi, 25.2) and Jerome (Prologus galeatus to the Books of Samuel) and a vernacular account by Josephus of the *Jewish War* addressed by him to Eastern Jewry (*BJ* i.3). However, since neither of these has actually survived, it is impossible to assess to what extent they correspond to the extant Greek version.

48. Bikerman, *RB* 59, 1952, p. 47.

49. Momigliano, *Terzo contributo alla storia degli studi classici e del mondo antico* I, 1966, pp. 237–38 (reproducing a paper from the *Bulletin of the School of Oriental and African Studies*, 1965, pp. 447–51.

50. Josephus, *Contra Apionem* i.41.

Chapter 1 is reproduced by kind permission of the Liberal Jewish Synagogue and Chapters 2–4, originally given as the Riddell Memorial Lectures, with the permission of the University of Newcastle-upon-Tyne.

Bibliography

Abrahams, I., *Studies in Pharisaism and the Gospels*, I–II, 1917.
Alexander, P. S., Review of G. Vermes, *Post-biblical Jewish Studies*, JTS 27, 1976, p. 172
Allegro, J. M., *Discoveries in the Judaean Desert* V, 1968
Baillet, M., *Discoveries in the Judaean Desert* III, 1962
Banks, Robert, *Jesus and the Law in the Synoptic Tradition*, 1975
Barr, James, *The Semantics of Biblical Language*, 1961
— *Fundamentalism*, 1977
Barthélemy, D., and Milik, J. T., *Discoveries in the Judaean Desert* I, 1955
Becker, Joachim, *Messianic Expectation in the Old Testament*, 1980
Betz, Otto, *What do we know about Jesus?* 1968
Bishop, E. E., *Jesus of Palestine*, 1955
Black, M., *An Aramaic Approach to the Gospels and Acts*, [3]1967
— *The Scrolls and Christian Origins*, 1961
Black, M. (ed.), *The Scrolls and Christianity*, 1969
Bornkamm, G., *Jesus of Nazareth*, 1960
Borsch, F. H., *The Son of Man in Myth and History*, 1967
Bousset, Wilhelm, *Die Religion des Judentums im späthellenistischen Zeitalter*, [2]1926
Brandon, S. G. F., *Jesus and the Zealots*, 1967
Braude, W. G., *Pesikta Rabbati* I–II, 1968
Braun, Herbert, *Qumran und das Neue Testament* I–II, 1966
Buber, Martin, *Two Types of Faith*, 1951
— *Israel and the World – Essays in a Time of Crisis*, 1963
— *The Kingship of God*, 1967
Büchler, Adolf, *Types of Jewish Palestinian Piety from 70 B.C.E. to 70 C.E.*, 1922
Bultmann, Rudolf, *Jesus*, 1926 = *Jesus and the Word*, 1934, 1958
— *The History of the Synoptic Tradition*, 1963
— *Theologie des Neuen Testaments*, [5]1965 = *Theology of the New Testament* I–II, 1952–55
Burchard, Chr., 'Das doppelte Liebesgebot in der frühen christlichen Überlieferung', *Joachim Jeremias Festschrift*, 1970, pp. 39–62
Caird, G. B., 'Chronology of the NT', *IDB* I, 1962, pp. 601–2
Carlston, C. E., 'Form Criticism', NT, *IDBS*, 1976, pp. 345–48

Carmignac, Jean, *Recherches sur le 'Notre Père'*, 1969
Casey, Maurice, *Son of Man: The Interpretation and Influence of Daniel 7*, 1979
Cassidy, Richard J., *Jesus, Politics and Society*, 1978
Catchpole, D. R., *The Trial of Jesus*, 1971
Charles, R. H., *The Apocrypha and Pseudepigrapha of the Old Testament* I–II, 1912–13
Charlesworth, James H., *The Pseudepigrapha and Modern Research*, 1976, ²1981
— (ed.) *John and Qumran*, 1972
Colson, F. H. and Whitaker, G. H., *Philo* I–X, 1929–62
Conzelmann, Hans, *An Outline of the Theology of the New Testament*, 1969
Coppens, J., *Le Fils de l'Homme néotestamentaire*, 1981
— *Le Fils de l'Homme vétéro- et intertestamentaire*, 1983
Cranfield, C. E. B., *The Gospel according to St Mark*, 1959
Cullmann, O., *The Christology of the New Testament*, 1959
Dalman, Gustaf, *Jesus-Jeschua*, 1922 = *Jesus-Jeshua: Studies in the Gospels*, 1929, 1971
— *Die Worte Jesu* ²1930 = *The Words of Jesus*, 1902
Danby, H., *The Mishnah*, 1933
Daube, D., *The New Testament and Rabbinic Judaism*, 1956
Davidson, Robert, and Leaney, A. R. C., *Biblical Criticism*, 1970
Davies, W. D., *The Setting of the Sermon on the Mount*, 1964
Davies, P. R. and Chilton, B. D., 'The Aqedah: A Revised Traditional History', *CBQ* 48, 1978, pp. 514–46
Delcot, M. (ed.), *Qumrân. Sa piété, sa théologie et son milieu*, 1978
Derrett, J. M. D., *Law in the New Testament*, 1970
Dodd, C. H., *The Parables of the Kingdom*, 1935, 1978
— *The Founder of Christianity*, 1970, 1971
Dunn, James D. G., *Christology in the Making*, 1980
Dupont-Sommer, A., *The Dead Sea Scrolls. A Preliminary Survey*, ET 1952
— *The Jewish Sect of Qumran and the Essenes*, ET 1954
— *The Essene Writings from Qumran*, 1961
Eissfeldt, Otto, *The Old Testament: An Introduction*, 1965
Evans, O. E., 'Kingdom of God, of Heaven', *IDB* II, 1962, pp. 17–26
Feliks, J., 'Mustard', *Enc. Jud.* 12, 1971, p. 720
Fiebig, P., *Der Menschensohn*, 1901
Fitzmyer, J. A., *The Dead Sea Scrolls. Major Publications and Tools for Study*, 1977
— *The Genesis Aprocryphon of Qumran Cave* I, ²1971
— *Essays on the Semitic Background of the New Testament*, 1971
— 'The Matthean Divorce Texts and some new Palestinian Evidence', *Theological Studies* 37, 1976, pp. 197–226
— 'Another View of the "Son of Man" Debate', *JSNT* 4, 1979, pp. 58–68
— *A Wandering Aramean: Collected Aramaic Essays*, 1979

Foerster, W., '*Epiousios*', *TDNT* V, pp. 590–99
— '*Exousia*', *TDNT* V, pp. 562–75
Fortna, R. T., 'Redaction Criticism, NT', *IDBS*, 1976, pp. 733–35
Freyne, Seán, *Galilee from Alexander the Great to Hadrian*, 1980
Friedrich, G., '*Prophētēs*', *TDNT* VI, pp. 848–55
Gerhardsson, Birger, *Memory and Manuscript: Oral Tradition and Written Transmission in Rabbinic Judaism and Early Christianity*, 1961, ²1964
— *Tradition and Transmission in Early Christianity*, 1964
— *The Origins of the Gospel Tradition*, 1977
Goodblatt, D. M., *Rabbinic Instruction in Sasanian Babylonia*, 1975
Goodenough, E. R., *Introduction to Philo Judaeus*, ²1962
Goodman, Martin D., Review of A. Oppenheimer, *The 'Am Ha-Aretz*, *JJS* 31, 1980, pp. 248–49
Grant, Michael, *Jesus: An Historian's Review of the Gospels*, 1977
Grässer, E., *Das Problem der Parousieverzögerung in den synoptischen Evangelien und in der Apostelgeschichte*, ²1960
Gray, J., *The Biblical Doctrine of the Reign of God*, 1979
Green, William S., 'What's in a Name? The Problematic of "Rabbinic Biography"', *Approaches to Ancient Judaism: Theory and Practice*, 1978, pp. 77–96
— 'Palestinian Holy Men: Charismatic Leadership and Rabbinic Tradition', *Aufstieg und Niedergang der römischen Welt*, ed. W. Haase, II. *Principat. 19.2 Religion (Judentum: Palästinisches Judentum)*, 1979, pp. 619–47
Hahn, F., *The Titles of Jesus in Christology*, 1969
Hamerton-Kelly, R., *God the Father: Theology and Patriarchy in the Teaching of Jesus*, 1979
Hanson, P. D., *The Dawn of Apocalyptic*, 1975
Harvey, A. E., *God Incarnate: Story and Belief*, 1981
— *Jesus and the Constraints of History*, 1982
Hayward, Robert, 'The Present State of Research into the Targumic Account of the Sacrifice of Isaac', *JJS* 32, 1981, pp. 127–50
Heinemann, J., *Prayer in the Talmud; Forms and Patterns*, 1977
Hengel, Martin, *Judaism and Hellenism*, I–II, 1974
— *Die Zeloten*, ²1976
Hering, J., *La royaume de Dieu et sa venue*, 1959
Higgins, A. J. B., *The Son of Man in the Teaching of Jesus*, 1980
Hübner, H., *Das Gesetz in der synoptischen Tradition*, 1973
Idelsohn, A. Z., *Jewish Liturgy and its Development*, 1932
Isaac, J., *Jésus et Israël*, 1946
Jackson, B. S., 'Legalism', *JJS* 30, 1979, pp. 1–22
Jacobs, Louis, *A Jewish Theology*, 1973
Jeremias, Joachim, '*Grammateus*', *TDNT* I, pp. 740–42
— *New Testament Theology* I, 1971
— *The Parables of Jesus*, ²1972
— *The Prayers of Jesus*, 1977

Jongeling, B., *A Classified Bibliography of the Finds in the Desert of Judah: 1958–1969*, 1971

Joüon, P., *L'évangile de Jésus-Christ*, 1930

Judéo-Christianisme. Recherches historiques et théologiques offertes en hommage au Cardinal Jean Daniélou, 1972

Käsemann, E., *Essays on New Testament Themes*, 1964

Kautzsch, E., *Die Apokryphen und Pseudepigraphen des Alten Testaments* I–II, 1900

Kittel, G., and Friedrich, G., *Theologisches Wörterbuch zum Neuen Testament* I–X, 1933–76 = *Theological Dictionary of the New Testament* I–X, 1964–76

Klassen, W., 'Love in the NT', *IDBS*, 1976, pp. 557–58

Klausner, J., *Jesus of Nazareth*, 1925

Klein, Charlotte, *Anti-Judaism in Christian Theology*, 1978

Klostermann, E., *Das Markusevangelium*, ⁴1950

Knibb, M. A., *The Ethiopic Book of Enoch* I–II, 1978

Kohler, K., *Jewish Theology*, 1918

Kümmel, W. G., *Promise and Fulfilment*, 1957

— *The Theology of the New Testament*, 1969

— *The New Testament: The History of the Investigation of its Problems*, ²1970

— *Introduction to the New Testament*, ²1975

— 'Ein Jahrzehnt Jesusforschung', *Theologische Rundschau* 40, 1975, pp. 283–336; 41, 1976/77, pp. 198–258, 295–363

— 'Jesusforschung seit 1965', *Theologische Rundschau* 43, 1978, pp. 105–61, 232–65; 45, 1980, pp. 48–84, 293–337

Ladd, G. E., *The Presence and the Future*, 1974

Lagrange, M.-J., *L'évangile de Jésus-Christ*, 1929

Lehmann, Paul, *The Transfiguration of Politics: Jesus Christ and the Question of Revolution*, 1975

Leo XIII, *Providentissimus Deus*, 1893

Lietzmann, H., *Der Menschensohn*, 1896

Lindars, Barnabas, *Jesus Son of Man*, 1983

Lohse, E., 'Rabbi, Rabbouni', *TDNT* VI, pp. 961–65

— 'Sabbaton', *TDNT* VIII, pp. 21–26

Machoveč, Milan, *A Marxist looks at Jesus*, 1976

McKnight, E. V., *What is Form Criticism?*, 1975

Maier, J., *Geschichte der jüdischen Religion*, 1972

Manson, T. W., *The Teaching of Jesus: Studies of its Form and Content*, 1931, ²1935

Marmorstein, A., *Studies in Jewish Theology*, 1950

Metzger, Bruce M., *The Early Versions of the New Testament*, 1977

Meyer, A., *Jesu Muttersprache*, 1896

Meyers, Eric M., and Strange, James F., *Archaeology, the Rabbis and Early Christianity*, 1981

Milik, J. T., *The Book of Enoch: Aramaic Fragments of Qumran Cave 4*, 1976
— *Discoveries in the Judaean Desert* I, 1955; III, 1962
— 'Milkî-sedeq et Milkî-reša' dans les anciens écrits juifs et chrétiens', *JJS* 23, 1972, pp. 95–144
Millar, Fergus, 'The Background of the Maccabean Revolution: Reflections on Martin Hengel's "Judaism and Hellenism"', *JJS* 29, 1978, 1–21
Moore, A. L., *The Parousia in the New Testament*, 1966
Moore, G. F., *Judaism in the First Centuries of the Christian Era* I–III, 1927–30
Moule, C. F. D., *The Origin of Christology*, 1977
Mowinckel, S., *He That Cometh*, 1956
Murphy-O'Connor, J. (ed.), *Paul and Qumran*, 1968
Neill, S. C., *The Interpretation of the New Testament 1861–1961*, 1963
Neusner, Jacob, *The Rabbinic Traditions about the Pharisees* I–III, 1971
— 'The Present State of Rabbinic Biography', *Hommage à Georges Vajda*, ed. G. Nahon and Ch. Touati, 1980, pp. 85–91
— 'Judaism after Moore: A Programmatic Statement', *JJS* 31, 1980, pp. 141–56
— *Judaism: The Evidence of the Mishnah*, 1981
Oepke, A., '*Parousia*', *TDNT* V, pp. 858–71
Oppenheimer, Aharon, *The 'Am Ha-Aretz*, 1977
Otto, Rudolf, *The Kingdom of God and the Son of Man*, 1943
Parkes, J., *The Conflict of the Church and the Synagogue*, 1934
Perrin, Norman, *The Kingdom of God in the Teaching of Jesus*, 1963
— *Rediscovering the Teaching of Jesus*, 1967
— *The New Testament: An Introduction*, 1974
What is Redaction Criticism? 1969
— *Jesus and the Language of the Kingdom*, 1976
Piper, John, '*Love your Enemies': Jesus' Love Commandment in the Synoptic Gospels and the Early Christian Paraenesis*, 1979
Ploeg, J. van der, *La secte de Qumrân et les origines du christianisme*, 1959
— et al., *Le Targum de Job de la grotte XI de Qumrân*, 1971
Przybilski, B., *Righteousness in Matthew and his World of Thought*, 1980
Quell, G., and Schrenk, G., '*Patēr*', *TDNT* V, pp. 959–82
Riches, John, *Jesus and the Transformation of Judaism*, 1980
Rigaux, B., *Les épîtres aux Thessaloniciens*, 1956
Rivkin, Ellis, 'Pharisees', *IDBS*, 1976, pp. 657–63
— *A Hidden Revolution*, 1978
Russell, D. S., *The Method and Message of Jewish Apocalyptic*, 1964
Safrai, S., 'The Teaching of Pietists in Mishnaic Literature', *JJS* 16, 1965, pp. 15–33
— 'Education and Study of the Torah', *The Jewish People in the First Century* II, 1977, pp. 945–70
Sanders, E. P., *Paul and Palestinian Judaism*, 1977
Schäfer, P., *Der Barkokhba-Aufstand*, 1981

Schechter, S., *Some Aspects of Rabbinic Theology*, 1909
Schlatter, A., *Der Evangelist Matthäus*, 1929
Schlosser, J., *Le Règne de Dieu dans les dits de Jésus* I–II, 1980
Schlüsser, Fiorenza, E., 'Eschatology of the NT', *IDBS*, 1976, pp. 271–77
Schnackenburg, Rudolf, *New Testament Theology Today*, 1963
— *The Moral Teaching of the New Testament*, 1965
Schneider, J., '*Kraspedon*', *TDNT* III, p. 904
Schoeps, Hans Joachim, *Theologie und Geschichte des Judenchristentums*, 1949
— *Urgemeinde, Judenchristentum, Gnosis*, 1956
Schrenk, G., see Quell, G.
Schürer, Emil, *Geschichte des jüdischen Volkes im Zeitalter Jesu Christi* I–III[3/4]1901–9
Schürer, E., Vermes, G., Millar, F., *The History of the Jewish People in the Age of Jesus Christ* I, 1973
Schürer, E., Vermes, G., Millar, F., Black, M., *The History of the Jewish People in the Age of Jesus Christ* II, 1979
Schürmann, H., 'Eschatologie und Leibesdienst in der Verkündigung Jesu' *Vom Messias zu Christus*, ed. K. Schubert, 1964, pp. 203–32
Schweitzer, Albert, *Von Reimarus zu Wrede*, 1906 – *The Quest of the Historical Jesus*, 1910, [3]1954
Segal, J. B., 'Popular Religion in Ancient Israel', *JJS* 27, 1976, pp. 1–22
Simon, Marcel, *Verus Israel*, [2]1964
— 'Réflexions sur le Judéo-Christianisme', *Christianity, Judaism and Other Greco-Roman Cults* II, ed. J. Neusner, 1975, pp. 53–76
Simon, Marcel, *et al.*, *Aspects du Judéo-Christianisme*, 1965
Simon, Marcel, and Benoit, A., *Le judaïsme et le christianisme antique*, 1968
Smith, Morton, *Jesus the Magician*, 1978
Souter, A., *Text and Canon in the New Testament*, 1913
Spicq, C., *Agapè dans le Nouveau Testament* I–III, 1958–9
Stauffer, E., *New Testament Theology*, 1955
Stendahl, K., *The School of St Matthew*, 1954, [2]1968
— *The Scrolls and the New Testament*, 1958
— 'Biblical Theology', *IDB* I, 1962, 418–32
Strack, Hermann, and Billerbeck, Paul, *Kommentar zum Neuen Testament aus Talmud und Midrasch* I–IV, 1922–28
Strange, James F., see Meyers, Eric M.
Strobel, A., *Untersuchungen zum eschatologischen Verzögerungsproblem*, 1961
Swetnam, James, *Jesus and Isaac*, 1981
Talmage, F. E., *Disputation and Dialogue: Readings in Jewish-Christian Encounter*, 1975
— *Kerygma und Apokalyptik*, 1967
Tödt, H. E., *The Son of Man in the Synoptic Tradition*, ET 1965
Ullendorff, Edward, *Ethiopia and the Bible*, 1968

Urbach, E. E., *The Sages: Their Concepts and Beliefs* I–II, 1975
Vermes, Geza, 'Hanina ben Dosa', *JJS* 23, 1972, pp. 28–50; 24, 1973, pp. 51–64 = *Post-biblical Jewish Studies*, pp. 178–214
— *Jesus the Jew: A Historian's Reading of the Gospels*, 1973, 1981, 1983
— *Post-biblical Jewish Studies*, 1975
— *The Dead Sea Scrolls in English*, ²1975
— *The Dead Sea Scrolls: Qumran in Perspective*, 1977, rev. 1981
— 'A Summary of the Law by Flavius Josephus', *NT* 24, 1982, pp. 289–303
Vermes, Pamela, *Buber on God and the Perfect Man*, 1980
Volz, Paul, *Eschatologie der jüdischen Gemeinde im neutestamentlichen Zeitalter*, ²1934
Weber, Ferdinand, *Jüdische Theologie*, 1897
Wellhausen, Julius, *Einleitung in die drei ersten Evangelien*, 1905
Westerholm, Stephen, *Jesus and Scribal Authority*, 1978
Winter, Paul, *On the Trial of Jesus*, 1961, ²1974
Wrede, Wilhelm, *Messiasgeheimnis in den Evangelien*, 1901 = *The Messianic Secret*, 1971
Wilcox, Max, '"Upon the Tree" – Deut 21:22–23 in the New Testament', *JBL* 96, 1977, pp. 85–99
Yoder, J. H., *The Politics of Jesus*, 1972

Index

27 chek
169
181